Council Democracy

The return to public assemblies and direct democratic methods in the wave of the global "squares movements" since 2011 has rejuvenated interest in forms of council organisation and action. The European council movements, which developed in the immediate post-First World War era, were the most impressive of a number of attempts to develop workers' councils throughout the twentieth century. However, in spite of the recent challenges to liberal democracy, the question of council democracy has so far been neglected within democratic theory. This book seeks to interrogate contemporary democratic institutions from the perspective of the resources that can be drawn from a revival and re-evaluation of the forgotten ideal of council democracy.

This collection brings together democratic theorists, socialists and labour historians on the question of the relevance of council democracy for contemporary democratic practices. Historical reflection on the councils opens our political imagination to an expanded scope of the possibilities for political transformation by drawing from debates and events at an important historical juncture before the dominance of current forms of liberal democracy. It offers a critical perspective on the limits of current democratic regimes for enabling widespread political participation and holding elites accountable.

This timely read provides students and scholars with innovative analyses of the councils on the 100th anniversary of their development. It offers new analytic frameworks for conceptualising the relationship between politics and the economy and contributes to emerging debates within political theory on workplace, economic and council democracy.

James Muldoon is a lecturer in political science at the University of Exeter. His main research interests are in democratic theory, socialism and the history of political thought. His work has appeared in *History of Political Thought*, *Political Studies*, *Theory, Culture & Society*, *Constellations* and *Critical Horizons*.

Routledge Advances in Democratic Theory
Edited by David Chandler and Paulina Tambakaki
(both University of Westminster)

Democracy is being rethought almost everywhere today: with the widespread questioning of the rationalist assumptions of classical liberalism, and the implications this has for representational competition; with the Arab Spring, destabilizing many assumptions about the geographic spread of democracy; with the deficits of democracy apparent in the Euro-zone crisis, especially as it affects Greece and Italy; with democracy increasingly understood as a process of social empowerment and equalization, blurring the lines of division between formal and informal spheres; and with growing demands for democracy to be reformulated to include the needs of those currently marginalized or even to include the representation of non-human forms of life with whom we share our planet.

Routledge Advances in Democratic Theory publishes state of the art theoretical reflection on the problems and prospects of democratic theory when many of the traditional categories and concepts are being reworked and rethought in our globalized and complex times.

The series is published in cooperation with the *Centre for the Study of Democracy*, University of Westminster, London, UK.

6. **Negativity and Democracy in the Critical Theory Tradition**
   Dialectics from Karl Marx to Open Marxism
   Vasilis Grollios

7. **Democratic Theory and the Enlarged Mentality**
   Stephen Acreman

8. **Council Democracy**
   Towards a Democratic Socialist Politics
   Edited by James Muldoon

CENTRE FOR THE
STUDY OF
DEMOCRACY

Council Democracy

Towards a Democratic Socialist Politics

Edited by James Muldoon

Routledge
Taylor & Francis Group
New York London

First published 2018
by Routledge
52 Vanderbilt Avenue, New York, NY 10017

and by Routledge
2 Park Square, Milton Park, Abingdon, Oxon, OX14 4RN

First issued in paperback 2020

Routledge is an imprint of the Taylor & Francis Group, an informa business

Library of Congress Cataloging-in-Publication Data
Names: Muldoon, James, 1985– editor.
Title: Council democracy : towards a democratic socialist politics / edited by James Muldoon.
Description: New York, NY : Routledge, 2018. |
Series: Routledge advances in democratic theory ; 8 |
Includes bibliographical references and index.
Identifiers: LCCN 2018009637 | ISBN 9780815383697 (hardback) |
ISBN 9781351205627 (webpdf) | ISBN 9781351205610 (epub) |
ISBN 9781351205603 (mobipocket/kindle) | ISBN 9781351205634 (master)
Subjects: LCSH: Works councils. | Labor union democracy. |
Direct democracy. | Socialism.
Classification: LCC HD5650 .C68 2018 | DDC 322/.2–dc23
LC record available at https://lccn.loc.gov/2018009637

ISBN 13: 978-0-367-66594-4 (pbk)
ISBN 13: 978-0-8153-8369-7 (hbk)

Typeset in Times New Roman by
Out of House Publishing

Contents

Contributors

Dario Azzellini is a visiting research fellow at the Industrial and Labor Relations (ILR) School, Cornell University and holds a PhD in political science and a PhD in sociology. His teaching, research and writing focuses on democracy, Labour Studies, worker and local self-management, social movements, Global Studies and Latin American Studies. He has published several books, journal articles and documentaries. His latest books are *Communes and Workers' Control in Venezuela: Building 21st Century Socialism from Below* (Brill, 2017) and *Vom Protest zum sozialen Prozess: Betriebsbesetzungen und Arbeiten in Selbstverwaltung* (VSA, 2018). He has also co-authored *They Can't Represent Us: Reinventing Democracy from Greece to Occupy* (Verso, 2014). He is co-editor of *The Class Strikes Back: Self-Organised Workers' Struggles in the Twenty-First Century* (Brill, 2018) and *Ours to Master and to Own: Workers' Control from the Commune to the Present* (Haymarket, 2011), and the editor of *An Alternative Labour History: Worker Control and Workplace Democracy* (Zed Books, 2015). Azzellini is a founding member of workerscontrol.net. As a documentary filmmaker he has filmed in Latin America and Europe. Together with Oliver Ressler he produces *Occupy, Resist, Produce*, a series of documentaries on recuperated factories under workers' control in Europe.

David Ellerman has written about the theory and practice of worker co-operatives and other forms of workplace democracy for over 40 years. He is the author of *Property & Contract in Economics: The Case for Economic Democracy* (1993) and *The Democratic Worker-Owned Firm* (1989). He also co-founded the American NGO, the Industrial Cooperative Association, in the late 1970s that adapted the Mondragon model of a worker co-operative to the American legal system. He was speech-writer and senior advisor to Joseph Stiglitz when Stiglitz was Chief Economist at the World Bank. His most recent book is *Helping People Help Themselves: From the World Bank to an Alternative Philosophy of Development Assistance* (2005). He is now doing full-time research and writing, dividing his time between Riverside, California (winter) and Slovenia/Croatia (summer).

Donny Gluckstein is a lecturer in history at Edinburgh College and the author of several books including: *The Western Soviets: Workers' Councils versus Parliament, 1915–1920* (1985), *A People's History of the Second World War* (2012), *The Tragedy of Bukharin* (1994), *Marxism and Trade Union Struggle: The General Strike of 1926* (with Tony Cliff) (1986), *Fighting on All Fronts: Popular Resistance in the Second World War* (ed.) (2015), *The Paris Commune: A Revolution in Democracy* (2011), *Nazis, Capitalism and the Working Class* (2012) and *The Labour Party: A Marxist History* (with Tony Cliff) (1996). He is an active trade unionist in the EIS and member of the Socialist Workers' Party.

Christopher Holman is an assistant professor in the School of Social Sciences at Nanyang Technological University, where he works on contemporary democratic theory and the history of political thought. His most recent book, *Machiavelli and the Politics of Democratic Innovation*, will be published in 2018 by the University of Toronto Press. He has also written a variety of scholarly articles in journals such as *European Journal of Political Theory*, *Contemporary Political Theory*, *Theory and Event*, *Telos*, *New German Critique*, *New Political Science* and more.

Gaard Kets studied history and political theory and is currently affiliated to Radboud University as a PhD candidate. His research focuses on the relation between intellectual leaders and the working class in the formation of council communist ideology during the council revolution in Germany, 1918–19.

Shmuel Lederman holds a PhD in political science from the University of Haifa, Israel. He teaches at the Department of History, Philosophy and Judaic Studies at the Open University of Israel, and at the Weiss-Livnat International MA Program in Holocaust Studies at the University of Haifa. He also serves as a research fellow at the Forum for Regional Thinking: an Israeli research institute dedicated to a critical examination of the Middle East. His research interests include the political thought of Hannah Arendt, Leo Strauss and John Stuart Mill, as well as genocide studies and the Israeli–Arab conflict. He is currently working on a book on Hannah Arendt and participatory democracy.

John Medearis is Professor and Chair of Political Science at the University of California, Riverside. His writings focus on questions involving democracy, social movements and political economy. His most recent book, *Why Democracy Is Oppositional*, explores democratic action in relation to phenomena of domination and alienation. He is also the author of *Joseph Schumpeter's Two Theories of Democracy* and *Joseph A. Schumpeter*. He received his PhD from the University of California, Los Angeles.

James Muldoon is a lecturer in political science at the University of Exeter. His main research interests are in democratic theory, socialism and the history of political thought. His work has appeared in *History of Political Thought*, *Political Studies*, *Theory, Culture & Society*, *Constellations* and *Critical Horizons*.

Benjamin Ask Popp-Madsen is a PhD student at the Department of Political Science at the University of Copenhagen. He is currently finishing his thesis on the role of the council system in the political thought of Hannah Arendt, Cornelius Castoriadis and Claude Lefort, as well as working on issues of the constituent power and the democratic exception. Benjamin has recently published a Danish anthology with primary texts from the Russian Revolution as well as published on issues of democratic thinkers in Danish as well as international journals.

Michael J. Thompson is Associate Professor of Political Theory in the Department of Political Science at William Paterson University. His next book, *Political Judgment and the Crisis of Modernity*, is forthcoming with SUNY Press.

Nicholas Vrousalis is Assistant Professor in Political Philosophy at Leiden University. His main research areas are distributive ethics, Marxism and the philosophy of social science. Vrousalis' work has appeared in *Philosophy and Public Affairs*, *Journal of Ethics*, *Politics, Philosophy & Economics*, *Southern Journal of Philosophy* and *Ethical Theory and Moral Practice*. His monograph, *The Political Philosophy of G. A. Cohen*, was published by Bloomsbury in 2015.

Gabriel Wollner is Junior Professor at the Department of Philosophy of Humboldt-Universität zu Berlin. He studied Philosophy, Politics and Economics (BA) and Political Theory (MPhil) at the University of Oxford and Public Policy (MPP) at Harvard University, and obtained his doctorate in Philosophy (PhD) from University College London. Prior to joining Humboldt-Universität he was Assistant Professor in Philosophy at the London School of Economics. His academic interests are in political philosophy and ethics, and the application of these inquiries to various issues in public policy and political economy.

1 Council Democracy

Towards a Democratic Socialist Politics

James Muldoon

Introduction

Capitalism and democracy have long been uncomfortable bedfellows. But with the ascendancy of a neoliberal rationality of governance, the expansion of corporate power and the increase of income and wealth disparities, the uneasy interaction between the two has gradually led to a hollowing out of democracy by powerful economic interests. Today, not only is policy- and law-making in most advanced industrial democracies dominated by a wealthy elite, but a marketplace rationality has seeped into governing institutions and the practices of daily life, undermining the very fabric of democracy as collective self-rule.[1] These developments reflect the influence of Friedrich Hayek's theory that markets should be freed from excessive political regulation and government intervention in order to deliver maximum productivity and efficiency. The post-Second World War belief in a mixed economy and the necessity of a strong role for government in economic planning has been replaced by a neoliberal consensus concerning the dangers of government intervention in the economy. Democracy, understood in the minimalist sense as the presence of free and fair elections, is viewed as having no place in the economic sphere due to the dangers democratic controls pose to individual freedom.

The response of the mainstream Left to the rise of neoliberal ideology has been largely to capitulate and adapt to liberal democratic capitalism as the unsurpassable horizon of modern politics. The collapse of the Soviet Union and mounting criticisms of the Marxist imaginary led to the development of a host of other theoretical interests focused on civil society, new social movements, deliberative mini-publics and participatory co-governance schemes. At a time when powerful economic actors were increasing their control over political processes – undermining the very basis of liberal democracy – theorists of democracy were turning away from an interest in the economic sphere and a concern for the obstacles that capitalist market forces posed to democratic renewal. In their seminal text published in 1992, *Civil Society and Political Theory*, Andrew Arato and Jean Cohen constructed a new justification of civil society and self-limiting democratisation movements.[2] Their focus on strengthening democratic culture through participation in civil society was based on a rejection of the Marxist strategy of striving for an emancipated, self-managed society. While Arato and Cohen made an important contribution to theorising a pluralist and differentiated society, their new Habermas-inspired political agenda came at the expense of an adequate theorisation of the contradictory relationship between capitalist relations of production and democracy.

In an era of ongoing erosion of democracy by corporate power, there is an urgent need to reconsider the necessary underlying conditions of democratic government. Scholars concerned with the strengthening of democratic practices and the redesign of democratic institutions should consider the significant threat posed by capitalist market relations. Among other concerns, the sheer concentration of private power in capitalist firms can undermine the capacity of democratic governments to realise collective democratic aims that may be against corporate interests. Capitalist firms also remain predominantly undemocratic authority structures in which workers must spend large amounts of their time and over which they exercise little control. The question of democracy within the workplace and broader economic institutions has been a marginal concern within democratic theory.[3] Of those radical democratic scholars interested in transformative politics, ontological theorising has often taken precedence over an analysis of the material conditions of democratic societies.[4]

Council democracy is a project of deepening democracy which includes the decentralisation of the state, democratisation of the economy and solidarity with similar international struggles for self-government. Council democrats view capitalist market relations as having to be not only *tamed*, but *transformed* in a manner which alters the underlying relationship between capital and labour and eliminates capitalists' controlling power over workers and the state. The aim of this book is to place the idea of council democracy in dialogue with contemporary democratic theory in order to interrogate the lessons that could be learned and resources that could be gained for strengthening democracy against the threat of capitalist market relations. Although contributors to this volume differ in their proposals for the principles, strategies and design of democratic institutions, they all seek to deepen democratic forms of governance and extend these to broader spheres of the economy and society.

In the wake of the chaos and calamity of the First World War, workers and soldiers across Europe organised into democratic councils in order to challenge existing social hierarchies and strive towards self-government and workers' control over production. The European council movements arose with little planning or foresight through the spontaneous organisational tendencies of workers in opposition to capitalist alienation, political domination and bureaucratic control. The programme of the council movements was for democracy, social reforms, pacifism, the socialisation of the economy and a transformation of the hierarchical systems that oppressed them. Council democrats strived for a deepening of democracy in existing political institutions and an extension of democratic principles throughout society including to workplaces and other economic institutions. They sought to defend important political rights embedded in a democratic republic, while furthering a programme of democratisation through the socialisation of the economy and the introduction of democratic control mechanisms into authoritarian institutions.

Inspired by the Paris Commune and the councils formed during the 1905 Russian Revolution, the council movements of the interwar period were the most impressive of a number of attempts at instituting workers' control over economic institutions throughout the twentieth century.[5] The councils experienced a rapid rise and dramatic fall with most of the energy and mass support behind the movements dissipated by 1920. In Russia, soviets arose and assumed de facto power alongside the Provisional Government in March 1917 during a period of dual power before the October Revolution. Workers' councils also emerged across Germany during November 1918, following a sailors' mutiny at Kiel, which led to the abdication of the Kaiser and a political struggle over the future form of the German state. A number of short-lived council republics were also established in Bavaria, Austria and Hungary in addition to workers' councils arising in Italy and the United Kingdom. While these council experiments were brief, they achieved remarkable lasting successes, including contributing to ending the First World War, bringing down the Russian and German monarchies, introducing the eight-hour workday and instituting women's suffrage in Germany.[6]

The classic image of council democracy consisted of a federal structure of councils that would exercise political and economic functions with a socialist system of co-operative production. The central institutional features of the council system were joint executive and legislative powers, a federal structure of local and regional councils leading to a national council and recallable delegates operating under imperative mandate.[7] However, as the councils developed during a period of revolution and crisis, there was much debate over their proper role and relation to existing institutions such as unions, parties and the state. In particular, there was a critical ambiguity concerning whether the councils would exist alongside, transform or replace state apparatuses.[8] The more radical elements of the movement were inclined to view the councils as complete alternatives to state institutions, while more moderate factions tended to conceptualise ways the existing state could be democratised and transformed.

While there was significant disagreement between council democrats, they were united by the underlying position that socialism could only be achieved through a deepening and extension of democracy into broader spheres of society. Rather than rejecting democracy as a bourgeois sham or advocating for a top-down legislation of socialism from above, council democrats sought to create a democratic socialist society based on participatory councils integrated into a federal structure of self-government and economic self-management. This started with a dissolution of the army and police and their replacement by a people's militia, the replacement of state bureaucrats by elected officials, and the institution of workers' management of factories. In practice, the council movements attempted to transform oppressive institutions and enact wide-reaching democratic reforms. This involved collective mobilisation to develop a countervailing power against existing authority structures. They realised that to implement thoroughgoing processes of democratisation they would require significant resources, organisation and ideological development in addition to strong support from the general population. Their underlying strategy was to extend democratic principles from the political sphere to other domains of society where democracy-resistant institutions and forces remained embedded, including the army, government bureaucracy and workplace.

Partly as a result of their short and contentious existence, the political experiences of the council movements have been inadequately incorporated into the history of political thought. They have fallen between the cracks of the interpretive frameworks of orthodox Marxism and liberalism and been misunderstood as either a form of top-down social democracy or council dictatorship. On the one hand, the council movements were disregarded by many German social democrats as a period of uncertainty and chaos before the establishment of liberal institutions and the Weimer Republic.[9] The councils were also misunderstood in the former Soviet Union because they were taken over and incorporated within one-party Bolshevik rule. Political theory has failed to acknowledge what is original and distinctive about council democracy and to take stock of the valuable contribution participants in the council movements have made to political thought and practice.

This volume explores different aspects of a discontinuous tradition I have called council democracy on account of its theorists' commitments to socialism, democracy and some role for workers' councils, either in a period of transformation or as organs of a future democratic socialist polity. It draws upon the practices and writings of council communists, social democrats, libertarian socialists, anarcho-syndicalists and radical liberals who were critical of the domination and exploitation of both top-down state socialism and liberal democracy. Many would have positioned themselves as internal critics of communism, while some sought to push social democracy or liberalism to their emancipatory horizons. In this council democracy tradition one could count Rosa Luxemburg, Richard Müller, Ernst Däumig, Anton Pannekoek, Otto Rühle, Herman Gorter, Max Adler, Otto Bauer, Sylvia Pankhurst, Karl Korsch and Antonio Gramsci, among others. By no means did these theorists agree on a set of doctrines, but they were informed by shared animating concerns and were similarly placed in their general outlook on the limitations and possibilities of radical politics. The political experience of workers' councils continued to exercise an influence over later theorists of the twentieth century and played a key role in the development of the political thought of Hannah Arendt, Claude Lefort, Cornelius Castoriadis, Miguel Abensour, C. B. Macpherson and members of the Frankfurt School.

The examination of council democracy as a set of principles and strategies of democratic socialist reform provides new conceptual insight into our understanding of democracy. Council democrats contested the institutional structure of liberal democracies, drawing attention to the insufficiencies of national elections for holding elites to account, maintaining substantive equality and ensuring widespread participation. The presentation of the striking differences between council democracy and current forms of democratic politics reveals our troubling distance from a more substantive vision of democracy. Drawing from debates and events at an important historical juncture before the dominance of current forms of liberal democracy opens up a broader horizon of our political imagination and provides an expanded scope of the possibilities for transformation. While contributors to this volume adopt a variety of political positions, many share the conviction that the council movements could provide a germ and catalyst that inspires theorisation of new institutional forms and practices for democratic self-government in the present.

This collection also reveals the subterranean influence of the experience of the council movements on the history of political thought. Although the history of the councils has been a neglected area within political theory, the model of a council democracy remains an important touchstone for a variety of emancipatory theoretical projects.[10] A return to the council tradition also opens new pathways to the interpretation of thinkers on the margins of the Marxist, socialist and anarchist canons – thinkers whose work has been disregarded or is difficult to classify within existing theoretical frameworks. The volume also seeks to cast light on the complex interrelationship between these traditions and challenge conventional accounts of their antagonistic relationship. In the process, it hopes to engender fresh reflection on the necessary conditions of a democratic socialist polity and effective strategies of political transformation.

Liberal democratic institutions face mounting challenges from technocratic and elitist forms of rule on the one hand, and authoritarianism and exclusionary forms of populism on the other. Citizens are increasingly sceptical not simply of particular political parties and governments, but of the system of parliamentary democracy itself.[11] In this climate, it is instructive to turn to past examples of how political collectives organised to deepen and extend democracy and struggle against the private power of wealthy elites and corporations. Engaging with the historical practices of the council movements enables political theory to examine a contextualised account of the problematic influence of capitalism and the modern state in democratic societies.[12] The return to public assemblies and direct democratic methods in the wave of the global "squares movements" since 2011 has rejuvenated interest in libertarian socialist and council thought.[13] Despite their significant differences from the early-twentieth-century council movements, political protest movements such as Occupy Wall Street and the Spanish and Greek *indignados* have used general assemblies and spokes councils to organise and co-ordinate their actions, thus potentially reawakening forms of council organisation and action. Following the hundredth anniversary of the emergence of council movements, contributors to this volume argue for a revised understanding of the councils' historical role and a new appreciation of their contemporary significance.

Theorising the Councils

Difficulty arises in attempts to theorise the council form due to the lack of agreement within the council movements over the councils' proper tasks and structure. Even in the Dutch and German council communist tradition of the 1920s, theorists adopted a wide range of positions on the role of the councils and their relationship to trade unions, political parties and parliaments. Nevertheless, certain political problems and tendencies arise that assist in mapping the major theoretical elements of council democracy.

The most important feature of the councils, and that which distinguishes them most profoundly from other movements and institutions, is their attempt to overcome the division between the political and the economic by instituting workers' control over the production process.[14] All council theorists shared a desire to extend democratic principles of accountability and control beyond the political state to broader spheres of social life, including workplaces and major economic institutions. Council theorists argued that private property and parliamentarianism enabled the bourgeoisie to dominate society by granting formal political equalities to all citizens, but failing to address material inequalities in ownership and control over economic resources.

Council theorists challenged liberalism's naturalised view of the economic sphere as a private realm of exchange between free agents and highlighted the pervasive structural inequalities that existed between workers and capitalists. Support for this view can be located in Marx's criticisms of liberal democracy in "On the Jewish Question."[15] Here, Marx argued that liberal democracy implicitly supported exploitation and domination due to the private ownership of the means of production and the vastly unequal distribution of resources. By leaving relations of subordination and domination in the economic sphere intact, Marx argued that liberal democracy failed to achieve a more complete social emancipation that would institute workers' self-management over production. Drawing on Marx's later insight that the underlying source of class antagonisms was the exploitation of labour by capitalists, council democrats called for a reorganisation of the fundamental relation between capital and labour such that the very need for a separate political state to rule over civil society would disappear. Many council democrats were inspired by the vision of the Paris Commune, theorised by Marx in "The Civil War in France" as "the political form at last discovered for the emancipation of labour."[16] One of the major differences between this view and a Leninist model of economic production was that the former entailed bottom-up workers' control over individual workplaces integrated into a broader system of a rationally planned economy and a self-determining democratic society.

Council theorists differed, however, on how this would be achieved in practice. The problem, as formulated by the German council democrats, was how to socialise the economy in a manner which avoided two equally problematic outcomes. At one end of the spectrum, Leninist versions of state socialism seemed to lead to a "bureaucratic despotism," since ownership of the means of production passed exclusively into the hands of state officials. At the other end, if the exclusive ownership of factories passed to workers, as in the syndicalist model, then non-workers and the rest of society would be denied an equal say in social production. Call this the socialisation dilemma. Differences existed within the council movements over the most effective strategies and the proper institutional framework to solve this problem.

According to the "pure council system" of Ernst Däumig and Richard Müller, councils should be organised in a pyramidal structure of local, regional and national councils.[17] The system had a central council at its apex beneath which stood parallel economic and political structures: the economic councils were elected in workplaces, and the political councils in territorial constituencies. Lower-level councils in both structures were elected directly and upper councils were composed of delegates elected from the lower councils. Workplaces would be placed under joint control of a workplace council and regional council to allow for more effective co-ordination across the system and a balancing of interests between individual enterprises and the needs of society as a whole. The model sought to ensure that co-ordination and mediation existed between the councils. It is notable for its attempt to chart a middle path between the federalism of anarcho-syndicalism and the centralisation of models of Leninism and social democracy.[18] It is unclear in this basic sketch what the precise distinction would be between political and economic issues or how disputes would be resolved between different levels of the council system. The model has been criticised for its overly schematic design and for its mixture of territorial and workplace councils.[19] Pannekoek, for example, was critical of all attempts to organise councils according to territorial units, which he considered as "artificial groupings" distinct from the organic development of workplace councils.[20]

Another example of an attempt to solve the socialisation dilemma was offered by Karl Korsch, who proposed a model in which capitalist ownership would be eliminated and three different types of council would have an equal say in determining production. He considered that certain controls over management and production should be exercised at the level of the individual factory, but that factory-level self-determination should be integrated with consumer-group councils to represent the interests of consumers and of representatives of the state (a "council of councils") to adopt the perspective of society as a whole.[21] This model sought to balance the needs of workers to exercise self-determination in their workplace with the interests of the community in co-ordinating production between individual units and across industries. Regardless of the final institutional plan, a majority of workers within the council movements were in favour of increasing workers' control over workplaces and of socialising most industries. In Germany, for example, the national congress of councils voted unanimously for the government to implement immediate plans for socialisation.[22]

A second and related aspect of council democracy was how council institutions would relate to existing state apparatuses. For the radical theorists, namely the Spartacus League, Revolutionary Shop Stewards and the left wing of the Independent Social Democrats (USPD), council democracy aimed to replace rather than supplement a liberal parliament. This can be differentiated from the position of council delegates from the Social Democratic Party (SPD), who believed existing institutions could be transformed in order to implement socialist policies.[23] For the more radical theorists, there were three main grounds for claiming a qualitative difference between the proletarian character of council institutions and bourgeois parliamentary institutions. First, council institutions exercised legislative and executive functions and were considered a "working institution" that would directly create and administer laws. Pannekoek argued that this format would prevent the development of career politicians and bureaucrats because there would be no need for political parties or large, permanent, unelected bureaucracies.[24] Second, delegates were directly elected from workplaces and could be immediately recalled if they did not follow the directions of workers. This was thought to prevent the rise of a bureaucratic class. Third, they were considered to be class-specific organs that would represent the interests of workers. We have good reason to doubt whether councils would have been able to overcome the problems of bureaucracy and political separation identified in council theorists' criticisms of liberal institutions. In practice, wherever councils took on a large amount of political and administrative tasks the executive organs of these councils tended to undertake most of the work with only occasional oversight from the main council bodies.[25]

Proposals also existed to combine a parliament with councils in various ways. Karl Kautsky believed that the question of "national assembly or council system?" need not be framed as an either/or issue. Kautsky proposed integrating a system of councils with a national parliament. The workers' councils would represent workers' interests and act as a pressure from below on elected representatives to ensure the implementation of socialist policies. Heinrich Laufenburg believed that a parliament could be integrated within a broader council system, although under the sovereign authority of workers' and soldiers' councils.[26] Claude Lefort would later read into the Hungarian Revolution of 1956 plans to integrate a system of workers' councils with a parliament and workers' unions to represent individual workers' interests. Various other propositions existed within the council movements to combine different aspects of these systems. Proposals to draw elements from the council system, while retaining key aspects of a representative government, legal system and constitutional state, have proved more influential among contemporary theorists inspired by the council tradition.

A third question concerned the proper role of the councils and whether they could be considered temporary organs of revolutionary struggle, embryonic institutions of a post-capitalist society or an initial stage in a longer process of revolutionary transformation. While the Bolsheviks (post-October Revolution) and SPD considered the councils as temporary organs to be replaced by one-party rule or a centralised social democratic state, council democrats tended to view the councils as ideal organs of revolutionary struggle that would play some role as more permanent institutions in a post-capitalist society. A "structure versus process" divide can be discerned in the literature. On the one hand, those who believed the councils contained an essentially proletarian structure, such as Däumig and Müller, conceived of them as the institutional basis of a post-capitalist polity. For these theorists, the councils were governing institutions that should be directly democratic, enable workers to participate in decision-making and exercise control over major industries in a rationally planned economy. On the other hand, for Karl Korsch the essential aspect of the councils lay not in any determinate institutional form, but in the openness of the councils to transformation and their ability to begin a process of institutional development beyond the confines of the state towards new experiments in organising social production.[27] Theorists such as Pannekoek and Castoriadis occupied a middle ground, at times advocating for the importance of specific features of the councils as genuinely proletarian in character, while also supporting the importance of the councils as an open form capable of transformation and development. While there is no necessary opposition between the two poles, it does indicate genuine differences in why theorists valorised the councils.

Fourth, council theorists also claimed that the councils enacted a fundamentally different conception of representation than that practised within parliamentary democracy. Council theorists were generally suspicious of representation and desired for people to take direct action within their spheres of competence. In circumstances where representatives were logistically necessary, council theorists argued they should remain in constant contact with their electors and be subject to immediate recall. A major theme of political writing on the councils is the proletarian character of directly elected delegates subject to immediate recall. Theorists from Marx to Müller and Pannekoek to Castoriadis all viewed recallable delegates elected by workers from within their factory organisations as a superior form of representation to parliamentary elections.[28] First, the delegate model was believed to enable a more direct expression of the interests of workers due to the delegates' organic connection to workers within their factory. Second, delegates were viewed as less likely to form a separate class that could potentially become distant from and dominate those who elected them. In this regard, the feature of immediate recall provided an extra measure of accountability, which was occasionally exercised, for example, when Russian delegates voted for a "Liberty Loan" to assist the Provisional Government to continue the war.[29] The principle of delegation was also commonly reported to have arisen naturally or spontaneously from workers' organisations without much need for discussion. As Anderson notes, "no one ever questioned the principle that delegates to the Central Councils should be revocable, at all times. The principle became an immediate reality."[30] According to Appel's account of the formation of councils, the workers viewed the delegation model as "a means of control from the bottom up."[31]

Although this system was often touted as a more direct form of democracy and unmediated expression of the will of the people, as delegates were selected to sit on progressively higher levels of councils, ordinary participants in the council movements began to exercise only an indirect influence over the decisions of higher council delegates. The reality of many council systems during their brief existence was that executive organs gradually took on more power and responsibility, although lower councils still retained a right of recall. Their theory of delegation remains vulnerable to long-standing criticisms of delegation theories of representation such as the difficulties of representing a plurality of interests and in engaging in meaningful deliberative processes of transformation.

Fifth, council democracy sought to reconcile two fundamentally distinct principles: workers' control over production, and a universal conception of democracy. Democracy aims to realise certain goals for all citizens such as equality under the law, voting equality and equal rights of participation.[32] As organisations representing the interests of workers, the council movement embodied the working-class struggle against the oppression of capitalists; but as a movement aiming to put an end to capitalist relations of exploitation and domination, council delegates sought to create a free and equal order in which all individuals could flourish as part of a self-determining society. In Marx's famous formula, the proletariat was a class with a "universal character" whose emancipation would put an end to class-based systems of oppression, thus liberating all those who did not live off the exploitation of the labour of others.[33] However, in practice, the council movements struggled to balance the tension between these sometimes competing principles, which led to different responses to the problem of democratic inclusion, transitional political strategies and questions of membership of the councils.

One example of this dilemma was the debate over whether "workers" or "the people" was a more appropriate political subject of emancipation. Delegates within the SPD tended towards more universalist formulations, drawing from the Erfurt Program to affirm that they opposed "all forms of exploitation and oppression, whether it is directed at a class, a party, a gender, or a race."[34] In a *Vorwärts* article, Friedrich Stampfer argued that a government must be elected by a broader section of the population than simply the workers and soldiers, which necessitated calling a constituent national assembly as soon as possible.[35] Even Karl Kautsky argued that the councils suffered from serious limitations of democratic inclusion, for it was not simply the bourgeoisie who were potentially excluded from the councils but any individual who was not actively engaged in paid labour in a workplace.[36] While radical council delegates agreed that white-collar workers and members of the intelligentsia could rightly form councils, their theorising and actions led to the exclusion of women engaged in unpaid reproductive labour, the unemployed, peasants and even certain workers outside of major industrial centres. Questions were raised about this problem in various meetings of councils, but no consensus was ever reached about how to resolve these issues.[37]

If tensions did exist between workerist and universalist aspirations of the councils, there were theorists prepared to resolve these primarily in favour of workers to ensure the proletarian character of new institutions. By council democracy, Pannekoek understood "workers power to the exclusion of the other classes."[38] On balance, Pannekoek considered that the necessity of establishing workers' control over production to ensure economic justice trumped the democratic principle of universality and democratic inclusion:

> If it is true that each person has a natural right to participate in politics, it is no less true that the whole world has a natural right to live and not to die from hunger. And, if to assure the latter, the former must be curtailed, then no one should feel that their democratic sensibilities have been violated.[39]

For Pannekoek, "whoever does not work as a member of a production group is automatically barred from the possibility of being part of the decision-making process."[40] Richard Müller supported both manual and intellectual workers in council institutions, but scoffed at the idea that members of the ruling classes should be allowed to form their own representative councils.[41] Rosa Luxemburg, however, was more sensitive to questions of exclusion and believed in the importance of broad alliances across oppressed classes. For Luxemburg, "Social Democracy has always contended that it represents not only the class interests of the proletariat but also the progressive aspirations of the whole of contemporary society. It represents the interests of all who are oppressed by bourgeois domination."[42] While no less supportive of the working-class character of the revolution than other council theorists, Luxemburg was more attentive to the universal demands of democratic socialist politics.

Finally, there were significant limitations to certain aspects of the council movements' vision of politics. For many council theorists, the overcoming of exploitative capitalist relations of production was the primary problem of politics. This led to difficulties in conceptualising how power operated along different axes such as gender, race and identity. It obscured the operation of other problematic social hierarchies, even ones that existed within their own movements. This narrow vision of the scope of political conflict then contributed to their overly optimistic view of the management of conflict in a post-capitalist society. Due to their focus on capitalism as the principal foe to be overcome, they tended to downplay the possibility of the persistence of significant political conflict after the revolution. Their often utopian picture of post-revolutionary society was supported by an underlying assumption of a homogeneity of values and interests of workers. They underestimated the extent to which workers could still have deep disagreement both on ideological matters and on basic practical problems of how society should be organised. Their theorising tended to rely on the utopian desire for a fundamental transformation of human nature and sociability through a long process of cultural and ideological development. From our vantage point, it is apparent that the council movements were misguided in their belief that political conflict would be significantly curtailed in a post-capitalist society. As a result, there is little attention to the social institutions that would create and enforce laws (if any) or how conflict between individuals or councils would be managed. One is struck by the radical underdetermination of the institutional dimensions of the council literature on this point. The neglect of theorising processes that would protect civil liberties and the absence of an independent judiciary in most proposed council systems raises questions about the capacity of these systems to safeguard basic civil liberties of minority and dissident groups.

One possible objection to my characterisation of the tradition of council democracy is that I have made reformists out of revolutionaries and obscured certain council communists' desires to abolish capitalism, eliminate class divisions and usher in a completely emancipated society. Within the council movements there were certainly radical elements who held such objectives, but council delegates supported a wide variety of competing principles and aspirations. While I believe we should emphasise the council movements' transformative potential, this need not imply fixed ideas about how democratic politics should intervene in economic relations or a schematic design for the final form of a future democratic socialist society. I do not believe the most useful and important aspects of council theory and practice lie in the more utopian demands for a complete transformation of human beings and society. Instead, we should seek to learn from their attentiveness to the corrosive effects of capitalism and inequalities in power, and their focus on active citizenship and widespread mobilisation as a pathway to democratic reform.

The Councils and Democratic Theory

While democratic theory has drawn extensively from other historical periods such as ancient Rome, ancient Greece, the Italian Renaissance and revolutionary France and America, the European council movements of the interwar period have failed to gain canonical status within the democratic theory literature. Leading democratic theorist, John Dryzek, considered council democracy a "dead duck" with few theorists or followers.[43] At the edges of the discipline, certain theorists have begun to return to the related concepts of economic democracy and workplace democracy, popularised in the 1980s by Robert Dahl, among others.[44] Recent historical scholarship has also provided new translations of primary sources on the councils, analysis of key historical actors and a compelling account of the continuity of attempts to develop workers' councils.[45] However, no existing work connects this historical scholarship with current debates in democratic theory or explores the implications of the political struggles of the councils for contemporary democratic regimes. This introduction provides a preliminary theoretical sketch of council democracy's relationship with the major strands of democratic theory.

Democratic theory has traditionally been concerned with the arrangement of political institutions and has viewed economic relations as related to but outside of its central considerations. The democratic organisation of workplaces and economic institutions has been examined by a number of theorists, but as the majority of mainstream democratic theory is liberal, it accepts liberalism's defence of the economic sphere as a private realm of exchange that need not be organised along similar principles to the political sphere. Another major barrier to further engagement with the council movements has been the mischaracterisation of the councils by some of their most prominent commentators. John Medearis has demonstrated that the legacy of the councils within political theory has been heavily biased by the interpretations of figures such as Lenin, Arendt and Schumpeter.[46] After originally considering the councils as temporary organs of insurrection, Lenin altered his view in 1917 – following the councils' rise in power – to support the councils as the emergence of "a state of the type of the Paris Commune," only to change his perspective once again – after the October Revolution – to subordinate the councils to the will of the Bolshevik Party.[47] The transformation of workers' councils from democratic organs into administrative apparatuses of a communist state in the Russian Revolution has created strong associations of the council movements with Bolshevik one-party rule, leading to difficulties disambiguating council theory from state socialism and Leninism. The dominant, although disputed, interpretation of historians sympathetic to the council movements is that Lenin adopted a cynical strategy of supporting the councils until the Bolshevik Party gained power, after which he moved to curtail their democratic agency and autonomy.[48] Furthermore, Lenin's criticisms of left-wing and council communists in "Left-Wing Communism: An Infantile Disorder" contributed to the neglect of these figures within Leninist and Trotskyist circles and ensured council theory a heretical status within orthodox Marxism.[49]

Within democratic theory, Hannah Arendt is perhaps the most influential supporter of council democracy and one of the principal sources of transmission of the council tradition. Numerous commentators have pointed out the distortions of Arendt's representation of the council movements, including her disregard for their socialist ideology and their concern for the democratisation of the economy.[50] For Arendt, the councils presented an alternative to the party system and representative democracy as institutionalised spaces for citizen participation, deliberation and action. Arendt's mythologised historiography of the councils placed workers' councils alongside Jefferson's sketches of a ward system, New England town-hall meetings, revolutionary societies and other instances of grass-roots democracy in a discontinuous tradition stretching back to the French Revolution. Her interpretation of the councils through her division between "the political" and "the social" has led to misunderstandings and lost opportunities – both for her and her interpreters – which has prevented democratic theorists' engagement with the tradition of the council movements.[51]

Minimal Democracy

In relation to the major current conceptions of democracy, council democracy is most manifestly opposed to minimal or elitist versions of democratic theory espoused by theorists such as Joseph Schumpeter and Adam Przeworski.[52] The demanding vision of council theorists of an active and self-managed society stands in stark contrast to the minimal requirements of a competitive struggle between elites for votes, which liberal minimal theorists contended was best able to render elites accountable and uphold civil liberties. For council theorists, the normative value of democracy was based on the ideals of substantive political equality, self-government and all citizens participating in self-determining institutions. Council theorists were critical of forms of politics based on the actions of elites and the passivity of ordinary citizens as they believed this robbed citizens of the capacity to determine their own existence and to defend their interests. Council democracy relies on a fundamentally different appreciation of human beings' capacities, and their limits, as political actors. Unlike elite theorists, council democrats did not believe that the basic political psychology of voters rendered them unable to make sound political judgements. They were more optimistic with regard to the capacities of ordinary citizens and the possibility of them adapting to a more active and engaged political culture. Pannekoek believed this would require that citizens "see themselves changed into new men with new habits, into men who feel closely united with their comrades as integral parts of a body animated by one and the same will."[53]

On one point, however, council theorists agreed with Schumpeter and other so-called "realist" democratic theorists. They too acknowledged that at its basis, politics was structured by a struggle for power. In a report by the Executive Council of the Workers' and Soldiers' Councils of Great Berlin, Richard Müller reminded delegates that "[a]ll political questions remain, in the end, questions of power."[54] In the determination of political strategies, Pannekoek believed that consideration should come back to a single question: "here is the criterion for every form of action, for tactics and methods of fight, for forms of organisation: do they enhance the power of the workers?"[55] Central to the council movements' conception of politics was that success lay in a realistic assessment of how a movement could effectively develop and deploy political power. An appreciation of their attentiveness to the underlying distribution of power between social groups reveals an under-acknowledged "realist" side of their political thought, in spite of their reputation for utopian thinking.

Participatory Democracy

Overall, the council movements' ideas resonate most clearly with the concerns of participatory democrats such as Carole Pateman and Benjamin Barber.[56] Participatory democracy arose in the 1960s on the back of the student movements and the emergence of the New Left in Europe and North America. As democratic and libertarian critics of state socialism, council democrats prefigure participatory democracy's critiques of bureaucracy, representative democracy and the separation of leaders from the masses, in addition to their emphasis on mass participation, cultural transformation and education. Both theories give citizens a central role in decision-making and promote self-determination and active citizenship, inspired by earlier civic republican ideals of self-rule and civic virtue. Participatory democracy rejuvenated these basic themes of council democracy and diversified its concerns through a theoretical extension from class struggle to multiple forms of oppression and a greater emphasis on new social movements, student radicalism and Third World liberation movements.

Participatory democrats were dissatisfied with the lack of opportunities for participation in representative democracy and with the broad array of undemocratic authority structures that controlled citizens' lives. The project for a participatory society, shared by participatory and council democrats, is an attempt to both democratise the state but also to extend participatory democratic mechanisms to other structures of authority within society. Early-twentieth-century socialists sought to defend the gains of a democratic republic as "the indispensable political basis of the new commonwealth" and "consistently develop it in all directions."[57] Council theorists advocated a project of the democratisation of authority structures including the bureaucracy, civil service, army, workplace and other social institutions. They also considered that this project would require "a dedicated attempt to make and keep the German people politically active" through education and development so they would "get used to self-management instead of governance."[58] Their version of bottom-up socialism was based on a vision of active citizens in a participatory society.

The workplace is a crucial institution for both theories, but here significant differences emerge in terms of their political analyses and normative ideals. Pateman draws on a variety of sources – including Mill, Rousseau, G. D. H. Cole's theory of guild socialism and the practical experiments of workers' self-management in Yugoslavia – in order to demonstrate the viability of participatory democracy with a particular emphasis on the workplace as a primary site of socialisation and development. Yet the priority is the moral transformation of individuals who take part in co-operative forms of industrial organisation. For Pateman, "the major function of participation in the theory of participatory democracy is therefore an educative one."[59] The workplace is an institution in which individuals could be educated, "including both the psychological aspect and the gaining of practice in democratic skills and procedures," to foster an active citizenry and democratic culture.[60]

Council democracy offers two major points of contrast. First, for council democrats, the priority is not simply on altering workplace hierarchies for the benefit of an individual's political education, but on challenging structures of power and changing the underlying dynamic between capital and labour. This more transformative aspect of the council democracy programme falls out of the purview of most participatory democrats.[61] Second, council democrats wish to intervene at the level of the individual workplace to institute worker self-management, but also at the level of the economy as a whole to place democratic controls over the production and distribution of goods. Council democracy seeks to integrate self-managed workplaces into a broader framework of economic democracy in which productive assets would be placed under democratic control. Participatory democracy lacks an adequate conception of the barriers that capitalist relations of production place in the way of democratic reforms, which leaves it without theoretical resources to address forms of economic domination. Living in a more unequal world, the council movements were more attuned to the concentration of private power and the political and economic domination arising within capitalist systems. They contended that the conditions of a truly participatory society required the transformation of state institutions and the reorganisation of the underlying economic relations between capitalists and workers.

Radical Democracy

Council democracy stands in an ambiguous relation with regard to the various radical approaches to democracy. On the surface, radical democracy's project of questioning and seeking to change the fundamental nature of liberal democracy in more emancipatory and egalitarian directions appears aligned with the ambitions of council democrats. However, there are also significant differences in terms of ontological presuppositions, theoretical framework and political programme which set them apart. Radical democracy is a broad category that includes a range of theorists from agonistic pluralists (Mouffe, Honig),[62] radical liberals (Connolly, Wolin)[63] to post-Marxists (Laclau, Rancière),[64] and can even include those who do not necessarily identify with the name and are perhaps better described as some form of communists or Marxists (Žižek, Badiou, Negri and Hardt).[65] Typically, radical approaches to democracy are characterised by their attention to fundamental differences and divisions within the body politic, the ineliminable character of contestation and the pursuit of an open and responsive political order. They are strongly influenced by various post-structuralist theories of language, identity and representation and often stake out their differences with competing theories at an ontological level.[66] Significant variations exist between radical democratic theory in terms of ontological commitments (abundance/lack; transcendence/immanence) and different modalities of political change (reform, renewal, reactivation, revolution).[67]

On one level, radical democracy provides a welcome critique of forms of closure and exclusion that pervade political theory, including that of council democracy. Their attention to radical differences and their openness to sites of political contestation and emerging forms of subjectivity offers a necessary antidote to the essentialism, teleology and economic determinism of certain orthodox approaches to Marxism. But while radical theorists offer important lessons on uncovering contingency, undecidability and pluralism, council democrats provide a stronger programme of political organisation and democratic transformation. Council theory was mostly written from the perspective of theorists organically connected to powerful workers' movements with a view to how this theory could be applied to practical questions of political struggle.[68] As a result, it has a more practical orientation and immediate material concerns, focusing on how movements should organise, develop their power and overcome concrete obstacles through the deployment of effective strategy. In contrast, radical democratic theory often unfolds at an abstract ontological level with unclear payoffs in terms of concrete commitments and practical political strategy. Supplementing radical democratic theory with insights from the council democratic literature offers an opportunity not simply to acknowledge agonism and remain open to difference, but to construct a positive political programme and engage with the central institutions of society in order to democratise and transform them.[69]

Certain varieties of radical democratic theory, most notably those of Wolin and Rancière, but also Abensour, Tully and Negri, contain an unwarranted anti-institutional bias which inhibits their capacity to effect long-term political change. These radical democrats tend to focus on moments of rupture and transgression, which leads to a vision of politics as insurrectionary, episodic and essentially non-institutionalisable. This tragic view displaces our gaze from contestation over central political and economic institutions to the margins of political life in search of momentary political experiences that remain subterranean in mass bureaucratic societies. Often, such a theory results in a binary and Manichaean schema involving a true form of politics pitted against that which passes for politics in contemporary quasi-oligarchic political structures (i.e. politics/the police, the political/politics, insurgent democracy/the State, revolution/constitutionalism, constituent power/constitutional politics, the multitude/Empire etc.). However, this unwarranted rejection of institutions as important sites of political struggle forecloses the possibility of challenging institutional power and embedding emancipatory logics in institutions for lasting political change.

Council democrats recognised the importance of institutions as possible sites of emancipation and developed a more useful and convincing account of the dynamics of institutional struggle. They were acutely aware of the essential role the state, bureaucracy, army, media and industry played in protecting and enhancing the power of the bourgeoisie. They targeted these institutions through an interventionist and transformative approach, which sought to challenge the concentration of private power and extend democratic principles of accountability and citizen control into democracy-resistant institutions from which citizens' voices had been excluded. Rather than circumventing institutions that make collective decisions, council democrats sought to reclaim and democratise them, utilising their strategic position as vehicles for liberation. In response to the problem of the bureaucratisation of institutions of power and the growth of an inevitable divide between institutions and citizens, council democrats proposed more strict democratic mechanisms of accountability such as the election of all public officials, the revocability of delegates, a workers' wage paid to all officials and the decentralisation of decision-making to local bodies. They also insisted that institutions should have strong connections to an active and mobilised citizenry capable of patrolling them and holding them accountable. In this way, council democrats direct attention back to the central issues of politics and provide missing elements of a coherent political programme.

Agonistic Democracy

Within the broad tradition of radical democracy, there are other theorists, such as Chantal Mouffe and Bonnie Honig, who adopt an agonistic conception of democracy, which, contrary to the anti-institutional theorists, emphasises the importance of engaging with institutions. Mouffe advocates a Gramscian "war of position" within institutions through the construction of a counter-hegemonic project via the creation of a democratic "chain of equivalence" between different struggles leading to the creation of a new democratic collective will. Mouffe's radical democratic project is perhaps the modality of political change closest to that of the council democrats, albeit with a stronger emphasis on liberal institutions, pluralism and an abandonment of "all hopes for a 'true democracy', a perfectly reconciled society, a perfect consensus."[70] Yet they would dispute her assumption of the sufficiency of a liberal democratic framework for this task. For Mouffe, the political principles of "liberty and equality for all," inherent within the liberal democratic tradition, should be radicalised and expanded.[71] Liberal democratic societies already view these as morally applicable principles; they simply need to be put more robustly into practice.

What is missing from her position is a sustained analysis of the significant barriers capitalist relations of production pose to such democratic transformations. The problem is not simply that liberal democratic societies do not act on their principles, but that these political principles exist alongside even more influential economic principles of competition, privatisation and accumulation, which, due precisely to the institutional framework of liberal democracy, are able to subvert and erode democratic politics. While at certain points in history the tensions between capitalism and democracy were moderated by the compromises of the welfare state, more recently, neoliberal variations of capitalism have hollowed out democracy while retaining its form. Mouffe underestimates the extent to which her project to "reinscribe socialist goals within the framework of a pluralist democracy" would require engagement with and radical transformation of existing institutions beyond the framework of liberal democracy through the socialisation of the economy.[72] To be sure, the council democrats are not very far from Mouffe's own project. But she tends to bracket out material concerns and her theorising of differences lacks a coherent account of how capitalist relations of production could be effectively transformed within liberal democracy. In her 2013 work, *Agonistics*, Mouffe has very little to say about transforming capitalist relations, and instead is concerned with criticising neoliberal ideology and strengthening systems of representative democracy and alternative party politics.[73]

Deliberative Democracy

Since the deliberative turn in the 1990s, deliberative democracy has become not only the dominant approach in democratic theory, but, according to John Dryzek, "the most active area of political theory in its entirety."[74] Its focus, even in the most recent "systemic turn" of deliberative theory, is on ensuring the legitimacy of decision-making through authentic dialogue and debate.[75] Deliberative theorists cast deliberation as a potential source of rejuvenation of democracy and a panacea for the current separation of governments from their citizens.

Council democrats understand the importance of deliberation, but they would question whether it should be considered *the* perspective from which to interrogate democratic politics. Consider the challenges currently faced by democratic states: rising levels of economic inequalities, governments dominated by special interests and private lobby groups, a dismantling of the welfare state by powerful corporations on the advance, and supra-national governance structures run by unaccountable technocratic elites. It is difficult to see which of these problems could be adequately addressed through the establishment of a deliberative forum or a higher quality of debate in current discussions.

The council movements were confronted with more immediate problems relating to other non-deliberative parts of the political process. Moreover, it was the councils' emphasis on these aspects that are of importance for contemporary politics. For the councils, the most crucial task was mobilisation of opposition forces against the institutional hierarchies of the old regime. What gave the councils their decisive influence was not the sophistication or eloquence of their arguments but the legitimacy generated through the mobilisation of large segments of the population in support of a transformative democratic programme with the political power to enforce it. Democratic politics for the councils involved the ongoing challenge to hierarchies that continually threatened to reassert themselves. The challenge of restraining elites who threaten to dismantle democratic controls cannot be met by introducing greater levels of deliberation within democratic institutions. The framing of the central political questions in terms of reaching a mutually amenable agreement was a strategy of the elites to create parliamentary institutions that they could then dominate.

At certain points in the political process, citizens seeking "fair terms of cooperation" in which to "reason together" is an important goal, but so too are actions that achieve substantive results in implementing democratic forms of control.[76] A narrow focus on how decisions are made and how citizens communicate with each other risks missing what is, from a council democracy perspective, the substantive activity of politics, i.e. collective action that challenges consolidated hierarchies and equalises power between citizens.[77] Such issues can simply not be adequately addressed within the framework of procedural reforms to decision-making. An examination of the history of the councils provides a revealing example of the limitations of the deliberative perspective and the necessity of broadening the study of democratic practices to a variety of other approaches.

Overview of Chapters

In Chapter 2, Donny Gluckstein offers a historical overview of the development of councils in Russia and Europe following the First World War. He argues that soldiers and workers spontaneously developed councils during crises brought on by the breakdown of the old regimes and the awakening of hopes for political transformation. Although the councils first arose organically, their continued development was a result of conscious efforts of organised sections of the working class with decades of experience in political activity and organising. The councils developed in a similar manner in different countries, revealing a certain naturalness of this organisational form to political actors at the time. Gluckstein views these councils as potential alternatives to state power, as radical elements within the councils strived to assert council democracy as a new form of political organisation. Gluckstein's historical analysis sets the stage for later theoretical discussions.

In Chapter 3, Gaard Kets and James Muldoon analyse the political experiences of actors directly engaged in the council movements in the early days of the German Revolution. They examine the minutes of meetings of the Workers' and Soldiers' Council of Hamburg from November 1918 to March 1919 in order to shed light on the development of council theory during a formative stage of revolutionary activity. They explore the political tensions that existed within the councils through a historical reconstruction of key debates, which reveals a more complex picture of council communism than that which currently predominates. On the topics of democratic inclusion, the relationship of the councils with old institutions and the role of political parties and trade unions, no clear consensus emerged from within the councils as to the best strategy for the political movement. Decisions made by the councils often reflected pragmatic compromises and immediate responses to urgent problems rather than a stable and coherent council ideology.

The next section of the book turns to theoretical questions in the tradition of council democracy. In Chapter 4, Gabriel Wollner seeks to address two prominent complaints about the democratic deficits of capitalist economic relations through a modified theory of council democracy. The first complaint relates to the absence of democracy within the workplace and the lack of workers' control over their own workday and over the activities of their firm. The second complaint concerns the barriers that powerful economic actors place to implementing democratic decisions. Drawing from Karl Korsch's theory of "industrial autonomy," Wollner argues for a fundamental transformation in property rights towards a system in which different rights formerly exercised by capitalist owners would be distributed to workers and consumers in order to enhance the level of democratic control over the economic sphere. In this sense, council democracy would simultaneously work towards democratising the workplace and enhancing the power of democratic politics over economic actors.

Chapter 5 addresses the issue of how we might transition from current capitalist relations of production and consumption to a democratic association of producers based on workers' councils. Nicholas Vrousalis analyses two competing answers to the question of socialisation that have dominated since the Russian Revolution, and seeks to map out a third alternative which avoids the pitfalls of either extreme. On the one hand, statism associates socialisation with ownership of the means of production passing from private hands to exclusive control by the state and its agents. On the other hand, syndicalism associates socialisation with the workers taking exclusive ownership of the means of production. Vrousalis discusses a way out of this dilemma proposed by Karl Kautsky and then criticises it for the subordinate role workers' councils play in his proposals. Vrousalis argues for what he terms a "Madisonian" solution based on a workers' parliament, which overcomes the issues plaguing the statist and syndicalist alternatives.

Michael J. Thompson criticises a romantic tendency of the council tradition which proposes a radical anti-statist vision of politics based on an expressivist view of human nature. In Chapter 6, Thompson proposes that we replace this desire to abolish the state with a more mature position that seeks to expand the democratic potential of the modern state and extend the underlying principles of democracy into the economy. He defends a position of "council republicanism" which integrates workers' councils into the institutional framework of the modern constitutional state in order to promote a democratic socialist form of politics. It is only the centralised institutions of the modern state that enable the maximisation of the principle of non-domination in social relations and enhance the democratic control of social and economic activity. Council republicanism therefore promotes a more substantive vision of democratic politics than that provided by liberal democracy or pure theories of council democracy.

In Chapter 7, Christopher Holman analyses Castoriadis' engagement with the council tradition. Starting with Castoriadis' early theorisation of the councils within the context of his critique of bureaucratic management, Holman traces the influence of the council tradition into Castoriadis' later writings on creativity, autonomy and self-institution. While previous commentators have tended to isolate the influence of the councils to Castoriadis' early writings, Holman argues that the institutional form of the councils presents a concrete space for the expression of creative desire that is so essential to Castoriadis' later philosophical anthropology. Furthermore, Castoriadis' unique reinterpretation of the tradition seeks to emphasise the role of human creativity within the councils. For

Castoriadis, Holman claims, the councils are more than an attempt to rationally organise the economy according to some fixed political schema. Instead, the councils are the institutional means through which human beings can enact and affirm their own underlying autonomy and creativity.

Shmuel Lederman discusses in Chapter 8 the reinterpretation of the council tradition by Hannah Arendt. Beginning from Arendt's famous distinction between "the social" and "the political," Lederman uncovers a distortion of the council tradition in Arendt's work which sought to ignore or downplay the socialist tendencies that lay within it. Yet at the same time, Lederman argues that this distortion enables Arendt to contribute an original dimension to the tradition. For Arendt, the councils enabled citizens to speak and act together, which created a space for political freedom to emerge. Arendt's reinterpretation of the council tradition can be seen as a radical critique of liberal democracy due to the emphasis it places on direct participation and citizen empowerment.

Benjamin Ask Popp-Madsen returns in Chapter 9 to Claude Lefort's two different interpretations of the council tradition. Following the Hungarian Revolution of 1956, Lefort theorises the councils in a similar manner to Castoriadis and other prominent members of Socialism or Barbarism. However, in 1976 Lefort offers a very different portrait of the Hungarian councils as representing a self-limiting form of power which sought to distribute political and economic power across a parliament, councils and trade unions. Lefort's reformulation of the council tradition seeks to institutionalise conflict within a political regime in order to protect it against totalitarian tendencies. Popp-Madsen places this theory in the context of Lefort's writing on democracy as instituting an empty space of power and theories of a mixed regime. He argues that we should interpret this theory as an argument for a socialist democracy which can be differentiated from both the liberal democratic and radical democratic interpretations of Lefort's work.

John Medearis seeks to examine the history of workers' councils in order to advise on strategies of transforming contemporary institutions in the present. In Chapter 10, he locates a number of central principles of the council movements that guided their programme of economic democratisation. Yet, tracing some of the technological, economic and social transformations that have occurred over the last century, Medearis questions whether democratising the factory, or workplaces more generally, offers the most effective strategy for transforming the broader political economy. The factory, which occupied a crucial position in early-twentieth-century economic life, has now been superseded by other forms of organisation. The altered nature of such relations means that to draw the right lessons from the council movement would mean dramatically transforming their political strategy to suit contemporary circumstances.

In Chapter 11, David Ellerman offers a theoretical justification for a form of workplace democracy. He argues that a philosophical defence of workers' control of workplaces and the products of their labour is possible outside of the lineage of Marxist and communist theory. In place of the common theoretical tradition of the council movements, Ellerman turns to principles drawn from the abolitionist, democratic and feminist movements in order to construct a novel defence of self-managed workplaces.

In the concluding chapter of the volume, Dario Azzellini examines how the legacy of the council movements has been furthered in contemporary social movements. In particular, he turns to worker-recuperated companies (WRCs) and political collectives striving for local self-government. Workplace occupations became widespread in Argentina in the 2001 crisis and then spread to other South American countries. Practices then developed in Europe and North Africa, employing the principles of self-determination, co-operative production and direct action. Local self-administration through direct democracy was most prominently practised by the Zapatistas in Chiapas, Mexico, but in this chapter Azzellini focuses on more recent examples in Venezuela and Rojava, Kurdistan. He analyses how communities formed local councils and constructed political organisations that drew from different socialist and councilist currents of political thought. While the circumstances are very different from those faced by the council movements a century ago, Azzellini argues that the principles and tactics of some of these contemporary social movements can be considered in the same tradition of council democracy.

Contributors to this volume all seek to interrogate the tradition of council democracy from different historical and theoretical perspectives. On the hundredth anniversary of the formation of councils in Germany, Austria and Hungary, historical circumstances have considerably altered the conditions which first gave rise to the council form. The following chapters seek to provide answers to the question of the ongoing significance of the councils and how they should motivate and guide political actors in the present.

Notes

1 Martin Gilens and Benjamin I. Page, "Testing Theories of American Politics"; Wendy Brown, *Undoing the Demos*.
2 Andrew Arato and Jean Cohen, *Civil Society and Political Theory*.
3 David Ellerman, "The Workplace," 51; For theories of economic democracy, see Carole Pateman, *Participation and Democratic Theory*; Robert Dahl, *A Preface to Economic Democracy*; David Schweickart, *After Capitalism*; Joshua Cohen and Joel Rogers, *On Democracy*.
4 Lois McNay, *The Misguided Search for the Political*.
5 For other cases, see Immanuel Ness and Dario Azzellini (eds), *Ours to Master and to Own*.
6 See Ralf Hoffrogge, *Working-Class Politics in the German Revolution*.
7 For an overview, see ibid., 108–16.

8 This ambiguity reflected long-standing debates within Marxism about whether the state would need to be "smashed," "dissolved," "seized" or whether it would "wither away." See, for example, Lenin's discussion in "The State and Revolution."
9 Karl Dietrich Erdmann, "Die Geschichte der Weimarer Republik als Problem der Wissenschaft."
10 See, for example, the examination of the influence of the councils on the political theories of Castoriadis, Lefort and Arendt in this volume.
11 Roberto Stefan Foa and Yascha Mounk, "The Danger of Deconsolidation."
12 Jonathan Floyd and Marc Stears (eds), *Political Philosophy versus History?*
13 Alexandros Kioupkiolis and Giorgos Katsambekis (eds), *Radical Democracy and Collective Movements Today*.
14 See Alex Demirovic, "Council Democracy, or the End of the Political," in Dario Azzellini (ed.), *An Alternative Labour History*.
15 Karl Marx, "On the Jewish Question."
16 Karl Marx, "The Civil War in France."
17 Ernst Däumig and Richard Müller outlined their schematic ideas for a "pure council system" in the journal *Der Arbeiter Rat* (The Workers' Council) and other publications. Some of these writings were reprinted in Dieter Schneider and Rudolf Kuda, *Arbeiterräte in der Novemberrevolution*. For an excellent account of the pure council system, see Hoffrogge, *Working-Class Politics in the German Revolution*, 108–16.
18 Hoffrogge, *Working-Class Politics in the German Revolution*.
19 Karl Korsch, *Karl Korsch: Revolutionary Theory*, 200.
20 Anton Pannekoek, "Social Democracy and Communism."
21 Karl Korsch, "What Is Socialization?"
22 Rudolf Hilferding, "Closing Address to Congress, 20 December 1918" [Congress Report], 341–4.
23 Karl Korsch, "Evolution of the Problem of the Political Workers Councils in Germany."
24 Pannekoek, "Social Democracy and Communism."
25 Oskar Anweiler, *The Soviets*, 112.
26 Korsch, "Evolution of the Problem of the Political Workers Councils in Germany."
27 Karl Korsch, "Revolutionary Commune."
28 Pannekoek, "Social Democracy and Communism"; Marx, "The Civil War in France."
29 David Mandel, *The Petrograd Workers and the Fall of the Old Regime*, 73.
30 Andy Anderson, *Hungary '56*.
31 Jan Appel, "Origins of the Movement for Workers' Councils in Germany."
32 Robert Dahl, *Democracy and Its Critics*.
33 Karl Marx, "A Contribution to the Critique of Hegel's Philosophy of Right."
34 The German Social Democratic Party, "The Erfurt Program."
35 Richard Müller, "Democracy or Dictatorship," in Gabriel Kuhn (ed.), *All Power to the Councils!*, 65.
36 Karl Kautsky, "National Assembly and Council Assembly," in John Riddell (ed.), *The German Revolution and the Debate on Soviet Power*.
37 For a historical exploration of this issue, see the contribution of Kets and Muldoon in Chapter 3, this volume.

38 Pannekoek, "Social Democracy and Communism."
39 Ibid.
40 Ibid.
41 Richard Müller, "Democracy or Dictatorship," 64.
42 Rosa Luxemburg, "Marxism or Leninism?," in *Reform or Revolution and Other Writings*, 94.
43 John Dryzek, "Democratic Political Theory," in Gerald F. Gaus and Chandran Kukathas (eds), *Handbook of Political Theory*, 143.
44 Robert Dahl, *A Preface to Economic Democracy*; Schweickart, *After Capitalism*; Tom Malleson, *After Occupy*.
45 Gabriel Kuhn (ed.), *All Power to the Councils!*; Hoffrogge, *Working-Class Politics in the German Revolution*.
46 John Medearis, "Lost or Obscured?"
47 V. I. Lenin, "The Dual Power." See also Anweiler, *The Soviets*, 165; cf. Lars Lih, *Lenin Rediscovered*.
48 Ibid., 161–5.
49 V. I. Lenin, "'Left-Wing' Communism."
50 John Sitton, "Hannah Arendt's Argument for Council Democracy," in Lewis P. Hinchman and Sandra K. Hinchman (eds), *Hannah Arendt*; James Muldoon, "The Origins of Hannah Arendt's Council System."
51 See, for example, Jeffrey Isaac's argument for increased civic participation and Andreas Kalyvas' theory of a "derevolutionized constituent power," both of which draw on Arendt's theory of council democracy, but overwrite rather than contribute to a council tradition. Jeffrey Isaac, "Oases in the Desert"; Andreas Kalyvas, *Democracy and the Politics of the Extraordinary*.
52 Schumpeter famously describes democracy as "that institutional arrangement for arriving at political decisions in which individuals acquire the power to decide by means of a competitive struggle for the people's vote." Joseph Schumpeter, *Capitalism, Socialism, and Democracy*, 269; Adam Przeworski, "Minimalist Conception of Democracy," in Ian Shapiro and Casiano Hacker-Cordon (eds), *Democracy's Value*.
53 Anton Pannekoek, "The Tactical Differences in the Labour Movement." Quoted in Serge Bricianer, *Pannekoek and the Workers' Councils*, 101.
54 Richard Müller, "Report by the Executive Council of the Workers' and Soldiers' Councils of Great Berlin," in Kuhn (ed.), *All Power to the Councils!*, 31.
55 Anton Pannekoek, *Workers' Councils*, 104.
56 Pateman, *Participation and Democratic Theory*; Benjamin Barber, *Strong Democracy*.
57 Karl Kautsky, "Guidelines for a Socialist Action Programme."
58 Ernst Däumig, "The National Assembly Means the Councils' Death," in Kuhn (ed.), *All Power to the Councils!*, 45.
59 Pateman, *Participation and Democratic Theory*, 42.
60 Ibid.
61 Cf. Joshua Cohen, "Economic Foundations of Deliberative Democracy."
62 Chantal Mouffe, *Agonistics*; Bonnie Honig, *Political Theory and the Displacement of Politics*.
63 William Connolly, *Pluralism*; Sheldon Wolin, "Fugitive Democracy," in Seyla Benhabib (ed.), *Democracy and Difference*.

64 Ernesto Laclau and Chantal Mouffe, *Hegemony and Socialist Strategy*; Jacques Rancière, *Disagreement*.
65 Slavoj Žižek, *Living in the End Times*; Alain Badiou, *The Rebirth of History*; Michael Hardt and Antonio Negri, *Declaration*.
66 See, for example, Lars Tønder and Lasse Thomasson (eds), *Radical Democracy*.
67 See Paulina Tambakaki, "Agonism Reloaded," 577–88.
68 Antonio Gramsci, *Selections from the Prison Notebooks*.
69 In this respect, council democrats are closest to the radical democratic theory of Chantal Mouffe, who is also critical of other varieties of agonistic theory for the absence of a theory of hegemonic struggle to supplement their understanding of plurality and agonism.
70 Chantal Mouffe, *The Return of the Political*, 94.
71 Chantal Mouffe, "Preface: Democratic Politics Today," 1–2.
72 Mouffe, *The Return of the Political*, 90.
73 Mouffe, *Agonistics*.
74 John Dryzek, "Theory, Evidence and the Tasks of Deliberation," in Shawn W. Rosenberg (ed.), *Deliberation, Participation and Democracy*, 239.
75 John Parkinson and Jane Mansbridge (eds), *Deliberative Systems*.
76 Amy Gutmann and Dennis Thompson, *Why Deliberative Democracy?*, 3.
77 This problem is recognised by many deliberative democrats. See, for example, Cohen and Rogers, *On Democracy*.

References

Anderson, Andy. *Hungary '56*. London: Phoenix Press, 1964.

Anweiler, Oskar. *The Soviets: The Russian Workers, Peasants, and Soldiers Councils, 1905–1921*. New York: Pantheon Books, 1974.

Appel, Jan. "Origins of the Movements for Workers' Councils in Germany." *Commune* 5 (2008).

Arato, Andrew and Jean Cohen. *Civil Society and Political Theory*. Cambridge, MA: The MIT Press, 1992.

Badiou, Alain. *The Rebirth of History: Times of Riots and Uprisings*. London and New York: Verso, 2012.

Barber, Benjamin. *Strong Democracy: Participatory Politics for a New Age*. Berkeley, CA: University of California Press, 1984.

Bricianer, Serge. *Pannekoek and the Workers' Councils*. St. Louis, MO: Telos Press, 1983.

Brown, Wendy. *Undoing the Demos: Neoliberalism's Stealth Revolution*. New York: Zone Books, 2015.

Cohen, Joshua. "Economic Foundations of Deliberative Democracy." *Social Philosophy and Policy* 6, no. 2 (1989): 25–50.

Cohen, Joshua and Joel Rogers. *On Democracy: Toward a Transformation of American Society*. Harmondsworth: Penguin, 1983.

Connolly, William. *Pluralism*. Durham, NC: Duke University Press, 2005.

Dahl, Robert. *Democracy and Its Critics*. New Haven, CT: Yale University Press, 1989.

———. *A Preface to Economic Democracy*. Berkeley, CA: University of California Press, 1985.

Demirovic, Alex. "Council Democracy, or the End of the Political." In *An Alternative Labour History: Worker Control and Workplace Democracy*. Edited by Dario Azzellini, translated by Joe Keeny. 31–66. London: Zed Books, 2015.

Dryzek, John. "Democratic Political Theory." In *Handbook of Political Theory*. Edited by Gerald F. Gaus and Chandran Kukathas. 143–54. London: SAGE Publications, 2004.

———. "Theory, Evidence and the Tasks of Deliberation." In *Deliberation, Participation and Democracy: Can the People Govern?* Edited by Shawn W. Rosenberg. 237–50. New York: Palgrave Macmillan, 2007.

Ellerman, David. "The Workplace: A Forgotten Topic in Democratic Theory?" *Kettering Review* 27, no. 2 (2009): 51–7.

Erdmann, Karl Dietrich. "Die Geschichte der Weimarer Republik als Problem der Wissenschaft." *Vierteljahrshefte für Zeitgeschichte* 3 (1955): 1–19.

Floyd, Jonathan and Marc Stears (eds). *Political Philosophy versus History? Contextualism and Real Politics in Contemporary Political Thought*. Cambridge: Cambridge University Press, 2011.

Foa, Roberto Stefan and Yascha Mounk. "The Danger of Deconsolidation: The Democratic Disconnect." *Journal of Democracy* 27, no. 3 (2016): 5–17.

German Social Democratic Party. "The Erfurt Program." Accessed at www.marxists.org/history/international/social-democracy/1891/erfurt-program.htm.

Gilens, Martin and Benjamin I. Page. "Testing Theories of American Politics: Elites, Interest Groups, and Average Citizens." *Perspectives on Politics* 12, no. 3 (2014): 564–8.

Gramsci, Antonio. *Selections from the Prison Notebooks*. New York: International Publishers, 1971.

Gutmann, Amy and Dennis Thompson. *Why Deliberative Democracy?* Princeton, NJ: Princeton University Press, 2004.

Hardt, Michael and Antonio Negri. *Declaration*. New York: Argo Navis Author Services, 2012.

Hilferding, Rudolf. "Closing Address to Congress, 20 December 1918." In *Allgemeiner Kongreß der Arbeiter- und Soldatenräte Deutschlands vom 16. bis 21. Dezember 1918 im Abgeordnetenhause zu Berlin. Stenographische Berichte* [Congress Report]. Berlin, 1919.

Hoffrogge, Ralf. *Working-Class Politics in the German Revolution: Richard Müller, the Revolutionary Shop Stewards and the Origins of the Council Movement*. Leiden: Brill Publishers, 2014.

Honig, Bonnie. *Political Theory and the Displacement of Politics*. Ithaca, NY: Cornell University Press, 1993.

Isaac, Jeffrey. "Oases in the Desert: Hannah Arendt on Democratic Politics." *American Political Science Review* 88, no. 1 (1994): 156–68.

Kalyvas, Andreas. *Democracy and the Politics of the Extraordinary: Max Weber, Carl Schmitt, and Hannah Arendt*. Cambridge: Cambridge University Press, 2008.

Kautsky, Karl. "Guidelines for a Socialist Action Programme." Accessed at www.marxists.org/archive/kautsky/1919/01/guidelines.html.

———. "National Assembly and Council Assembly." In *The German Revolution and the Debate on Soviet Power. Documents: 1918–1919 Preparing the Founding Congress*. Edited by John Riddell. 94–107. New York: Anchor Foundation, 1986.

Kioupkiolis, Alexandros and Giorgos Katsambekis (eds). *Radical Democracy and Collective Movements Today: The Biopolitics of the Multitude versus the Hegemony of the People*. London: Routledge, 2014.

Korsch, Karl. "Evolution of the Problem of the Political Workers Councils in Germany." Accessed at www.marxists.org/archive/korsch/1921/councils.htm.

———. *Karl Korsch: Revolutionary Theory*. Edited by Douglas Kellner. Austin, TX: University of Texas Press, 1977.

———. "Revolutionary Commune." Accessed at www.marxists.org/archive/korsch/1929/commune.htm.

———. "What Is Socialization? A Program of Practical Socialism." *New German Critique* 6 (1975): 60–81.

Kuhn, Gabriel (ed.). *All Power to the Councils! A Documentary History of the German Revolution of 1918–1919*. London: PM Press, 2012.

Laclau, Ernesto and Chantal Mouffe. *Hegemony and Socialist Strategy: Towards a Radical Democratic Politics*. London: Verso, 1985.

Lenin, V. I. "The Dual Power." Accessed at www.marxists.org/archive/lenin/works/1917/apr/09.htm.

———. "'Left-Wing' Communism: An Infantile Disorder." Accessed at www.marxists.org/archive/lenin/works/1920/lwc/.

———. "The State and Revolution." Accessed at www.marxists.org/archive/lenin/works/1917/staterev/.

Lih, Lars. *Lenin Rediscovered: What Is to Be Done? In Context*. London: Haymarket Books, 2008.

Luxemburg, Rosa. "Marxism or Leninism?" In *Reform or Revolution and Other Writings*. Mineola, NY: Dover Publications, 2006.

McNay, Lois. *The Misguided Search for the Political: Social Weightlessness in Radical Democratic Theory*. Cambridge: Polity Press, 2014.

Malleson, Tom. *After Occupy: Economic Democracy for the 21st Century*. Oxford: Oxford University Press, 2014.

Mandel, David. *The Petrograd Workers and the Fall of the Old Regime: From the February Revolution to the July Days, 1917*. London: Macmillan Press, 1983.

Marx, Karl. "The Civil War in France." Accessed at www.marxists.org/archive/marx/works/1871/civil-war-france/index.htm.

———. "A Contribution to the Critique of Hegel's Philosophy of Right: Introduction." Accessed at www.marxists.org/archive/marx/works/1843/critique-hpr/intro.htm.

———. "On the Jewish Question." Accessed at www.marxists.org/archive/marx/works/1844/jewish-question/.

Medearis, John. "Lost or Obscured? How V. I. Lenin, Joseph Schumpeter and Hannah Arendt Misunderstood the Council Movement." *Polity* 36, no. 3 (2004): 447–76.

Mouffe, Chantal. *Agonistics*. London: Verso, 2013.

———. "Preface: Democratic Politics Today." In *Dimensions of Radical Democracy*. Edited by Chantal Mouffe. 1–14. London: Verso, 1992.

———. *The Return of the Political*. London: Verso, 1993.

Muldoon, James. "The Origins of Hannah Arendt's Council System." *History of Political Thought* 37, no. 4 (2016): 761–89.

Ness, Immanuel and Dario Azzellini (eds). *Ours to Master and to Own: Workers' Control from the Commune to the Present*. Chicago: Haymarket Books, 2011.

Pannekoek, Anton. "Social Democracy and Communism." Accessed at www.marxists.org/archive/pannekoe/1927/sdc.htm.

———. *Workers' Councils*. London: AK Press, 2003.

Parkinson, John and Jane Mansbridge (eds). *Deliberative Systems: Deliberative Democracy at the Large Scale*. New York: Cambridge University Press, 2012.

Pateman, Carole. *Participation and Democratic Theory*. Cambridge: Cambridge University Press, 1975.

Przeworski, Adam. "Minimalist Conception of Democracy: A Defense." In *Democracy's Value*. Edited by Ian Shapiro and Casiano Hacker-Cordon. 23–55. Cambridge: Cambridge University Press, 1999.

Rancière, Jacques. *Disagreement: Politics and Philosophy*. Minneapolis, MN: University of Minnesota Press, 1999.

Schneider, Dieter and Rudolf Kuda. *Arbeiterräte in der Novemberrevolution. Ideen, Wirkungen, Dokumente*. Frankfurt: Suhrkamp Verlag, 1968.

Schumpeter, Joseph. *Capitalism, Socialism, and Democracy*. New York: Harper & Brothers, 1942.

Schweickart, David. *After Capitalism*. London: Rowman & Littlefield, 2002.

Sitton, John. "Hannah Arendt's Argument for Council Democracy." *Polity* 20, no. 1 (1987): 80–100.

Tambakaki, Paulina. "Agonism Reloaded: Potentia, Renewal and Radical Democracy." *Political Studies Review* 15, no. 4 (2017): 577–88.

Tønder, Lars and Lasse Thomassen (eds). *Radical Democracy: Politics Between Abundance and Lack*. Manchester: Manchester University Press, 2005.

Wolin, Sheldon. "Fugitive Democracy." In *Democracy and Difference: Contesting the Boundaries of the Political*. Edited by Seyla Benhabib. 31–45. Princeton, NJ: Princeton University Press, 1996.

Žižek, Slavoj. *Living in the End Times*. London and New York: Verso, 2011.

Part I

The Councils in Historical Perspective

2 The Development of Workers' Councils

Between Spontaneity and Organisation

Donny Gluckstein

"Behind every strike lurks the hydra of revolution."[1]

The workers' and soldiers' councils that emerged during and after the First World War did not follow a pre-determined blueprint to replace the bourgeois state or overthrow capitalist society. They initially represented a working-class response to the effects of war and capitalist competition. Competition between capitalist nations was being waged using the blood of millions of ordinary people. Carnage abroad was accompanied by economic dislocation and assaults on basic freedoms at home. With conventional channels of parliamentary democracy and official trade union action suspended due to the "national emergency" of the war, there was no alternative for the victims of this imperialist tragedy but to improvise a collective answer. The choice, according to Rosa Luxemburg, was between "socialism or regression into barbarism."[2]

Councils (or soviets in Russian) arose in countries as far apart as Russia, Germany, Britain, Hungary, Ireland, Austria, Indonesia and Italy. Even though their origins lay in very specific circumstances linked to particular locations and industrial sectors, this did not diminish their universal potential for united class action and social reconstruction. Thus, while the first councils grew organically from the economic base of society – the workplace – they nonetheless developed an effective democratic political power. Indeed, it was through the grounding of politics in the unified power of producers that it became possible to transcend a major flaw in bourgeois parliamentary democracy – that real influence is left in the hands of the capitalists and their supporters.

The structure of the councils was based on workplace elections with delegates directly elected and subject to immediate recall. As a consequence the political composition could evolve as mass consciousness changed. Petrograd operated a system of one delegate per 1,000 workers (and one per army company). In Berlin, Hamburg and Bremen it was one per 1,000, 600 and 180 workers respectively.[3] In Glasgow and Sheffield the Workers' Committees were controlled from below by an assembly of elected shop stewards, as were Turin's factory committees.

Composed of workers' delegates accountable to, and recallable by, their electors, councils also posed a challenge to existing labour movements. Social democratic political parties and bureaucratic trade unionism did not pose a fundamental alternative to conventional power structures as they had adapted to working within existing systems. This weakness was further accentuated by their full compliance with belligerent governments on the grounds that all dissent should be submerged in a (fictitious) wartime "common interest."

Although the councils' sudden emergence and wide geographical spread suggests an element of spontaneity, their path was inevitably influenced by the ideological beliefs of their participants. The delegates who formed the early movement held a variety of attitudes towards imperialist war, but in many cases, councils were initiated by conscious revolutionaries who were prepared to defiantly swim against the stream and lead resistance against the war.

With the overthrow of Tsarism and rise of Bolshevism in 1917, revolution began to spread and the soviet model was widely emulated. Yet at the very moment the council was poised to become much more than an assembly of delegates and constitute the building block of a new kind of state on an international scale, a powerful current emerged to oppose this idea. Social democracy, which was hostile to any long-term role for workers' councils, became the dominant force in this second phase. Even though immediate circumstances led the Social Democrats to become involved in the revolution, the majority of delegates, moulded in the previous period, still shared a reformist faith in parliament's capacity to overcome the capitalist system. Therefore, only in Bolshevik Russia was the workers' council more than a fleeting phenomenon. It did not take long before the tide had turned and councils had disappeared, even though the name persisted in the Union of Soviet Socialist Republics (USSR). While the councils were not the result of any pre-given party programme, they were certainly a forum in which parties competed for influence and power.

This chapter examines the key issues of the relationship between objective and subjective preconditions, politics and economics, workers' parties and councils, organisation and spontaneity, leadership and the masses, and form and content. Although it might appear that these factors were mutually exclusive and could not be transcended, I argue that they were dialectically interconnected and that the council was a key nexus that linked them together. Finally, due to space constraints, the focus of this chapter is on the most important period of development for the councils from 1915 to 1920.

Precursors: Paris and Saint Petersburg

In 1843, Marx questioned previous attempts by utopian socialists to predict future society:

> everyone *will* have to admit to himself that he has no exact idea what the future ought to be. On the other hand, it is precisely the advantage of the new trend that we do not dogmatically anticipate the world, but only want to find the new world through criticism of the old one.[4]

It was not until the appearance of the Paris Commune in 1871 that he concluded there was now a "political form at last discovered under which to work out the economical emancipation of labour."[5]

While the Commune was a precursor of the workers' councils, it differed in important respects. In 1871, workplaces in the French capital tended to be minuscule due to fears that large factories would be the seedbed of revolution. The Commune only became possible because siege conditions during the Franco-Prussian war shut down most industry. Unemployed workers were then enrolled into the Parisian National Guard. In this way, they acquired the organisational framework for daily debate and delegate accountability that lies at the heart of council democracy.

After its bloody suppression, the significance of 1871 was forgotten, and the workers' movement's efforts went into building the Second International. Social democratic parties operated inside bourgeois parliaments while a new trade union officialdom bargained over economic goals. Therefore, when the Saint Petersburg Soviet appeared during the 1905 Russian Revolution, the Bolshevik Central Committee saw it as a needless distraction. It warned against "the danger of politically amorphous and socialistically immature workers' organisations created by the spontaneous revolutionary movement of the proletariat."[6] Unfortunately, this formulation of an opposition between the council form and political parties misunderstood the roles of both.

The 1905 Revolution was ultimately unsuccessful, but the council idea lived on as a memory of how political transformation could be achieved. Furthermore, the lessons of this episode were theorised by leading Russian socialists. Lenin thought: "the Soviet of Workers' Deputies should be regarded as the embryo of a *provisional revolutionary government*."[7] Trotsky, who had been president of the Saint Petersburg Soviet, developed his groundbreaking theory of permanent revolution on the basis of his experiences. Having seen the rapid pace at which workers' power could be developed, he rejected the Second International's view that there was a fixed sequence of social development: from feudalism to capitalism and then to socialism. He envisioned an economically backward Russia leapfrogging the capitalist stage if supported by revolutions elsewhere.

The Objective Conditions for Council Development: Social Crisis

Despite the manifest profiteering, oppression, injustice and gross inequality produced by capitalism, it survives because the masses broadly accept that there is no alternative. This trick is accomplished by a combination of force and persuasion. Labour movement institutions like social democratic parties and trade unions can acquiesce in this process. They embody an ideology, a structure and a practice that operate within the system by channelling the aspirations of its supporters through the established institutional framework and balancing capital's needs against the hopes of labour. Reformist parties operate in parliament, while unions engage in collective bargaining which leaves workers divided along the lines of industries or individual companies. In both scenarios the terms of subjugation are negotiated rather than ended.

However, there are elements within capitalism that generate instability, the chief of these is the exploitation of the working class and competition between rival units of capital. During the period 1914 to 1918, these two features were taken to a new level when competition took the shape of an unprecedented total war and success became intertwined with a dramatic intensification of exploitation on the home front. This was deeply disruptive to established patterns and thus set the scene for the rise of the workers' council.

Yet more was needed. History is littered with wars in which the only outcome was death and misery. Only after the First World War was a comprehensive working-class alternative to the existing state and society posed on an international scale. War, and particularly defeat in war, had undermined the legitimacy of the capitalist state, but also jeopardised the basis for social democracy. Between 1914 and 1918, with European nation-states fighting for their own survival, their respective ruling classes demanded total subservience to the "cause" – their cause. Since a reformist strategy relies on capitalism being successful enough to pay for reforms, social democracy felt it had no choice but to give in to this appeal and abandon any talk of positive change "for the duration." This semi-critical, semi-independent position that social democracy sought to occupy became untenable.

In Germany, the mighty Social Democratic Party (SPD) joined the Kaiser's *Burgfrieden* (peace within the fortress); in France the socialists joined the *Union Sacrée* (Sacred Union of the nation); in Britain Labour MPs threw over their leaders (Hardie and MacDonald) to join Lloyd George's coalition. Even where formal capitulation was refused, opposition to the imperialist war was restrained in practice (with the exceptions of Russia and Bulgaria). Thus, Italy's Socialist Party declared "neither support nor sabotage," which amounted to doing nothing. Russia's Mensheviks dropped criticism of the First World War once the tsar had gone, and they enthusiastically backed the provisional government's policy of "defencism." Very few leading Social Democrats agreed with Karl Liebknecht, the only German SPD deputy to vote against war credits on 4 August 1914, that "the main enemy is at home."

Official trade unionism also failed to act decisively against the war. Even France's prominent anarcho-syndicalists in France decided upon wartime class collaboration. Their failure to address political issues left them defenceless when, on political grounds, a truce was demanded over economic class struggle. In Britain, Arthur Henderson, a trade union leader, took over the Labour Party and accepted a ministerial appointment. This collaboration of official trade unions was also reinforced by direct state intervention. Britain's Defence of the Realm Act shelved civil liberties, while the Munitions Act outlawed strikes in engineering. Germany copied its enemy by introducing equivalent legislation, the Law of Siege and the Auxiliary Service Law. Russia already had only minimal civil liberties and its War Industry Committees also targeted engineering, as did Italy's Industrial Mobilisation System.

Closure of traditional channels for dissent occurred at a time of rapidly worsening conditions. For example, by 1918 the death rate in Turin (behind the lines) was 49 per cent above its pre-war level.[8] During the war, inflation in Britain reached 205 per cent; in Germany 300 per cent; Italy around 400 per cent; while the Russian figure topped 1,000 per cent.[9] Even when money was available the diversion of food to front-line soldiers created shortages and even famine. Germany endured a "turnip winter" in 1916/1917 when virtually nothing else was available to eat. In Russia, the lack of food precipitated the downfall of the tsar in February 1917.

The Subjective Conditions: Metalworkers as Pioneers

While the council movement had universal significance for working-class democracy, its initial development depended on a specific set of conditions. Although council structures spread right across Russia, Germany, Austria, Britain, Hungary and Italy, they almost always began in centres of metalworking. These included Petrograd, Berlin, Glasgow, Vienna, Budapest and Turin.

It might be expected that such an institution would first appear among the most downtrodden sections of society. Yet many of the pioneers did not fit that description. They were relatively well-paid skilled men who were sometimes dubbed an "aristocracy of labour." This was not only the case in long-established engineering factories such as those in Clydeside or Berlin. A recently arrived unskilled worker in the most militant factory in Petrograd, the Putilov works, described attitudes in this way: "Alongside the textile workers, the metalworkers appeared to be a race apart … Soon I began to feel that the workers in the engineering shop – fitters and turners – looked down on me."[10]

Why did that comparatively privileged group play such a leading role in forging class unity? Even before 1914, there was a distinctive feature to working-class organisation in this industry. Metalworking factories tended to produce a wide and fluctuating variety of items, and this involved numerous distinct work teams. As a result engineering workers bargained or battled at workshop level with supervisors over issues such as piece rates. Such detailed interactions could not be managed by union officials external to the workshop, and so shop-floor representatives were established. They were a distinct group of individuals who were simultaneously part of the union organisation (if it existed), but also were more closely connected to the rank and file than the union head office. Though details varied, these individuals tended to be directly elected and accountable, sharing the same conditions and experiences as the rank and file that worked alongside them. In Britain, they were called shop stewards; *starosti* in Russia; *Obleute* in Germany; delegates of the *commissioni interni* in Italy. The directly democratic and bottom-up organisational power embodied in the workers' council, which made it an alternative to trade unions and reformist parties, was dependent on links to the working class at the point of production. If such well-rooted representatives combined across factories, then local industries, then towns and eventually across whole countries, the power wielded by the working class was immense.

Another part of the explanation relates to how different elements of society were affected by the First World War. Though engineers were exempt, vast numbers of men were drawn into armies. At 16 million, Russia had the largest of these, while Germany fielded 13 million, Italy almost six million and Britain five million. Battlefields generated a huge increase in demand for metalworking products – artillery, vehicles, ships and planes. Domestically the First World War was therefore seen as an "engineers' war."

The reach of such shop-floor representatives was dramatically extended after 1914. During the conflict, the number of British metalworkers rose by 34 per cent to 2.4 million. In Germany the increase was by 44 per cent to three million. The majority of Russian engineers were located in Petrograd (formerly called Saint Petersburg), which, by 1917, saw 150,000 workers added to its pre-war total of 243,000.[11] The arrival of firms like Fiat in Turin in 1899 had already made it a major manufacturing centre. Such was the growth in the need for engineers there that, as the employers' organisation put it: "[c]arpenters, masons, simple labourers were trained and in a few months were baptised as mechanics."[12] Turin's factory workforce doubled during 1918. It is significant that most of those killed on Berlin's revolutionary barricades were born outside the city.[13] Added to this was the concentration of munitions workers. Most other industries had smaller and more dispersed production units, which made the chances of their workers pioneering a mass institution like the soviet less likely. By 1917, Berlin had 37 engineering factories with over 1,000 workers.[14] This was only topped by Petrograd, which had the strongest council movement of all. Here 38 major plants employed over 2,000 workers each while metalworkers formed two thirds of the industrial workforce.[15]

The intense demand for metalworkers, and their relative immunity from the threat of punitive conscription, potentially enhanced their bargaining position in relation to management. But this merely encouraged the bosses and state to try to bind the manacles of employer and state control all the more tightly since nothing less than total servitude and maximum exploitation was acceptable. Thus repressive legislation such as Britain's Munitions Act aimed to prevent dissatisfied workers not only from striking, but even from changing their employers. Working hours were extended to the limit of physical endurance. At Fiat in Turin, 75 hours a week was the norm. In Berlin, the working day went from 8.5 to 11 hours for six days per week with additional compulsory labour on Sundays. Fourteen-hour shifts were common for Viennese metalworkers, while Petrograd and Glasgow experienced similar changes.

An additional radicalising factor was the introduction of vast numbers of women and young people into industry. In Russia, 43 per cent of industrial workers at the time of the revolution were female, with rates of 22 per cent in Italy and 20 per cent in France. More important were the large number of female workers in munitions. By 1917, they made up 70 per cent of the Italian munitions workforce, over half in Germany and Austria, and 37 per cent in France.[16] Not only did they suffer terrible working conditions, but in an atmosphere of sexism they were expected to continue to fill stereotypical roles such as feeding the family (when shortages were common) and providing customary care (despite the dramatic extension in factory hours), and all for a fraction of the wage given to their male counterparts. Consequently, they were often in the vanguard of the broader struggle. In Glasgow women led a rent strike movement during 1915 that drew a large segment of the munitions industry towards mass strike action. In May 1918, Hungarian officials were also alarmed because

> [w]omen workers not only frequently attempt to disrupt factories by interrupting production, but even deliver inflammatory speeches, take part in demonstrations, marching in the foremost ranks with their babies in their arms, and behaving in an insulting manner towards the representatives of the law.[17]

The following month the embryo of workers' councils was set up in Budapest after a strike outbreak. The single most important event, however, took place on International Women's Day in 1917 in Petrograd when a protest over the lack of bread led to a full-scale revolution that forced the tsar's abdication.

By employing low-wage female labour in the factories, capitalism was seeking to exploit gender division to achieve intensified exploitation. It might be true that for working-class women an engineering job was more financially rewarding than their previous employment (such as domestic service), but earning less for doing the same job as a man risked dragging everyone's pay down while profits soared. The influx of unskilled labour required new technology and ways of working that further undermined the exclusivity of skill (and therefore its bargaining power, job security and control). It was the issue of "dilution" of skills that led to the formation of the Clyde Workers' Committee in Glasgow, while class solidarity across genders such as the rent strike played a key role in the development of workers' councils there and elsewhere. The 1917 Russian Revolution was sparked not only by a women's protest over bread, but overlapped with a recently imposed lockout and strike at the 30,000-strong Putilov munitions works, probably the largest factory in the world at the time. The answer to the bosses' divide-and-rule tactics was class unity in action, and the workers' council offered this to an unprecedented degree.

One reason the 1905 Russian Revolution had failed was because the workers organised in the Saint Petersburg Soviet had been relatively isolated geographically, and lacked sufficient active support from broader segments of the population. Above all, these workers were unable to win over the soldiers who were used to repress the revolt. In February 1917, mutinous regiments sent delegates to council meetings. By 17 March 1917, 49 cities had soviets; by June the number was 519.[18]

The Council as Process: Spontaneous or Organised, Economic or Political?

What follows is a description of stages in the growth of workers' councils, but it should not be assumed that in every place this sequence was necessary or unfolded everywhere in the same manner. Trotsky's theory of permanent revolution, drawing on the experience of the 1905 Saint Petersburg Soviet, was based on a "law of uneven and combined development" which rejected "pedantic schematism."[19] This should also be applied to the growth of workers' councils. Nevertheless, it is possible to discern a continuum which began with immediate, day-to-day workers' struggles over superficially economic issues and stretched all the way to the constitution of workers' councils and a struggle over the future political form of the state. This also entailed a transition from instantaneous direct action to more organised and strategic decision-making; from class dispersal to unity; and from individual businesses or industrial sectors to cities, and ultimately entire countries. The developmental flow encompassing these numerous different factors is referred to here as *the council process*.

Workers' councils came into existence at the intersection of: (1) a widespread upsurge of workers' activity focused on resolving immediate issues; and (2) the efforts of political currents in the labour movement seeking to give this an organisational shape (in either a revolutionary or reformist direction). There was no clear opposition between spontaneity and organisation in the formation of councils, nor was there a clear separation at all times between economics and politics. The first workers' councils began as a spontaneous reaction by workers to wartime crisis and the consequent need for large-scale co-ordination. However, as Trotsky pointed out in relation to Russian events: "To the smug politicians of liberalism and tamed socialism everything that happens among masses is customarily represented as an instinctive process" but "the mystic doctrine of spontaneousness explains nothing."[20] Furthermore, it was one thing to protest or strike in large numbers, it was another to give this a permanent organisational form that endured long after the protest or strike had ended. At an organisational level, the workers' council therefore reflected the pattern identified by Rosa Luxemburg during the 1905 Russian Revolution:

> Political and economic strikes, mass strikes and partial strikes, demonstrative strikes and fighting strikes, general strikes of individual branches of industry and general strikes in individual towns, peaceful wage struggles and street massacres, barricade fighting – all these run through one another, run side by side, cross one another, flow in and over one another – it is a ceaselessly moving, changing sea of phenomena. And the law of motion of these phenomena is clear: it does not lie in the mass strike itself nor in its technical details, but in the political and social proportions of the forces of the revolution.[21]

We can now trace the history of the development of workers' councils in a number of contexts. The first step in this process was taken through workers improvising a tool for co-ordinating unofficial strike action. On 22 January 1905, Tsarist troops massacred unarmed demonstrators. This provoked a revolution, and in October the first workers' council, the Saint Petersburg Soviet, met to organise a political general strike. Trotsky described it

> as a response to an objective need – a need born of the course of events. It was an organisation which was authoritative and yet had no traditions, which could immediately involve a scattered mass of hundreds of thousands of people while having virtually no organisational machinery.[22]

In February 1917, with this experience still in mind, it took just two days to assemble the Petrograd Soviet after the revolution had begun. Although the establishment of soviets in both 1905 and 1917 was first proposed by the Mensheviks, during January 1918, the Bolsheviks gained a majority in Russia's soviets and established centralised council structures so as to bring independent strike committees under their control.

Glasgow appeared to be a world away from Petrograd in terms of economic, social and political development. Here there were legal trade unions, parliamentary democracy and no history of workers' revolution. Yet this city witnessed a workers' council, the Clyde Workers' Committee, during 1915. Here too the aim was to efficiently organise an engineering strike and the cause was both economic and political – the use of the Munitions Act to discipline or sack workers who had taken action over pay. Revolutionary socialism was very weak in Britain and represented by a clutch of tiny parties such as the British Socialist Party (BSP) and Socialist Labour Party (SLP). Yet the chair of the Clyde Workers' Committee was a BSP member, the treasurer was SLP, and other committee members included the former and current editors of the SLP newspaper. However, it is important to note that they were there as leading shop stewards and factory convenors, not as political functionaries.

The process of strike waves that eventually led to councils in Germany commenced in April 1917. The revolutionary overthrow of the Russian tsar, and a demonstration of women in Leipzig demanding bread, initiated urgent preparations for a stoppage in Berlin. This was disrupted by arrests, but in Leipzig the strike went ahead led by a committee of two metalworkers and two socialists. The demands the strike committees made were for bread and peace without annexations. In Germany, leadership of the strike waves and first attempts to build workers' councils came from the revolutionary *Obleute* (shop stewards) who were also members of the Independent Social Democrats (USPD), a left-wing wartime breakaway from the SPD. The most radical grouping, the Spartacists, were absent from this process.

In Austria, the drive towards workers' councils came when Daimler metalworkers in Vienna walked out for peace.[23] Between 3 and 25 January 1918 that stoppage grew to 700,000 workers.[24] A similar strike shook Hungary during December 1917. By January 1918, 150,000 marched through Budapest to the slogan, "[l]ong live the workers' councils!" and "[g]reetings to Soviet Russia."[25] In a conscious rejection of "the parliamentary cretinism of the social democracy," a call for councils in Hungary came from syndicalist shop stewards.[26]

In Turin, the workers' council movement (which adopted the title of "factory councils," but aimed to federate across all industries) took off in 1919. Italy's factory council movement originated from discussions in the pages of the *Ordine Nuovo* (New Order) socialist newspaper. Close collaboration between leading militants in the factories and Marxist theoreticians like Antonio Gramsci, who were nominally members of the Italian Socialist Party but would become founders of the Communist Party shortly after, led to the development of existing factory organisation into something far more ambitious.

Within workers' councils, political parties competed to shape the direction of events. Among the workers there existed different political currents, which was reflected in the presence of both revolutionaries and reformists. For the former, to set up workers' councils in the midst of global war, and at a time when strikes were illegal, implied a readiness to lead the proletariat in actively resisting state policies. In contrast, some reformist leaders oversaw the formation of workers' councils with exactly the opposite intention, to take the initiative and ward off Bolshevism, by keeping the masses under their control.

Seeing the councils as a process, rather than adopting a formalistic approach focusing on constitutions, or rules for elections and the like, makes it possible to grasp the points of similarity between various council movements across countries. As an aside, it is worth noting that not all explosions of working-class activity have led to the appearance of councils. These upsurges are a necessary, but not sufficient, basis for the formation of workers' councils. Europe in 1945 bore many of the hallmarks of 1918/1919 and yet workers' councils were not to be seen. Whereas the First World War seriously weakened social democracy and its customary organisational forms, the combined efforts of reformism and Stalinism in 1945 strangled the independent rank-and-file initiatives that made workers' councils possible the first time.

In Britain and Italy, for example, the shop stewards' and factory council organisations never extended beyond the sphere of metalworking. Even if the catalyst was the political situation, struggle remained focused on the economic impact of the war and its aftermath. On Clydeside the climax was reached in early 1919 when the prospect of mass unemployment for munitions workers loomed and a strike to cut the working week to 40 hours culminated in a riot. The British Cabinet was told: "it was a misnomer to call the situation in Glasgow a strike – it was a Bolshevist rising."[27] The movement was rapidly quelled when troops were sent in. Willie Gallacher of the Clyde Workers' Committee explained the defeat in these terms: "[w]e were carrying on a strike when we ought to have been making a revolution."[28] In Turin the battle focused on control of production rather than the state and the employers. In April 1920 a mass stoppage of 500,000 was broken by the army, with the assistance of union officials. Gramsci concluded:

> Turin is a garrisoned fortress. It is said that there are 50,000 troops in the city, that artillery is drawn up on the hills, that reinforcements are waiting on the outskirts of the town and armoured cars in the city. If there was still someone in our midst who created illusions … if anyone found difficulty in making that last step to the point where *power in the factory can be seen as just one element in relation to State power* – if such doubters, such deluded people still existed, then this lesson was for them.[29]

The experience of Glasgow and Turin indicates that while workers could choose to merge their economic struggles into political ones, the process was by no means automatic or inevitable. Revolutionary leaders such as John Maclean in Britain, or Gramsci in Italy, were critical of the fact that the council movement failed in practice to consciously take the economic struggle on to an explicitly political plane. Elsewhere there were no such limitations as council movements caught up in the revolutions that swept through Russia, Germany and the Hapsburg Empire could not fail to focus on political questions.

Dual Power

While it is useful to visualise the council as process, it does not follow that it was automatically propelled towards a clear end, or possessed a *telos* of its own. The council institution created a space beyond the hold of the earlier structures of the labour movement, but in one sense it served as a forum for discussion and decision, a *form without a determined content*. The way in which different delegates acted within the councils varied from case to case. The content of the leadership and direction of the councils was subject to change though democratic decision-making. Evidence for this was given by an American witness of Russian events, John Reed, in his article "Soviets in Action":

> No political body more sensitive and responsive to the popular will was ever invented. And this was necessary, for in time of revolution the popular will changes with great rapidity. For example, during the first week of December 1917, there were parades and demonstrations in favour of a Constituent Assembly – that is to say, against the Soviet power. One of these parades was fired on by some irresponsible Red Guards, and several people killed. The reaction to this stupid violence was immediate. *Within twelve hours the complexion of the Petrograd Soviet changed.* More than a dozen Bolshevik deputies were withdrawn, and replaced by Mensheviki. And it was three weeks before public sentiment subsided – before the Mensheviki were retired one by one and the Bolsheviki sent back.[30]

Democratic form and the developmental process described above could interact in different ways. In Glasgow and Turin it was relatively easy for a small number of politically radical or revolutionary individuals to stay at the helm even if the council movement served primarily as a vehicle for tackling economic concerns. Even if their views did not coincide with the majority of metalworkers, their daring leadership in the industrial field was deemed to justify their leadership positions. However, this was not the case when full-scale revolutions broke out and councils spread far beyond the engineering heartlands to embrace much larger portions of the working class and even the army. This happened in Russia, Germany, Austria and Hungary. In this entirely new situation (which amounted to a dramatic leap forward in the developmental process), the importance of a council's political direction was magnified since, as Lenin put it in April 1917: "[t]he basic question of every revolution is that of state power."[31]

Workers' councils provided an arena within which different currents fought for class leadership and political questions were voted on. If the majority of workers (and therefore their delegates) could be won to the notion that the council, rather than parliament, was the basis for genuine popular control of society then the council system could triumph. If, by contrast, the view persisted that the council was merely a temporary institution pending the arrival of post-war stability and bourgeois constitutional arrangements, then it was doomed to disappear.

The issue became particularly acute when the tsar, kaiser and Austrian emperor were toppled by mass uprisings. At that point councils constituted a power standing alongside the weakened, but still extant, capitalist state. Lenin defined this phenomenon as dual power: "The highly remarkable feature of our revolution is that it has brought about a *dual power* … Alongside the Provisional Government, the government of the *bourgeoisie, another government* has arisen … the Soviets of Workers' and Soldiers' Deputies."[32] Trotsky elaborated:

> no historic class lifts itself from a subject position to a position of rulership suddenly in one night, even though a night of revolution … [T]he class which is called to realise the new social system, although not yet master of the country, has actually concentrated in its hands a significant share of the state power, while the official apparatus is still in the hands of the old lords. That is the initial dual power in every revolution.[33]

Dual power offered the councils the opportunity to move the developmental process forward into creating a full democratic state form, yet paradoxically it also created a major difficulty. It was one thing for workers to use council organisation as a means to overcome divisions within the class or solve immediate problems. It was quite another to fully embrace the political conclusion that the council was the fundamental alternative to capitalism and the state. Unless the council was secured on this more ambitious basis its rival was bound to monopolise the position of state power. The revolutionary standpoint was held by a minority, and it quickly became evident just how small that minority was.

In Berlin, dual power was reflected by the co-existence of a Workers' and Soldiers' Council Executive alongside a provisional government of "People's Commissars" tied to the old state. At the National Congress of Workers' Councils a majority of the delegates were from the reformist SPD which wished to end the experiment of revolution as quickly as possible. Only ten delegates were Spartacists, but Karl Liebknecht, despite his record of opposing the war, was not even granted a seat. Another issue at the Congress was that the 179 workers among the delegates were outnumbered by full-time party and union officials.[34] The Congress's first decision was to abandon dual power in favour of a reconvened parliament, and the four years of revolutionary struggles that followed largely took place independently of council organisation.

Hungary's path to dual power involved a bitter battle between supporters of workers' council power and the politically dominant Social Democrat leaders who opposed them. A giant strike against the war in January 1918 only ended because the entire party executive resigned over the mass refusal to return to work. In response, Hungary's revolutionaries issued a leaflet saying: "The workers must realise their right of self-determination! ... [F]orm your workers' councils ... and subordinate the party's present leadership to the will of the proletariat."[35] When the Hapsburg empire collapsed at the end of the year, a workers' council was indeed formed, yet it was controlled by reformist politics, with 239 of the 365 delegates sent by trade unions. The newly formed Hungarian Communists could only muster ten delegates.[36]

Social Democrat leaders blocked an attempt to provide the council with its own decision-making structure and thus the party's own executive fulfilled this role.[37] By January 1919, reformist support in the Workers' Council was slipping away and before the majority was lost the Social Democrat leaders won a vote to expel the Communist delegates.[38] In the following month, the entire Communist leadership was arrested. External developments were driving things forward, however. A complicated twist in events in March 1919 saw Hungary's international position become critical and this was accompanied by further domestic radicalisation. At this point, the Social Democrats determined the Communists should be released and invited into government. The change was not brought about by the Workers' Council, which merely endorsed the Social Democrats' proposal. A brief Soviet Republic followed but was crushed with relative ease as mass support for it was insufficiently strong.

A similar situation occurred in Bavaria. Even though the workers' movement in this southern German state was relatively weak, a Council Republic was proclaimed during April 1919. The cobbled-together coalition of Social Democrats, Independents and anarchists who announced it were reacting to the assassination of a socialist leader and the formation of the Hungarian Soviet government. Communists expressed "profound suspicion" at an "attempt of bankrupt leaders to ingratiate themselves with the masses by a seemingly revolutionary action."[39] After just six days, power was handed to the Communists who attempted to lead the ill-fated Republic forward while simultaneously organising proper elections to the councils from which it could draw strength.[40] Soon after, the Bavarian Soviet Republic was crushed by social democratic forces.

In Austria, the Social Democratic Party Congress, held a week before the overthrow of the monarchy, called "on the workers and soldiers, in the current circumstances, to maintain calm, order and discipline."[41] However, a small group of left radicals had developed after the January 1918 strike and called for a Council Republic. With revolution in full flow they were strong enough to win the convocation of an all-Austrian Workers' Council Congress. That body duly announced that "the workers' council should represent all currents within the working class which recognize the goal of class struggle as being the emancipation of the proletariat and the achievement of the socialist order."[42] This statement was little more than left cover for the Social Democratic Party. The same Congress elected its leader, Friedrich Adler, to head the National Workers' Council Executive Committee. He promptly rejected an appeal for solidarity from the Hungarian Council Republic and wound the movement down as quickly as possible.[43]

The exception to this picture was Russia. Yet when the Petrograd Soviet first met after the February 1917 revolution the Bolsheviks, who had been the most active and consistent opponents of war, found they could muster only 65 delegates out of 2,800. The rest of the participants generally supported the Mensheviks and Social Revolutionaries. These parties rejected the notion of the Soviet replacing the bourgeois state. It took eight months of argument, plus dramatic events such as further disasters in war, the "July days" and Kornilov coup, for the popular mood to shift and the majority to swing behind the Bolshevik slogan of "all power to the soviets." Only then, in October 1917, did the Russian councils take over under Lenin and Trotsky's leadership. Council power was secured until outside pressures – foreign and civil war armies that physically decimated the working class and the economy – destroyed its very foundations. When Stalin took over in 1929 he continued to use the words "Soviet" and "Socialist" in the USSR's title, but the soviets had long since ceased to exist.

The different outcomes obtained in Russia compared to Germany, Austria and Hungary revealed both the strengths and the limitations of the workers' council. For the revolution to succeed, it requires a unified force in the form of a strong revolutionary party. Trotsky, who had presided over the first workers' council in 1905, would conclude in "The Lessons of October":

> Without a [revolutionary] party, apart from a party, over the head of a party, or with a substitute for a party, the proletarian revolution cannot conquer. That is the principal lesson of the past decade … We have paid far too dearly for this conclusion – with regard to the role and importance of a party in a proletarian revolution – to renounce it so lightly or even to minimize its significance.[44]

Conclusion

The experience of the First World War and its traumatic consequences moved millions to the Left. Through a process of developing organisation councils gave structural form to the upsurge of self-activity that followed. This simultaneously created a collective and democratic alternative both to the bourgeois state and to the labour movement institutions indelibly moulded by capitalism – reformist parties and trade unions. Councils merged spontaneity with organised leadership, free debate with centralised action, and were a reaffirmation of the perspective first laid down by Marx about the "political form at last discovered under which to work out the economical emancipation of labour."[45]

Notes

1 V. I. Lenin, "On Strikes."
2 Rosa Luxemburg, "The Junius Pamphlet."
3 Donny Gluckstein, *The Western Soviets*, 20, 109.
4 Karl Marx, "Letter to Ruge Kreuznach."
5 Karl Marx, "The Civil War in France."
6 Quoted in Tony Cliff, *Lenin 1: Building the Party (1893–1914)*.
7 Ibid.
8 *L'Avanti!* Turin edition, 13 January 1918.
9 Gluckstein, *The Western Soviets*, 50.
10 Quoted in Stephen Anthony Smith, *Red Petrograd*.
11 David Mandel, *The Petrograd Workers and the Fall of the Old Regime*, 44.
12 Mario Abrate, *La lotta sindacale nella industrializzazione in Italia, 1906–1926*, 66.
13 Dieter Baudis and Herman Roth, "Berliner Opfer der Novemberrevolution 1918/19," 109.
14 Ibid., 108.
15 Mandel, *The Petrograd Workers and the Fall of the Old Regime*, 44.
16 Chris Fuller, "The Mass Strike in the First World War," 145.
17 Alan Woods, "The Hungarian Soviet Republic of 1919."
18 Marc Ferro, *The Russian Revolution of February 1917*, 79.
19 Leon Trotsky, *The History of the Russian Revolution*, vol. 1.
20 Ibid.
21 Rosa Luxemburg, "The Mass Strike."
22 Leon Trotsky, *1905*, 122.
23 Fuller, "The Mass Strike in the First World War."
24 Erika Weinzierl and Kurt Skalnik (eds), *Österreich 1918–1938*, 35–6.
25 Rudolf Tokes, *Bela Kun and the Hungarian Soviet Republic*, 40.
26 Leaflet quoted in ibid., 37.
27 Quoted in Iain McLean, *The Legend of Red Clydeside*, 125.
28 Willie Gallacher, *Revolt on the Clyde*, 221.
29 Antonio Gramsci, *Selections from Political Writings, 1910–20*, 182.
30 John Reed, "Soviets in Action."
31 V. I. Lenin, "The April Theses."
32 V. I. Lenin, "The Dual Power."
33 Trotsky, *The History of the Russian Revolution*, 224.
34 Gluckstein, *The Western Soviets*, 142.
35 Quoted in Tokes, *Bela Kun and the Hungarian Soviet Republic*, 43.
36 They first attended in December 1918. See ibid., 113.
37 Ibid.
38 Ibid., 117.
39 Quoted in Rose Leviné-Meyer, *Levine: The Life of a Revolutionary*, 89.
40 Ibid., 97.
41 Quoted in Weinzierl and Skalnik (eds), *Österreich 1918–1938*, 70.

42 Ibid., 78.
43 Ibid.
44 Leon Trotsky, "The Lessons of October."
45 Marx, "The Civil War in France."

References

Abrate, Mario. *La lotta sindacale nella industrializzazione in Italia, 1906–1926*. Milan: Franco Angeli, 1967.

L'Avanti!, Turin edition, 13 January 1918.

Baudis, Dieter and Herman Roth. "Berliner Opfer der Novemberrevolution 1918/19." *Jahrbuch für Wirtschaftsgeschichte* 3 (1968): 73–149.

Cliff, Tony. *Lenin 1: Building the Party (1893–1914)*. Accessed at www.marxists.org/archive/cliff/works/1975/lenin1/chap07.htm.

Ferro, Marc. *The Russian Revolution of February 1917*. London: Prentice-Hall, 1972.

Fuller, Chris. "The Mass Strike in the First World War." *International Socialism* 145 (2015). Accessed at http://isj.org.uk/the-mass-strike-in-the-first-world-war.

Gallacher, Willie. *Revolt on the Clyde*. London: Lawrence & Wishart, 1936.

Gluckstein, Donny. *The Western Soviets*. London: Bookmarks, 1985.

Gramsci, Antonio. *Selections from Political Writings, 1910–20*. London: Lawrence and Wishart, 1977.

Lenin, V. I. "The April Theses." Accessed at www.marxists.org/archive/lenin/works/1917/apr/04.htm.

———. "The Dual Power." Accessed at www.marxists.org/archive/lenin/works/1917/apr/09.htm.

———. "On Strikes." Accessed at www.marxists.org/archive/lenin/works/1899/dec/strikes.htm.

Leviné-Meyer, Rose. *Levine: The Life of a Revolutionary*. Farnborough: Saxon-House, 1973.

Luxemburg, Rosa. "The Junius Pamphlet." Accessed at www.marxists.org/archive/luxemburg/1915/junius/.

———. "The Mass Strike." Accessed at www.marxists.org/archive/luxemburg/1906/mass-strike/.

McLean, Iain. *The Legend of Red Clydeside*. Edinburgh: John Donald Publishers, 1983.

Mandel, David. *The Petrograd Workers and the Fall of the Old Regime*. London: Macmillan, 1983.

Marx, Karl. "The Civil War in France." Accessed at www.marxists.org/archive/marx/works/1871/civil-war-france/index.htm.

———. "Letter to Ruge Kreuznach." Accessed at www.marxists.org/archive/marx/works/1843/letters/43_09.htm.

Reed, John. "Soviets in Action." *The Liberator* (1918). Accessed at www.marxists.org/archive/reed/1918/soviets.htm.

Smith, Stephen Anthony. *Red Petrograd: Revolution in the Factories 1917–1918*. Cambridge: Cambridge University Press, 2010.

Tokes, Rudolf L. *Bela Kun and the Hungarian Soviet Republic*. New York: Praeger, 1967.

Trotsky, Leon. *1905*. London: Allen Lane, 1971.

———. *The History of the Russian Revolution*. London: Pluto Press, 1977.
———. "The Lessons of October." Accessed at www.marxists.org/archive/trotsky/1924/lessons/ch8.htm.
Weinzierl, Erika and Kurt Skalnik (eds). *Österreich 1918–1938*. Graz: Styria, 1983.
Woods, Alan. "The Hungarian Soviet Republic of 1919: The Forgotten Revolution." Accessed at www.marxist.com/hungarian-soviet-republic-1919.htm.

3 Rediscovering the Hamburg Workers' and Soldiers' Councils

Gaard Kets and James Muldoon

Introduction

Council communism was a socialist current that first emerged within the German and Dutch sections of the Second International. Council communists were critical of the bureaucratisation of the Russian Revolution, adhered to a principle of the self-emancipation of the working class and advocated the establishment of workers' councils. This body of theory was developed by key figures such as Anton Pannekoek, Herman Gorter, Otto Rühle, Richard Müller and Ernst Däumig, and responded to the experiences of the Russian and German revolutions. In this chapter, we aim to shed new light on our understanding of the development of council theory through an analysis of the early political experiences of council delegates in Hamburg at a formative stage of revolutionary activity in Germany.

Council theory is little known beyond the narrow confines of a seemingly dogmatic ideology with rigid principles based on the rejection of hierarchies, mediation and substitutionism. Characteristic of this position, Gilles Dauvé has argued that although council theorists rightly emphasised the importance of worker self-activity and the dangers of bureaucratisation, council theory ultimately developed into a rigid ideology of "councilism."[1] While there are a number of excellent analyses of council thought that are exceptions to this general trend, it is unfortunately this stale image of councilism that predominates today.[2] One reason for this is that some of the principal sources of knowledge of the European council movements have been transmitted by their political opponents and critics. John Medearis has shown how V. I. Lenin, Hannah Arendt and Joseph Schumpeter produced distorted accounts of the councils and obscured their significance for contemporary politics.[3] One of the earliest and still most influential negative accounts of council theory was provided by Lenin in his polemic against what he portrayed as a form of ultra leftism and an "infantile disorder" of communism.[4] For Lenin, this position adhered to a "rigid doctrinairism," which rejected all forms of leadership, maintained a principled opposition to participation in parliamentary elections and trade union activity, and repudiated all political parties and party discipline. Lenin concluded that such "hopelessly muddled thinking" in fact led to an "incapacity for sustained effort, unity and organised action, which, if encouraged, must inevitably destroy any proletarian revolutionary movement."[5] The authority of such negative and misrepresentative accounts of the councils has added to their neglect within contemporary political theory.

In this chapter, we contribute to a more nuanced understanding of the development of council theory by reconstructing political debates within the meetings of council delegates during the early stages of the German Revolution of 1918–19. We examine the minutes of 76 meetings of the Workers' and Soldiers' Council of Hamburg from 6 November 1918 to 24 March 1919 in order to offer a rich portrait of a key moment in the development of council theory.[6] We focus on the period of the councils' greatest power and influence from the early days of November to the First National Congress of Workers' and Soldiers' Councils on 16 December 1918, at which point the councils voted for elections to a National Assembly to take place on 19 January 1919 (a vote which council delegate Ernst Däumig referred to as a "suicide club" for the councils). The choice of Hamburg is ideal because it was a major city of industrial production, a centre for strike activities and in close proximity to the sailors' revolt at Kiel at the end of October 1918. The selection of Hamburg, rather than the councils in Berlin, also allows us to gain an insight into one of the less studied regional centres outside of the capital.

Delegates within the councils faced the daunting task of pushing through a transformative programme in the interests of ordinary workers while maintaining the basic administrative functions of a failing government and crippled economy. Placing their debates in political context offers an opportunity to study these ideas in action, which helps dispel the myth of council ideology as a set of abstract and dogmatic principles. Council theory is perhaps best known through Anton Pannekoek's *Workers Councils*, which has a more speculative and utopian bent to it than other writings in the tradition. Council delegates within the Workers' and Soldiers' Council of Hamburg were concerned with immediate problems and debated how they would grapple with enacting their principles in the face of the realities of a complex environment. In the course of our analysis, we show that council delegates held a variety of positions on different issues and demonstrate how theoretical principles often succumbed to the necessity of pragmatic solutions.

Studying council debates also offers an important perspective due to the relative lack of theoretical elaborations of council ideology before the emergence of workers' councils in the Russian and German revolutions. As workers' councils arose spontaneously in mass strikes across Europe with little planning or knowledge of how they would be developed, the initial meetings of councils are important moments of political contestation that contain crucial debates concerning different interpretations of political challenges. An examination of these records provides insight into the mindset of participants, rather than of council theorists often writing well after the events themselves. While we have a number of excellent monographs on some of the major theorists of council theory such as Anton Pannekoek, Richard Müller and Rosa Luxemburg, there has been less published on local council delegates and the practices of political movements during the revolution.[7] We aim to contribute to filling this gap with a detailed examination of a short chapter in the history of the council movements. What we observe from the debates is that there is no single official position of council communism, but rather a set of shared underlying concerns and a number of different ways in which these ideas were put to work in different political contexts.

This chapter will proceed as follows. First, we introduce the political context of the formation of the Hamburg councils. The next section examines the first debates of the Hamburg Council concerning the relationship between councils and the institutions of the previous political order. This question would play a pivotal role in the formation of council communist ideology. Hamburg is a particularly interesting case for this question, because the council had to relate not only to the national assembly in Berlin, but also to the two representative institutions that had governed this relatively autonomous city-state during the past decades: the *Senat* (Senate) and the *Bürgerschaft* (Parliament). Third, we analyse debates concerning the relationship between councils, political parties and trade unions. Finally, we analyse the issue of membership and democratic inclusion. The councils faced questions of who should be included in their political organisation, in particular concerning women, peasants, intellectual labourers and the unemployed. We conclude by reflecting on the meaning of these instances of bottom-up political thought for the development of the council idea.

The Workers' and Soldiers' Council of Hamburg

In the final months of the war in 1918, German sailors mutinied and rebelled following an order from the naval command in Kiel for one final suicidal mission against the Allied forces. The hardships of the war and the growing radicalisation of workers and soldiers had created conditions fertile for revolution. Attempts by the government to make concessions, such as the appointment of Max von Baden as new *Reichskanzler* and the inclusion of social democratic ministers in his cabinet, proved unsatisfactory to German workers who increasingly called for the abdication of the kaiser. The first mutinies and strikes of October 1918 were crushed and political leaders were thrown into prison. On 3 November 1918, a series of demonstrations for the release of the prisoners led to the establishment of a soldiers' council, prompting a spread of strikes and the formation of councils across Germany.

On 5 November 1918, the Independent Social Democrats (USPD, an "anti-war" split-off of the SPD) organised a massive gathering in the *Gewerkschaftshaus* (trade union building), where sailors from Kiel were greeted with much enthusiasm leading to a solidarity strike.[8] Wilhelm Düwell, editor of SPD journal, *Vorwärts*, proposed a mass demonstration to take place on the next day and called for the establishment of a workers' and soldiers' council.[9] This call was answered by over 40,000 people who gathered on 6 November 1918 at the Heiligengeist field in Hamburg. Many of the participants were armed sailors, soldiers and workers who marched to strategic positions across the city and captured the army headquarters, various military barracks and the city newspaper, *Hamburger Echo*.

By the evening of 6 November 1918 the workers' and soldiers' provisional council was acknowledged (even by representatives of the local senate and parliament) as the highest political and military authority in Hamburg. Except for maintaining order and protecting the outcomes of the revolution, the main priority of this council was to organise elections for a more permanent workers' and soldiers' council. On 8 November 1918, elections took place in the factories and workshops for the *Großen Arbeiterrat* (Grand Workers' Council) of approximately 600 delegates. These industrial delegates gathered on 9 November 1918 to choose 18 delegates for the Workers' Council. The remaining 12 seats in the 30-seat Workers' Council were occupied by delegates from the three workers' parties (USPD, SPD and left radicals (mostly communists)) and delegates from the trade unions. The USPD and left radicals initially dominated the council, demonstrated by the fact that USPD member Heinrich Laufenberg was elected First Chairman.

Soldiers elected delegates to the Workers' and Soldiers' Council of Hamburg through their own council structures. From ships and barracks across the city, soldiers elected delegates to the "General Assembly of Soldiers' Councils of Hamburg-Altona and surroundings," which consisted of 350 members. From this group, 100 members were delegated to the "Delegates' Assembly," which was in turn led by a small executive committee of 15 (later 30) members called the "Soldiers' Council." Together the Soldiers' Council and Workers' Council formed the Workers' and Soldiers' Council of Hamburg with 60 members, as shown in Figure 3.1. This council existed until its final meeting on 24 March 1919, a day after the elections for the city parliament, which made it obsolete. Having lost all their influence in the first months of 1919, the red flag hung by the revolutionaries on 11 November 1918 over the town hall was finally removed and the Workers' and Soldiers' Council was dissolved.

The Councils and the Old Institutional Order

In some of the most well-known texts of council communism, by Pannekoek, Rühle and Korsch, for example, councils were envisaged as alternatives to

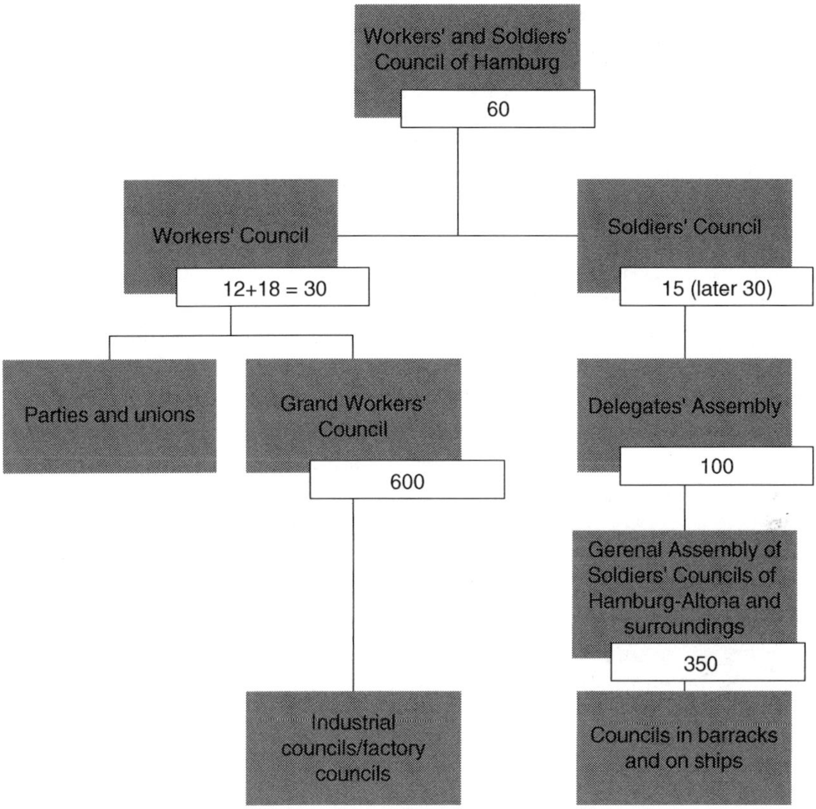

Figure 3.1 The Structure of the Workers' and Soldiers' Council of Hamburg

bourgeois state institutions.[10] Many council theorists considered workers' councils as proletarian organs that were distinct from bourgeois institutions due to their directly recallable delegates, system of voting from within the working class and workers' control over production. Many radical council delegates also imagined a council system as a complete break with the past. In a speech to the First National Congress of Workers' and Soldiers' Councils, Ernst Däumig declared: "[w]e have to abandon the entire old administrative machinery, on the federal, regional, and municipal level. The German people have to get used to self-management instead of governance."[11] However, in most cities in Germany outside of Berlin, councils exercised little more than a supervisory function over existing government apparatuses. As the latter offered no resistance to the councils, the whole administrative structure tended to remain in place.[12] Many of the older industrialists, state authorities and other elements of the bourgeoisie were suspicious of the councils, but they dared not risk directly attacking them.[13]

The revolutionaries perhaps naively underestimated the resilience of the old institutions and failed to foresee the difficulties of undertaking basic administrative duties without them. Ernst Däumig argued that "[t]he state apparatus had new men at its head but remained essentially unchanged."[14] Similarly, Karl Korsch also recorded that "[c]ouncils were in many if not most cases content with a very ineffective 'control,' when in reality they should have demanded full powers in the legislative, executive and judicial fields."[15] Only the Executive Committee of the Berlin council, headed by Richard Müller, demanded that full legislative and executive power should reside in the councils. However, even the Executive Committee conceded the necessity of maintaining certain existing government apparatuses, stating in a promulgation on 11 November 1918: "[a]ll the communal authorities of the various *Länder*, of the entire Reich, and of the army are to continue in their activities."[16]

The precise relationship between the new councils and the older institutions was subject to heated debate within the councils. The example of Hamburg provides an illustrative case study of the practical problems faced by many of the local councils arising across Germany. In this instance, the old institutions were abolished by decree for only a few short days before revolutionaries were forced to acknowledge how dependent they were on them for administrative support, which led to a desire for compromise and co-operation. The arguments between delegates in Hamburg are also instructive because they prefigure the main debate at the First National Congress of Workers' and Soldiers' Councils in Berlin: the choice between parliamentary democracy and proletarian democracy, between "national elections or the council system." Three main factors came into play in negotiations over the place of state administrative institutions alongside the councils. First, there were ideological differences between political parties over the role of the councils. While radical council delegates in the USPD and the radical Left believed that councils should form the basis of new state institutions, the SPD was reluctant to view the councils as genuine alternatives to a parliamentary system. SPD delegates used their position in the councils to retain or reform existing state structures. Second, there was a lack of understanding among the workers about the nature of a council system and ideological hesitations about creating a full council republic. Due to the propaganda efforts of the SPD, liberals and conservatives, the rallying cry for national unity around parliamentary elections was very strong and workers were not convinced that a council system presented a desirable alternative to parliamentary institutions. Third, pragmatic concerns also prevented the swift abolishment of state apparatuses because it would have been impossible to fulfil basic administrative duties that were so desperately needed to keep the country functioning. Thus, even when radical elements dominated the councils, they hesitated at completely removing key institutions of the bourgeois state.

Hamburg was governed by a senate in which a mayor, deputy mayor and 24 senators were (from 1860 onwards) elected by a parliament (citizens' council) and appointed for life. The Parliament did not consist of all citizens, but an elite based on wealth and social class. The provisional workers' and soldiers' councils that arose on 6 November 1918 did not immediately alter the official position of these old institutions, even after obtaining de facto power over the city. In the evening, delegates of the provisional workers' council marched on the town hall to meet with the senators. Delegates declared to the senators that "the workers and soldiers have taken political power into their hands, they will show that they are ready to use this power the right way."[17] However, the Senate was not abolished, but only commanded to secure the supply of paper for the declarations of the council. One newspaper even reported that although the councils had taken authority over police and military matters, the Senate and the Parliament would be able to function as usual.[18] In its first public announcement, the council declared that it had conquered "most of the political power," leaving the precise relation between the council and the old institutions unclear.[19]

On 12 November 1918, at the Presidium of the Workers' and Soldiers' Council of Hamburg, a unanimous proclamation was issued stating:

> The Workers' and Soldiers' Council has taken over the execution of political power in the state territories of Hamburg. The Senate and Parliament do not exist anymore. The Hamburg state territories will soon be part of the German People's Republic ... Public servants remain at their positions. Their wages will be paid ... The Workers' and Soldiers' Council will from now on meet in the town hall.[20]

The Presidium's desire to put an end to the old institutions is further emphasised by the fact that the meetings of the Council were now to take place in the town hall, the traditional home of the Senate and Parliament.

The meeting of the Workers' and Soldiers' Council of Hamburg followed directly after the meeting of the Presidium. The atmosphere of the meeting was *gewitterschwül* (ominous), with the door and room being guarded by armed sailors. Nobody was allowed to leave the room before the end of the meeting, and some members felt trapped.[21] Laufenberg started off the debate by reading the proclamation of the Presidium, but a political difference soon emerged between the radical delegates and those of the SPD. Louis Gruenwaldt, council delegate and chairman of the SPD faction in the Parliament, argued that authorities would not have to be removed by violence and that rather than replace the Parliament and Senate, their voter base should be expanded to universal suffrage. He was supported by Heinrich Schönberg, leader of the trade union cartel, who argued that social reform rather than revolution would be in the best interests of workers.[22] In his opinion, dismissing the Senate would lead to economic turmoil, which would anger the masses and turn them against socialism. The radical council delegates rejected these arguments as too conservative for the current revolutionary situation and considered that there was no time or capacity to hold municipal elections for a new parliament. The Council voted in favour of the proclamation of the Presidium with six dissenting votes (presumably SPD). Gruenwaldt concluded that the radicals had decided on a "very unpleasant undertaking."[23] However, this vote would not be the last word on the existence of the old institutions.

Following the council meeting, Laufenberg visited the Senate accompanied by armed sailors and explained to them that their institution no longer existed. He stated that "the past had been definitively emptied" and that there were no more "bridges between the past and the present left."[24] Nevertheless, he explained that the Council would still request the expertise and co-operation of individual former senators for the governance of the city. In a council meeting on 13 November 1918, it was decided that former senators could exercise their former offices under political control of the Council.[25] After some ambiguity about whether the senators could continue their work *as senators*, it was decided that the most prominent former senators could sit in a commission together with delegates from the Council, which would operate under political control of the Council.[26]

On 15 November 1918, the Council discussed its plans for the old parliament and the institutions that would replace it. The issue for the Council was that the Parliament was still required to pass finance bills that would allow government spending. The councils did not want to take on such functions and believed that a separate body should organise the city's finances such as wages for policemen, benefits for the unemployed and veterans, housing for the poor, food distributions, etc. Delegates discussed the possibility of establishing a new communal parliament with universal suffrage that would replace the Parliament. Gruenwaldt of the SPD argued that holding elections was impossible at this point, so there was no other option but to use existing institutions. Berthold Grosse, SPD, agreed and added that there would be democratic benefits of maintaining the Parliament and expanding the voting population of the city's representative body to include all classes. It was decided in the Council that, in spite of their previous proclamation, the Parliament would still function, now with universal suffrage, as would the Senate. This was a marked reversal of the Council's initial intentions and can be viewed as a concession in its attempt to grapple with the difficult political realities of governing a country still in turmoil.

To explain this new constellation of political powers to the public and to the old institutions, Grosse proposed that Laufenberg hold a rousing speech before the first meeting of the Parliament in which he would directly explain their new capacities and how these related to the sovereignty of the Council.[27] The next day, Laufenberg and four other delegates from the Council met with five representatives of the Senate to explain the new power relations between the Council and the old institutions.[28] Six main issues were raised.[29] First, political sovereignty remained firmly in the hands of the Council. In order to achieve this, the Council was granted veto power over all decisions and the old institutions should only deal with non-political issues. Second, the Council was to appoint four delegates with full participation rights in the Senate. Third, one of the Council delegates in the Senate would act as third chairman, on equal footing with the first and second chair. Fourth, a new parliament would be elected by popular vote based on universal suffrage as soon as possible. Fifth, the Council would participate in the financial commission of the Senate. The sixth and final issue related to a possible change in the names of the Senate and the Parliament as they were so closely associated with the old political order. Various proposal were submitted (*Rat* or *Magistrat* for the Senate, *Stadtverordnetenversammlung* for the Parliament), but none of them were agreed upon. The main reason for this was the fear that foreign allies and investors would withdraw their capital from Hamburg if the main institutions were renamed. It was argued that the chaos that would result from a renaming could be catastrophic for the financial situation of Hamburg. Hence, in order to secure continuity and the state's capacity to deliver basic services, the traditional names of the old institutions were maintained.[30] Although an idea of a more direct democracy nested in factories and barracks animated radical council delegates, the practical demands of administration cut short any possible experiment with a "pure" council system.

Political Parties and Trade Unions

Council communists are perhaps most well-known for their vehement rejection of participation in political parties and trade union activity. Their steadfast advocacy of the role of the masses over leaders and criticisms of the role of the Communist Party led Lenin to accuse them of "denying the necessity of the party and of party discipline" and of "completely disarming the proletariat in *the interests of the bourgeoisie*."[31] This anti-party position is most clearly presented in Otto Rühle's 1920 pamphlet, *The Revolution Is Not a Party Affair*.[32] Rühle was critical of the commanding role that leaders played in political parties and the depoliticising effect this had on the masses by decreasing their initiative and denying them effective agency. He also argued that the larger and more powerful a political party became, the more it would defend its power within the system at the expense of advocating for structural change and revolutionary activity. Rühle believed the separation between political parties and trade unions needed to be overcome by an organisation with a unified framework, which would be "neither a political party with parliamentary chatter and paid hacks, nor a trade union." He argued for a revolutionary organisation that was organised factory by factory such as the General Workers' Union

(AAU), which was formed after the German Revolution in opposition to the traditional trade unions.

However, this radical anti-party position was not initially shared by most council delegates, but instead slowly developed as a result of their disillusionment with traditional political parties following the Russian and German revolutions and the perceived betrayal of the working class by the Bolsheviks and the SPD. In 1918 at the height of the German council movements' power, although there was dissatisfaction with the SPD for their granting of war credits, and talk of the need for an "organisation of a new kind," there was only a limited anti-party discourse among council delegates. As late as 1920 in "World Revolution and Communist Tactics," Pannekoek still believed in the necessity of a well-disciplined revolutionary party in organising working-class consciousness.[33] Later, Pannekoek would grow more sceptical of traditional political parties and call for new organisations that would be "parties or groups based on opinions," which would act as "organs of the self-enlightenment of the working class."[34] Such educational groups would function mainly for propaganda purposes and would be organisations within which

> persons with the same fundamental conceptions unite for the discussion of practical steps and seek clarification through discussions and propagandize their conclusions, such groups might be called parties, but they would be parties in an entirely different sense from those of today.[35]

The idea that all political parties were bourgeois and that a revolutionary party was "a contradiction in terms" was a position that was developed later than 1918.[36]

Let us examine how events unfolded on the ground in Hamburg in relation to this issue. The initial formation of councils by sailors at Kiel and the solidarity strikes and councils in Hamburg were not organised through existing political parties. The emergence of soldiers' and workers' councils across Germany began as spontaneous actions that had their origins in strike committees and industrial councils rather than the traditional institutions of worker representation such as the SPD and trade unions. However, as soon as the councils arose political parties such as the SPD and USPD organised to take action within the councils and dominated initial meetings and discussions. In Hamburg, the USPD initially held an advantage over the SPD due to its closer ideological and organisational connections to the councils. Following the demonstration at the Heiligengeist field on 5 November1918, the first provisional workers' and soldiers' council consisted only of members from the USPD. At a meeting of *Vertrauensmänner* (trustees) organised by the SPD and trade unions, Hugo Haase proposed to ban party and trade union members from the councils, since "these people cannot represent the interests of the revolutionary proletariat."[37] His proposal was met with enormous resistance. During a meeting of the USPD on the same day, however, this proposal to exclude party and union representatives from the Council had more success: his proposal earned "warm applause."[38] When the leadership of the SPD and trade union cartel met on the morning of 7 November 1918, they were aware that they were about to miss the revolutionary boat, and it was decided that they must do everything in their power to regain their influence on the working masses.[39]

Although the USPD initially attempted to organise in the councils without the SPD and trade unions, the organisational power of the SPD and their threat to sabotage the councils by organising their own delegate assemblies led the USPD to compromise.[40] On the evening of 8 November 1918, representatives of the SPD, USPD, trade unions and left radicals gathered to discuss the composition of the Council. The radical parties demanded that the Council be the new sovereign body that would lead the revolution. While sceptical of the organisational form of the councils, the SPD and trade unions were willing to co-operate within the council structure on the condition of *Gleichberechtigung* (equal rights). This led to the executive of the Workers' Council consisting of three delegates from both the SPD and USPD.[41] Thus, while initial aspirations were for the councils to transcend party divisions, pragmatic concerns for unity and organisational power led to a balance of power between the parties within the councils. Council delegates were not opposed to parties per se. Although many of the radical delegates were critical of the direction of the SPD, they still belonged to a political party and saw a pivotal role for a mass workers' party in leading revolutionary activity. The idea of dissolving all parties within the councils was only appealing to those delegates who believed they could already exercise control over the direction of events.

The compromise between the two parties was very similar to the one reached in Berlin, where council delegates also tended to be elected by the parties rather than directly through factory organisations. Council delegates in Berlin voted for an interim cabinet of six members called the "Council of People's Deputies" (*Rat der Volksbeauftragten*), which consisted of three SPD members and the three USPD members. These two factions also disagreed over the proper role of the councils, leading to factional fighting and an increasingly difficult relationship between different council organs.[42] On the day of the First National Congress of Workers' and Soldiers' Councils in Berlin, both the SPD and USPD pre-caucused to organise voting, leading party membership to be the strongest determinant of how a delegate voted at the Congress.[43] This conflict reflected the deep underlying ideological disagreements about the role of the councils in a future German state held by the two parties.

Writing afterwards, council theorists who experienced events were critical of the role of political parties. Both Ernst Däumig and Karl Korsch argued that the infighting between the parties had a distorting effect on the development of working-class consciousness and organisation within the councils.[44] Däumig claimed that "[i]n many cases, the members of the workers' councils were simply appointed by the leadership of the two social democratic parties without even consulting the rank and file."[45] This increased the top-down nature of the councils, which prevented the rank and file from exercising adequate control over deputies. Second, factional strife between parties within the councils created a "conflict between 'party discipline' and 'proletarian duty'" whereby a delegate could be torn between remaining faithful to their party and voting in the interests of the working class.[46] Particularly in the case of delegates from the SPD, which did not have much faith in the councils, delegates could be prevented from acting as local representatives for their factories and workplaces.

Yet it is hard to imagine a political system without parties or how, without the oppressive apparatuses of a one-party state, they could be prevented from arising in a council system. The idea of a strict opposition between the "parties" on the one hand and the "councils" on the other ignores the extent to which organised political parties were able to exert their influence over the emergence of new political actors and institutions. It is impossible to demarcate between two separate "systems," since most actors within the councils were also party members and the dynamics of party politics played out within the councils. The council movements emerged without the organisational initiative of the main political parties but it was soon dominated by party factions. The position of the later council communists developed through a growing scepticism of the role of political parties, but even at the extreme end, theorists could not completely detach themselves from the necessity of an organisation that would co-ordinate and lead revolutionary activity.

Membership and Democratic Inclusion

The (self-)determination of any political community is defined though relations of inclusion/exclusion. The formation of a community requires a moment of closure in which a frontier is drawn defining who has membership and is able to participate in government. This closure and the resulting boundaries of the community can be contested and change over time. The revolutionary moment in Germany provided an opportunity to radically alter the power relations between classes and to redefine a new democratic collective. The empire under Bismarck had been a relatively conservative, hierarchical and closed society, which had resisted progressive pushes for reform from liberals and socialists. With the abdication of the kaiser and the councils' assumption of power in November 1918, the council movements faced a theoretical dilemma of reconciling their desire for the rule of the working class with their aspiration for an inclusive political community in a post-capitalist society. While their political programme was based on class struggle against a ruling elite, the final aim of socialism was the elimination of class-based oppression and the inclusion of all individuals as free and equal members of a self-determining society.

This tension was not always easily resolved and produced different accounts of socialist political organisation and objectives. For example, by council democracy, Pannekoek understood "workers power to the exclusion of the other classes," and he was critical of discourses of abstract universality insofar as they would empower "the war profiteers, black market speculators, landowners, moneylenders, rentiers, all those who live off the labor of others without doing any work themselves."[47] In a clash between the desire for democracy and workers' control over production, Pannekoek tended to come down on the side of the latter. Meanwhile Luxemburg, in one formulation, argued that "Social Democracy has always contended that it represents not only the class interests of the proletariat but also the progressive aspirations of the whole of contemporary society. It represents the interests of all who are oppressed by bourgeois domination."[48] Although she was no less aware of the dangers of counter-revolution, Luxemburg felt the importance of achieving socialism through democracy and reaching out to other marginalised groups. These positions represent different attempts at negotiating the often-conflicting demands of the need to organise for power and protect the revolution against counter-revolutionary tendencies, while fulfilling the underlying socialist goals of struggling for an egalitarian and inclusive society.

During the revolution, grappling with this theoretical problem entailed answering the practical question of who could be a member of the councils. This issue took on particular significance once councils assumed political power and membership of the councils involved the opportunity to actively participate in self-government. The debates within the Hamburg Workers' and Soldiers' Council provide the opportunity to analyse how council delegates faced challenges from three different partially excluded groups: women, peasants and the unemployed. Our analysis reveals that in the early days of the revolution, council delegates were relatively inattentive to how not only the bourgeoisie, but many of the lower classes were effectively excluded from participation in the councils. They confronted issues of democratic exclusion only when they were thrust upon them, and even then, often haphazardly and inadequately. These debates reveal many of the ideological limitations of the era and the failure to properly grapple with questions of internal power hierarchies and other forms of exclusion outside of the capital/labour relation.

Before addressing these three groups, there was one group, the bourgeoisie, whose removal from positions of structural power there was little disagreement about among socialists. The councils were recognised as class-specific institutions that were intended to counteract the bourgeoisie's economic and political power. As Müller addressed the National Congress:

> the people who produce must be in the councils, whether they are manual or intellectual workers – but not every parasite exploiting the labor of others! Comrades, be aware! We already have "landlords' councils." What's next? "Millionaires' councils"? Such councils we don't need.[49]

The council system would not allow members of the bourgeoisie to create their own centres of power in the form of councils because these would be aimed at oppressing workers and reinforcing class rule. As a result, Pannekoek considered that "the ruling class must be excluded from exercising any political influence whatsoever."[50] If a member of the bourgeoisie wished to give up their private ownership of capital and participate in the new society alongside workers then he could "make his voice heard in the factory assemblies" and "have the same decision-making power as any other worker."[51] The exclusion of the bourgeoisie was not a permanent ban on all individuals, but rather on a particular formation of political power designed to expropriate surplus labour from workers.

The exclusion of marginalised groups in society was partly due to the organisation of councils in workplaces. The council movements sought to eliminate the distinction between the political and the economic; in other words, to remove the need for a separate political sphere by workers directly administering the production process for the benefit of the community. This would place processes of self-government directly in workplaces as primary sites of production and socialisation. However, with political membership organised through workplaces rather than artificial electoral boundaries, participation in a political community became dependent on and conditioned by the size and type of an individual's workplace. Pannekoek recognised that "whoever does not work as a member of a production group is automatically barred from the possibility of being part of the decision-making."[52] Yet for those outside of the organised industrial labour in the cities (which was the majority of the population), this entailed a reduced capacity for participation in government.

The first example of exclusion is women who played a pivotal role in the organisation and maintenance of society during the war, working in the factories and providing the front and their families with resources. Moreover, these women had organised demonstrations and strikes (such as the one that had toppled the tsar in Russia in 1917) and were at the centre of the political struggle for universal suffrage. In spite of all this, women were both severely underrepresented within the councils as delegates and also as a class that was more likely to have undertaken unpaid reproductive labour outside of a workplace environment and was therefore excluded from participation in workplace-based councils.[53]

In the Hamburg Grand Workers' Council only three of the 600 members were women. In the smaller and more influential Hamburg Workers' and Soldiers' Council, this figure was reduced to just one, Erna Halbe. These figures reflected national trends, with only two female council delegates among the 489 who attended the National Congress.[54] There were also barely any women who acted as officials within the council movements when compared to the significant numbers within rank-and-file workers.[55] Efforts by advocates for women's rights to redress this vast inequality were never taken seriously. At a preparatory meeting of the *Vertrauensmänner* of the Hamburg workplaces on 9 November 1918, the membership and composition of the workers' council was discussed. While it was agreed that there would be representation from different categories of labour (i.e. metal, wood, coal, etc.), a proposal from two members to elect women to the executive of the council was neither discussed nor put to a vote and soon fell off the agenda.[56] On 19 November 1918, the issue was discussed once more because the council had received a letter from the Hamburg-Altona Organisation for Women's Rights concerning the establishment of a Women's Council to form part of the Hamburg Workers' and Soldiers' Council in order to defend women's interests. Their request was denied and as a consolation the women's organisation was allowed to elect a delegate to the socio-political commission of the council.[57] However, an invitation to this meeting never arrived and repeated efforts to rectify the matter fell on deaf ears.

It was clear that most council delegates believed that all workers, not simply factory workers, should be allowed to form councils and be part of the federal council system. Ernst Däumig argued that "the council system is not only relevant for the manual worker but also for the intellectual worker" as it should "build the necessary bridges uniting all proletarians."[58] In the meeting of the Hamburg Workers' and Soldiers' Council that took place on 13 November 1918, the announcement that public servants (teachers, policemen, fire fighters, etc.) were establishing their own councils was greeted with enthusiasm as it provided an opportunity for bureaucratic personnel sympathetic to the revolution to play a greater role in the city's governance.

On the question of peasants, the council movements were generally more hesitant. On the one hand, the imperative of the "Zusammenarbeit von Stadt und Land" (co-operation between city and country) was an important ideal for council delegates, yet they also expressed concerns over the conservatism of rural organisations.[59] When the topic of food shortages arose, it was immediately suggested that the best public speakers be sent to the surrounding villages to secure the delivery of food from the farmers to Hamburg. These speakers were to persuade the farmers to elect farmers' councils that would co-operate with the Workers' and Soldiers' Council in the city.[60] Delegates considered that even the existing liberal farmers' clubs could play a role, although there were fears that the empowerment of these peasant organisations could result in counter-revolutionary activities.

Ultimately, the immediate need to avoid food shortages overrode any ideological concerns and it was agreed that delegates would be sent.

A third example of the question of inclusion in the Hamburg Workers' and Soldiers' Council was the representation of the unemployed. Since council delegates were elected in the workplace, the unemployed had no direct influence on council politics. Nevertheless, in the Council's function as the governing body of the city, many decisions had to be taken with regard to questions of unemployment, rounds of discharges in industry (especially in relation to the military) and unemployment benefits. In the first weeks, there was no discussion within the councils about decisions concerning the unemployed being taken without their knowledge or input. It was only at the end of 1918, when a large number of unemployed workers gathered in front of the town hall and demolished the car of one of the delegates, that they were considered. Although these unemployed men and women did not demand membership of the council, eventually the council decided that representatives of the unemployed should be in permanent contact with the council through the establishment of a commission.[61]

As a sociological reality, the working class did not include all lower and oppressed classes in society. Radical labour leaders were generally sceptical of the capacity of peasants, petite bourgeoisie and other declassed individuals to exercise power in a manner that furthered the aims of the revolution. They had good reason to doubt whether certain other groups would follow their political programme, but the exclusion of such groups raises serious questions about the councils' democratic credentials. There was also a theoretical lacuna concerning members of society who were connected to the working class but not engaged in paid productive labour for various reasons. Certain council theorists adhered to a troubling connection between a conception of productive activity and political rights. Furthermore, while council delegates aimed to extend council forms of organisation to all productive workers, the reality was that only the major centres were included. In Berlin, for example, initial plans for the formation of workers' councils were drawn up without any consideration for the huge industrial and working-class neighbourhoods outside of Berlin's city limits.[62] The three examples of exclusion we have examined reveal a common theme: questions of membership were discussed only in response to problems raised by marginalised groups themselves rather than as a result of the desire to clarify the proper demos of these new democratic institutions and to establish adequate democratic principles of inclusion. Yet the democratic character of the councils meant that marginalised groups could voice their concerns and demand inclusion, even if these demands were handled arbitrarily and imperfectly.

In conclusion, revolutionaries wished to depart from existing repertoires of politics, but struggled to create new ones. The collapse of the legitimacy and authority of the old order and the organisation of councils into a force capable of taking de facto power created the possibility of radical transformation. Yet attempts to create a new society were impeded both by ideological hesitation and the practical realities of attempting to govern in a divided society and with the collapse of basic administrative functions. Existing political parties certainly did not make the revolution, but they were quick to seize opportunities to advance their programmes. The unfamiliar radical council ideas eventually gave way to a much more well-known programme of social democratic reforms that the SPD managed to find support for among a broad variety of moderate and conservative forces.

There were no clear blueprints for the political challenges faced by revolutionaries. The Russian Revolution, by and large, was seen as a cautionary tale. While some of the radical delegates believed that important lessons could be learnt from this experience, even Laufenberg sought to distance Germany from the Russian example. As a result, the actions of council delegates reflected a number of pragmatic compromises and the competing interpretations over the proper structure and role for the councils that existed among council delegates. Nevertheless, the experience of participating in workers' councils would inspire a generation of left intellectuals and activists, some of whom would continue to theorise the experience of workers' councils as a third path between the bureaucracy of state socialism and the inequalities and exploitation of capitalist democracy.

Notes

1 Gilles Dauvé, *Eclipse and Re-Emergence of the Communist Movement*, 95.
2 Exceptions include Oskar Anweiler, *The Soviets*; Phillippe Bourinet, *The Dutch and German Communist Left (1900–1968)*; Immanuel Ness and Dario Azzellini (eds), *Ours to Master and to Own*.
3 John Medearis, "Lost or Obscured?"
4 V. I. Lenin, "'Left-Wing' Communism."
5 Ibid.
6 We benefited from the recent publication of the source book, Volker Stalmann (ed.), *Der Hamburger Arbeiter- und Soldatenrat 1918/19* [*The Hamburger Workers' and Soldiers' Councils, 1918–19*].
7 John Gerber, *Anton Pannekoek and the Socialism of Workers' Self-Emancipation 1873–1960*; Ralf Hoffrogge, *Working-Class Politics in the German Revolution*; Paul Frölich, *Rosa Luxemburg*.
8 From 1917 to 1922 the SPD was called the *Mehrheitssozialdemokratische Partei Deutschlands* (MSPD) to distinguish it from the USPD. For simplicity, we use SPD in this chapter for this party throughout its history.
9 Stalmann (ed.), *Der Hamburger Arbeiter- und Soldatenrat 1918/19*, 126–8.
10 See, for example, Anton Pannekoek, *Workers' Councils*.
11 Ernst Däumig, "The National Assembly Means the Councils' Death," in Gabriel Kuhn (ed.), *All Power to the Councils!*, 48.
12 Walter Tormin, *Zwischen Rätediktatur und Sozialer Demokratie*, 89–90.
13 Ernst Däumig, "The Council Idea and Its Realization," in Kuhn (ed.), *All Power to the Councils!*, 53.
14 Ibid., 57.

15 Karl Korsch, "Evolution of the Problem of the Political Workers Councils in Germany."
16 Quoted in ibid.
17 Stalmann (ed.), *Der Hamburger Arbeiter- und Soldatenrat 1918/19*, 136–7.
18 Ibid.
19 Ibid., 143–4.
20 Ibid., 176–7.
21 Ibid., 180–2.
22 Ibid.
23 Ibid., 182.
24 Ibid., 187–9.
25 Ibid., 183–6.
26 Ibid., 189.
27 Ibid., 199–207.
28 Ibid., 215–22, 217.
29 For the debates of these issues, see the minutes of the meetings in ibid., 199–237.
30 Ibid., 208–14, 222–8, 223.
31 Lenin, "'Left-Wing' Communism," italics in original.
32 Otto Rühle, "The Revolution Is Not a Party Affair."
33 Anton Pannekoek, "World Revolution and Communist Tactics."
34 Anton Pannekoek, "General Remarks on the Question of Organisation."
35 Anton Pannekoek, "Party and Class."
36 Ibid.
37 Stalmann (ed.), *Der Hamburger Arbeiter- und Soldatenrat 1918/19*, 44.
38 Ibid., 126–8.
39 Ibid., 144–6.
40 Ibid., 148–9.
41 Ibid., 153–7.
42 Müller, "Democracy or Dictatorship," in Kuhn (ed.), *All Power to the Councils!*, 59.
43 Sabine Roß, *Biographisches Handbuch der Reichsrätekongresse 1918/1919*, 166.
44 Korsch, "Evolution of the Problem of the Political Workers Councils in Germany."
45 Däumig, "The Council Idea and Its Realization," 55.
46 Ibid., 55–6.
47 Anton Pannekoek, "Social Democracy and Communism."
48 Rosa Luxemburg, "Marxism or Leninism?" in *Reform or Revolution and Other Writings*, 94.
49 Müller, "Democracy or Dictatorship," 64.
50 Pannekoek, "Social Democracy and Communism."
51 Ibid.
52 Ibid.
53 The role of gender in the German Revolution is yet to be thoroughly studied. Although recent decades have seen some first steps in this direction, most notably Helga Grebing, *Frauen in der deutschen Revolution 1918/19*; Kathleen Canning, "Gender and the Imaginary of Revolution," in Klaus Weinhauer *et al.* (eds), *Germany 1916–23*, 103–26.

54 Roß, *Biographisches Handbuch der Reichsrätekongresse 1918/1919*, 209–12.
55 "The Unions and Women," 2; Grebing, *Frauen in der deutschen Revolution 1918/1919*.
56 Stalmann (ed.), *Der Hamburger Arbeiter- und Soldatenrat 1918/19*, 161–3.
57 Ibid., 248–52.
58 Däumig, "The Council Idea and Its Realization," 58.
59 Stalmann (ed.), *Der Hamburger Arbeiter- und Soldatenrat 1918/19*, 190–4.
60 Ibid., 183–6.
61 Ibid., 431–8.
62 Hoffrogge, *Working-Class Politics in the German Revolution*, 76.

References

Anon. "The Unions and Women." *Der kommunistische Gewerkschafter* 2 (1921).

Anweiler, Oskar. *The Soviets: The Russian Workers, Peasants, and Soldiers Councils, 1905–1921*. New York: Pantheon Books, 1974.

Bourinet, Phillippe. *The Dutch and German Communist Left (1900–1968): "Neither Lenin Nor Trotsky Nor Stalin!" – "All Workers Must Think for Themselves!"* Leiden: Brill Publishers, 2016.

Canning, Kathleen. "Gender and the Imaginary of Revolution." In *Germany 1916–23: A Revolution in Context*. Edited by Klaus Weinhauer, Anthony McElligott and Kirsten Heinsohn. 103–26. Bielefeld: Transcript Verlag, 2015.

Dauvé, Gilles. *Eclipse and Re-Emergence of the Communist Movement*. London: PM Press, 2015.

Frölich, Paul. *Rosa Luxemburg: Ideas in Action*. London: Pluto Press, 1994.

Gerber, John. *Anton Pannekoek and the Socialism of Workers' Self-Emancipation 1873–1960*. Dordrecht: Kluwer Academic Publishers, 1989.

Grebing, Helga. *Frauen in der deutschen Revolution 1918/19*. Heidelberg: Stiftung Reichspräsident-Friedrich-Ebert-Gedenkstätte, 1994.

Hoffrogge, Ralf. *Working-Class Politics in the German Revolution: Richard Müller, the Revolutionary Shop Stewards and the Origins of the Council Movement*. Leiden: Brill Publishers, 2014.

Korsch, Karl. "Evolution of the Problem of the Political Workers Councils in Germany." Accessed at www.marxists.org/archive/korsch/1921/councils.htm.

Kuhn, Gabriel (ed.). *All Power to the Councils! A Documentary History of the German Revolution of 1918–1919*. London: PM Press, 2012.

Lenin, V. I. "'Left-Wing' Communism: An Infantile Disorder." Accessed at www.marxists.org/archive/lenin/works/1920/lwc/.

Luxemburg, Rosa. "Marxism or Leninism?" In *Reform or Revolution and Other Writings*. Mineola, NY: Dover Publications, 2006.

Medearis, John. "Lost or Obscured? How V. I. Lenin, Joseph Schumpeter and Hannah Arendt Misunderstood the Council Movement," *Polity* 36, no. 3 (2004): 447–76.

Ness, Immanuel and Dario Azzellini (eds). *Ours to Master and to Own: Workers' Control from the Commune to the Present*. Chicago: Haymarket Books, 2011.

Pannekoek, Anton. "General Remarks on the Question of Organisation." Accessed at www.marxists.org/archive/pannekoe/1938/general-remarks.htm.

———. "Party and Class." Accessed at .

———. "Social Democracy and Communism." Accessed at www.marxists.org/archive/pannekoe/1927/sdc.htm.

———. *Workers' Councils*. London: AK Press, 1947.

———. "World Revolution and Communist Tactics." Accessed at www.marxists.org/archive/pannekoe/tactics/.

Roß, Sabine. *Biographisches Handbuch der Reichsrätekongresse 1918/1919*. Düsseldorf: Droste Verlag, 2000.

Rühle, Otto. "The Revolution Is Not a Party Affair." Accessed at www.marxists.org/archive/ruhle/1920/ruhle02.htm.

Stalmann, Volker (ed.). *Der Hamburger Arbeiter- und Soldatenrat 1918/19*. Düsseldorf: Droste Verlag, 2013.

Tormin, Walter. *Zwischen Rätediktatur und Sozialer Demokratie: Die Geschichte der Rätebewegung in der deutschen Revolution 1918/19*. Düsseldorf: Droste Verlag, 1954.

Part II

Councils, the State and the Problem of Socialisation

4 In Defence of Council Democracy

Gabriel Wollner

Introduction

Within contemporary political philosophy, two complaints about the democratic deficits of capitalism feature with particular prominence. The first complaint concerns economic production and identifies a lack of democracy at the workplace.[1] The second complaint concerns democratic politics and focuses on the limits that economic actors impose on the state's ability to put democratic decisions into practice.[2] I shall argue that a neglected institutional vision from the history of ideas succeeds in solving both these problems at once. A suitably modified version of council democracy, associated with the traditions of both council communism and anarcho-syndicalism, in which the autonomy of workers' councils is constrained by political democracy, and which distributes different incidents of property rights between the dimensions of economic production and political democracy, simultaneously realises the aims of democratising the workplace and re-establishing the effective sovereignty of democratic politics.

My argument proceeds in four steps. I present my preferred version of the two prominent complaints in as favourable and systematic a fashion as possible, introduce a general and a particular vision of council democracy, explain how the particular version of council democracy succeeds in addressing both problems, and conclude by briefly elaborating on both the force and the limits of my argument.

Two Democratic Complaints

Diagnoses of the deficits of democratic capitalism abound. I shall substantiate two prominent contemporary complaints about the failures of democratic politics by offering a general remark about democratic commitments, distinguishing between two types of complaints or democratic deficits, showing that two prominent contemporary complaints have a common root in private property and arguing that it is very difficult to address both of them simultaneously.

Democratic Commitments: Legitimacy and Authority

There are at least two ways in which it matters whether or not institutions are democratic.[3] Democracy matters for both the legitimacy and the authority of an institution. The question of legitimacy is about whether an institution has the right to perform the acts that it ordinarily performs, for example, to treat its members in particular ways.[4] Democrats believe that institutions have the right to perform certain acts in virtue of the fact that they are democratic. The state, for example, has the right to demand tax payments from its citizens in virtue of its democratic institutions, and there are certain acts, for example, threatening the use of force, that may only be performed by such institutions. The question of authority is about whether those subject to an institution's decisions and demands have a reason to accept the decision or comply with the demand, simply in virtue of the fact that it is the institution's decision or demand. Democrats believe that those subject to an institution have such a reason in virtue of the fact the institution is democratic.[5] The fact that a state makes decisions democratically gives its citizens a reason to comply, and more strongly, citizens have a reason to comply only if their state is democratic.[6]

Complaints about the democratic deficit of an institution may correspondingly be of two kinds. Relying on democracy's significance for the legitimacy of an institution, one may complain that because an institution is in relevant respects undemocratic, it lacks the right to perform the acts that it actually performs. Relying on democracy's significance for the authority of an institution, one may argue that because it is in important respects undemocratic, the institution in question lacks the reason-giving power associated with the idea of authority, and that its members either have no reason to comply with its demands, or at least no democracy-induced reason to comply with its demands.

Two Complaints Reconstructed

I believe that the two prominent diagnoses of the democratic deficits of capitalism should be understood as involving both a legitimacy complaint and an authority complaint. One complaint concerns economic production and identifies a lack of democracy at the workplace. There are different variants of this complaint in circulation, all of which share a common structure comprising three observations. The first observation is about the structure of the capitalist firm and identifies the characteristic features of the relationship between owners, managers and workers. While some authors focus on relationships of governance within firms and emphasise the difference between firms and markets as modes of organising economic activity,[7] others argue that states and firms resemble each other in important respects.[8] According to the second observation, the features characteristic of the firm give rise to a particular moral problem. The ways in which workers are treated stand in need of justification and the powers that superiors claim need to be grounded. The third observation concerns solutions to the problem posed by the existence of the firm. Democracy would offer one, if not the only, way of justifying the treatment of workers or grounding the powers of superiors.

In combination, these observations deliver the diagnosis of a democratic deficit and the demand for workplace democracy. The democratic deficit of the capitalist firm impairs both its legitimacy and its authority. The capitalist firm treats its members in ways that would be legitimate only if the firm was democratic. Without workplace democracy, the firm has no right to treat workers in the way they are currently treated. And superiors would have the moral power to generate demands, and inferiors a corresponding reason to comply, only if the firm was democratic. No managerial authority without workplace democracy.

Another complaint concerns democratic politics and focuses on the limits that economic actors impose on the state's ability to put democratic decisions into practice. While there are different variants of complaints focusing on the relationship between capitalism and democratic politics, they do again share a common structure.[9] First, they build on a diagnosis of the mechanism by which economic activity undermines the realisation of democratic decisions. While some emphasise the adverse impact that corporate activity may have on the feasibility of realising democratic aims, for example, when firms make just taxation impossible by relocating abroad in response to increased tax rates, others focus on how the mere threat of actions like relocation constrains policy options, while still others emphasise the structural limits on what the democratic state can do that are imposed by its financial dependence on capitalist economic activity. Second, the fact economic actors impose constraints on the state's ability to put democratic decisions into practice is understood as impairing democracy. Democratic institutions that cannot put democratic decisions into practice are in important respects deficient. Interpretations of how exactly this deficiency is to be understood will differ in at least two respects, offering different interpretations of what democratic norm is violated, which in turn depends on the reasons for valuing democracy, and exactly what wrong economic actors commit, including, for example, the violation of a duty to comply with democratic decisions.[10] And third, there are recommendations for how to overcome the democratic deficit. While some solutions identify the need for corporate self-regulation, appealing to firms' moral duty not to undermine democratic feasibility, other solutions insist on the need for regulation and politically restricting what economic actors can do.

Again, I believe that the democratic deficit diagnosed in the second observation is, even though less obviously than in the case of the workplace, understood as a legitimacy and an authority deficit of democratic political institutions. Begin with legitimacy. The inability of democratic institutions to put decisions into practice threatens their legitimacy because institutions have a right to rule only if they rule effectively. A state may have the right to treat its subjects in otherwise morally problematic ways to ensure compliance with a democratic decision, say to coerce citizens into supporting a scheme of health care provision, only if the state does indeed succeed in putting that democratic decision into practice, say by actually establishing a scheme of health care provision. A similar line of reasoning applies to the case of authority. It seems that a state cannot (even) generate a (pro tanto) reason for its citizens to act in order to realise an aim that has been decided democratically, if others have the right not to act on that reason, while the success of realising the aim depends on everyone's action. An army officer who orders her soldiers to attack does not give her soldiers a reason to attack if half the soldiers have a right not to act on her orders, while the attack depends on a sufficiently large number, say more than half the soldiers, attacking.

Two further arguments support my claim that the problem is a problem of both democratic legitimacy and democratic authority. According to the Failed Credentials Argument, the adverse impact that economic actors have on the ability to put democratic decisions into practice undermines the normative credentials that confer legitimacy and authority on institutions. Firms' and corporations' ability to affect the feasibility conditions of democratic decisions gives owners a greater effective say than non-owners, thus undermining the democratic principle that everyone should have an equal opportunity for influencing political outcomes.[11] Assuming that equal opportunity for influence is necessary for authority and legitimacy, the complaint about economic actors' adverse impact thus is a complaint about a lack of legitimacy and authority. And second, consider the Incompleteness Argument. It seems that an institution has a far-reaching and encompassing right of democratic rule, that is, the right to treat members in particular ways and the power to generate reasons vis-à-vis citizens, only if the institution has effective democratic control over a sufficiently large number of parameters within its domain. Otherwise the mechanism of democratic justification fails. One cannot argue that an individual has to perform a particular act because that act contributes to an outcome or state of affairs that has been decided democratically, if the outcomes or states of affairs to which the act would in fact contribute is not the one that has been decided democratically.

The Common Root of Private Property

I have argued that two prominent complaints about the democratic deficits of capitalism are best understood as complaints about the democratic legitimacy and authority of both the firm and the state. But what feature exactly accounts for this twofold deficit? I believe that both types of democratic deficit have their common root in private property rights in the means of production. Let me briefly sketch an uncontroversial account of property rights before explaining how different aspects of this account explain the respective democratic deficit.

The function of private property rights is to assign objects to persons, reflecting the organising idea that it is for particular individuals to decide how objects are to be used, as well as to benefit from their use.[12] The organising idea may be spelled out in different ways, depending on how property rights are justified, and on how exactly different individual rights are bundled into a set of property rights. The list of rights to be combined in particular set or conception of property rights includes the right to possess, the right to use, the right to income, the right to manage and the right to capital.[13] For present purposes, the latter two are of particular significance. The right to manage gives owners the power to decide how and by whom the objects of ownership are to be used. The right to capital gives owners the power to dispose, transfer and alienate the objects of ownership.

The right to manage is at the heart of the democratic authority and legitimacy deficit of the capitalist firm. The owner's right to decide how and by whom the means of production are to be used is incompatible with democratic decisions about these issues. The right to manage establishes a form of non-democratic governance at the workplace. Owners claim a right to treat workers in particular ways, tell them what to do and to threaten sanctions in case of non-compliance as instances of the right to manage. In practice, this right is enshrined in and supported by corporate law and labour law.[14] Advocates of the status quo will argue that property rights in general and the right to manage in particular establish the legitimacy of and authority within the capitalist firm. On the standards of democratic legitimacy and authority, they do not.

The right to capital is at the heart of the democratic authority and legitimacy deficit on the level of politics. The owner's right to dispose, transfer and alienate objects of ownership gives owners the power to adversely affect the feasibility conditions of democratic politics. The owners' right to sell their means of production, not to make use of them, or to transfer them across borders allows them to avoid being part of the realisation of democratically decided aims.[15] Advocates of the status quo will argue that firms can claim property rights as offering protection against the demands of democratic politics. Democratic critics will argue that property rights undermine the legitimacy and authority of democratic politics.

The Difficulty of Simultaneously Addressing Both Problems

How to overcome the twofold democratic deficit? Focusing on the democratic deficits of the capitalist firm and aiming to restore authority and legitimacy at the workplace, democratisation on the level of production is called for. Instead of giving owners the right to decide how the means of production are to be used, those actually using the means of production should make these decisions democratically. While there are different ways of realising these requirements, including, for example, workers' representation in a system of co-determination or worker-owned co-operatives, the animating spirit is the same. For economic production to meet the standards of legitimacy and authority, the control rights assigned to owners need to give way to democratic decision-making.

Focusing on the deficits of democratic politics and aiming to restore the authority and legitimacy of political actors, the curtailment or transfer of private property rights is called for. To reassert its effective power of putting democratic decisions into practice, the state needs to establish political control over economic life. Means to that end may take a variety of forms and come in degrees. Weak measures include regulation that eliminates certain options from the option set of owners, for example, the introduction of capital controls curtailing the right of owners to transfer assets across borders. Stronger measures include the transfer of property rights from individual owners to political actors, for example, through the socialisation or nationalisation of the means of production.

While each of these solutions possesses important merits, they also suffer from significant shortcomings.[16] The apparent shortcoming is that a solution to one problem does not solve the other. Democratising the workplace does not re-establish the authority and legitimacy of political actors at the state level. And transferring property rights to these political actors does not achieve legitimacy and authority at the workplace. But there is also a deeper problem. Solving one of the two problems in the way suggested makes solving the other problem impossible. This is for two reasons. First, each of the two solutions features a different answer to the question: Who decides how and to what ends the means of production are used? According to the first solution, the answer is workers. According to the second solution, the answer is citizens. Second, the first solution succeeds only if the answer is workers, and the second solution succeeds only if the answer is citizens. For the workplace to be legitimate, those who are treated in ordinarily questionable ways must have a democratic say, and for superiors to have reason-generating powers, those who give those reasons have to be democratically controlled. Giving everyone in a population a democratic say in how a small subset of that population is to be treated does not render that treatment legitimate. Those subject to the decisions ought to have a democratic say in making it. Similarly, the authority relationship will have to be established within the productive unit. And for democratic politics to be legitimate, all citizens subject to political rule and not just workers will have to have a democratic say. Giving only a subset of a population a democratic say over democratic aims which all citizens will have to comply with and support does not establish legitimacy.[17] And for democratic institutions to have the power to give reasons, the authority relationship will have to hold between political institutions and all citizens. The question of how to re-establish the democratic authority and legitimacy of both the firm and state, it seems, has no easy answer.

Council Democracy

Even though general questions of economic democracy have reappeared on the agenda of contemporary political philosophy, the particular vision of council democracy has not.[18] The present section thus sets the stage for my argument, that a suitably modified version of council democracy realises the aims of democratising the workplace and re-establishing the effective sovereignty of democratic politics, by offering an overview of the defining features of council democracy. I believe that the vision of council democracy is best understood as insisting on a number of mid-level organisational principles, which are associated with a particular tradition in the history of ideas and real-world experiments, justified as the most appropriate realisation of a number of moral demands, and compatible with various more detailed institutional proposals.[19] My exposition proceeds in four steps. I explain the animating spirit behind the vision of council democracy, elaborate on its intellectual ancestry and real-world attempts at realising it, discuss the organisational principles at its heart and remark on both justificatory and institutional pluralism.

The Animating Spirit of Council Democracy

The ideal of council democracy aims at filling a gap in socialist theory, turns against both the capitalist status quo and alternative versions of socialisation, and hopes to achieve direct democratic control over economic production. The socialist formula of the "socialisation of the means of production" is empty as it fails to identify and spell out the politico-economic principles and institutions of the preferred alternative to capitalism.[20] What exactly does the socialisation of the means of production entail? And along what lines and through which institutions is economic life beyond capitalism to be organised? In an attempt to overcome the reluctance of thinking about what a socialist society may actually look like, the vision of council democracy offers an answer to these questions. The theory of council democracy fills a gap in socialist theory by spelling out what Karl Marx refers to as the "political form at last discovered under which to work out the economic emancipation of labour."[21]

In doing so, council democracy turns against both the capitalist status quo and the alternative of state-led socialisation from above and simple nationalisation of the means of production. Its advocates object to the "feudalism of the factory," the hierarchy of the workplace and the power of owners that are characteristic of the capitalist status quo. At the same time, they recognise the limits of socialisation on the level of the state and express scepticism about centralisation. There are limits to what can be achieved by nationalising the means of production. In particular, socialisation from above fails to realise the self-governance of producers at the level of production.

To overcome the capitalist status quo while avoiding the shortcomings of nationalisation, advocates of council democracy defend a particular version of democratisation as a form of socialisation. The democratisation of economic life presupposes the expropriation of owners to enable the exercise of control by those directly involved in production. Council democrats go beyond indirect democratic control over economic production, for example, through political participation and state control of industry, and demand direct control over economic processes on all levels. The establishment of workers' councils on the level of the factory as the basic unit and a federal structure building on councils on the level of industries and the economy as a whole, ensures direct participation of producers in economic governance.

Intellectual Ancestry and Real-World Experiments

In one form or another, the animating spirit of council democracy finds expression in the history of its theory and practice. While a fully worked-out history is beyond the scope of my present argument, there are different intellectual strands or sources of council democracy, each influential in different historical periods and associated with different traditions in the labour movement.[22] An early intellectual strand or source is associated with libertarian socialism and anarcho-syndicalism of the late nineteenth century, featuring figures like Joseph Proudhon and Mikhail Bakunin.[23] Two later strands or sources find expression in British versions of guild socialism as formulated by G. D. H. Cole, as well as in council communist ideals formulated by Anton Pannekoek and Karl Korsch.[24] While there are important differences (see my discussion of justificatory and institutional pluralism below), there is sufficient convergence to speak of one broad tradition of council democracy (see my argument of the next section).

Associated with these different strands or traditions, there are many historical experiments initiated in various countries by different actors in the history of the labour movement. The council movement in the German Revolution of 1918/19, for example, was informed by and helped develop the theory of council communism.[25] The attempts to reorganise political and economic life in Catalonia during the Spanish Civil War are more closely associated with and influenced by anarcho-syndicalism.[26] But again there is sufficient unity and convergence on basic organisational principles and commitments to view all of them as instantiating a version of council democracy. The organisational principles of convergence are what I turn to next.

The Organisational Principles of Convergence

Council democrats converge on a number of mid-level organisational principles and commitments, which both express the theory's animating spirit and are featured in the history of its theory and practice. They concern the scope, the unit and the nature of democracy, as well as views on how units of democracy are vertically and horizontally integrated.

Just like advocates of other variants of economic democracy, council democrats are convinced that the scope of democratic decision-making properly comprises the most important economic functions and decisions. These decisions include micro-issues arising on the level of the firm, like working hours and organisation of the workplace, as well as macro-issues, including the questions of what is produced and how. Instead of having these issues settled by owners exercising property rights, decisions ought to be made democratically by those relevantly affected by or subject to the decisions.

Importantly, the primary unit of democratic decision-making is the individual factory, firm or other basic unit of production. This focus expresses the idea that council democracy is about workers' self-direction and control. Convictions about the importance of self-management not only grounds a bottom-up approach to socialisation but also limits the role that mediating organisations like parties and unions play within it. Instead of relying on party or union representatives, those involved in production should directly control the conditions and direction of their productive activity.

Consequently, the nature of council democracy is direct and participatory. Workers' councils ensure that producers make decisions directly and aim at full democratic participation.[27] Where feasibility considerations impose constraints that require representation or compromised forms of participation, there are requirements on the form that compromises and representation may take. Where representation cannot be avoided, an imperative mandate, permanent control and revocability of representatives, as well as resemblance in socio-economic characteristics between represented and representatives, are called for. Council democratic views on vertical integration develop this theme further. The significance of direct control is maintained by insisting on a federal structure for integrating different levels of the economy. The local unit of production, the local council, is the primary unit and any overarching structures for settling issues that can only be settled on a higher level, involving syndicates or councils of councils, arise from and are authorised by the basic and primary unit.

In addition to recognising the need for vertical integration, some council democrats recognise the need for horizontal integration, which arises on all levels, from local to state. While it is clear that economic governance arises as an independent dimension in its own right, triggering a concern for economic democracy that the vision of council democracy answers to, it is not clear how the dimension of economic governance relates to the dimension of political governance. While all council democrats insist on the independent significance of democratic economic governance, the link of the economic council structure to political organisation and governance is seen differently by advocates of different versions of council democracy.[28] Disagreement on these issues gives rise to one of the two kinds of pluralism next on my agenda.

Two Types of Pluralism

Having explained the shared ancestry and history, as well as the common aims and institutional principles of council democracy, it is also important to recognise two kinds of pluralism. There is justificatory pluralism because the vision of council democracy is compatible with a number of deeper moral commitments and justifications. Without covering the full range of values, and without going through the details of each justificatory argument, council democracy should be seen as motivated by at least six concerns. Council democracy could be motivated by a concern for ending exploitation. Replacing private property in the means of production with a council system will make it impossible for owners to take unfair advantage of non-owners. Council democracy could also be seen as a way of overcoming alienation. Producing under a council system will avoid alienation in the process of production, the alienation of workers from their product, and realise Marx's "association of free producers." It could further be seen as establishing the type of workers' control required to realise an ideal of collective self-determination. Alternatively, it could be seen as offering an institutional guarantee of freedom understood as non-domination, by ensuring that nobody is liable to the arbitrary interference of others. Council democracy could also be understood as a way of realising and maintaining egalitarian relationships within the sphere of economic production. Finally, and most importantly for my present argument, council democracy offers a way of ensuring the democratic legitimacy and authority of political and economic institutions. I believe that even if not all of these ideas have historically been invoked by advocates of council democracy, each of them offers an at least initially promising line of argument. Council democracy's animating spirit and the organisational principles of convergence are compatible with a number of deeper justifications.

The second type of pluralism concerns questions of institutional design. The organisational principles of convergence identified above are compatible with a number of more precise institutional proposals. Institutional details in which different variants of council democracy differ from each other concern in particular the issue of horizontal integration and include questions like these: Is the structure of economic councils the only framework for making collectively binding decisions? If democratic decision-making on the economic dimension is supplemented with an overarching political or territorial dimension, what form should political governance take? And what exactly is the relationship between the economic and the political/territorial dimensions? Strong versions of council democracy insist on the economic council structure as the sole dimension of making binding collective decisions,[29] while weaker or hybrid versions of council democracy propose a model in which the autonomy of councils is constrained by the institution of political/territorial democracy, which may or may not take a parliamentary form.[30] One particular version of the latter view will figure in my argument of the next section.

The Promise of Council Democracy

I believe that a suitably modified version of council democracy, in which the autonomy of councils is constrained and supplemented by institutions of political democracy, realises the aims of democratising the workplace and re-establishing the effective sovereignty of democratic politics. Let me briefly set out the particular vision that I have in mind before explaining how it promises to simultaneously solve the legitimacy and authority problems identified above.

The Particular Version

Karl Korsch advocates a vision of council democracy as "industrial autonomy,"[31] demanding the elimination of capitalist ownership from the process of production, and the unbundling and redistribution of property rights and their incidents between different dimensions and across different levels of economic production.[32] At the core of the proposal is the reorganisation of relations of production by assigning different property rights previously exercised by capitalist owners to workers and citizens, while simultaneously establishing democratic control over which rights are exercised by what group and at what level. The conception takes seriously the animating spirit behind council democracy and instantiates the principles of organisational convergence. Important property rights are assigned to producers organised in democratic councils at the level of the respective productive unit, other property rights are held by democratic economic or political institutions at a different level, for example, by a council of councils or bodies integrating the interests of producers and consumers, while decisions about what bundle of property rights is held where are made democratically. To illustrate the proposal, consider how the right to manage is divided between different dimensions and levels of democratic governance and how the right to capital is curtailed by democratic decisions, before looking at the issue of vertical and horizontal integration.

Under capitalist private property, owners decide how and to what end the means of production are used. Under the regime of industrial autonomy, the right to manage is unbundled and the democratised rights to make various decisions are distributed between different groups at different levels. While decisions about the processes and conditions of production will be made democratically by those directly involved in production, other decisions, for example what to produce, may be decided democratically at a different level, for example by a syndicate operating on an industry level, by a council of councils or by a body integrating the economic and political dimensions. The question of how decision rights are distributed between different levels and different groups is tricky and I will outline some guiding principles below when addressing the issue of integration. But importantly, there are a number of decisions, which were formerly subsumed under capitalist private property, that under industrial autonomy are made democratically at the level of workers' councils. And even decisions made at a higher level will reflect lower-level inputs, brought to the syndicate or other bodies through representation of workers' councils' decisions by imperative mandate.

While the right to manage illustrates how property rights are unbundled and exercised democratically, the right to capital illustrates how property rights are subject to democratic control. Capitalist private property entails the owner's right to alienate and transfer her assets. Under industrial autonomy, the right to alienate and transfer may be curtailed in virtue of decisions democratically made. It may be democratically decided that there just are certain things that right-holders, including democratic workers' councils, cannot do. Democratically imposed limits on the transferability of the means of production, for example, provide an important way in which council democracy in its industrial autonomy version achieves overall democratic control over economic production.

But which principles determine what rights go where and how democracy at the basic council level is integrated with independent political structures and higher levels of decision-making? Korsch's answer builds on the idea of "constrained autonomy."[33] The lowest-level unit, say the council on the firm or factory level, has the right to decide an issue democratically, subject to the constraint that where the interests of others are relevantly affected, the issue moves up or sideways. In cases of vertical integration, where the interests of other producers are affected, the issue moves up to the syndicate or the council of councils. In cases of horizontal integration, where the interests of non-producers are affected, the issue moves to structures that integrate economic and political democracy.

The Promise

This version of council democracy, in which the autonomy of workers' councils is constrained and supplemented by institutions of political democracy and which distributes different incidents of property rights between the dimension of economic production and the dimension of political democracy, simultaneously realises the aims of democratising the workplace and re-establishing the effective sovereignty of democratic politics. The original challenge is not only that workplace democracy fails to re-establish the authority and legitimacy of political actors, while indirect political control fails to achieve legitimacy and authority at the workplace, but that the solution of one problem makes a solution of the other one unlikely. Let me explain how council democracy as industrial autonomy solves the problem of legitimacy and authority on both the level of the firm and politics, and explain the mechanism in virtue of which, unlike more prominent alternatives, it succeeds in both these respects.

As argued above, for economic production on the level of the firm to meet the standards of legitimacy and authority, the control rights assigned to owners need to give way to democratic decision-making. In the model of council democracy as industrial autonomy, important control rights are exercised in a democratic fashion directly by producers. As also argued above, for the re-establishment of political sovereignty and legitimacy, the state needs to assume political control over economic life. In the model of council democracy as industrial autonomy, the state exercises such control not only through horizontal integration but also by imposing limits on the exercise of property rights.

There are three mechanisms in virtue of which council democracy as industrial autonomy succeeds in establishing legitimacy and authority in the political and economic dimension. First, it offers a way of unbundling and dividing up property rights that other approaches treat as unified and solitary. The control rights at the heart of legitimacy and authority can be distributed so as to meet both sets of requirements. Second, it incorporates both the democratic exercise and the democratic control of rights formerly considered private property rights. Whereas workers' councils and the structure building upon them are the locus of the exercise of rights, political institutions offer the mechanism of democratic control. And third, council democracy as industrial autonomy links the democratic control of rights back to the basic unit of economic production through institutions of vertical and horizontal integration.

Limits of the Argument and Open Questions

I have argued that council democracy ought to be reconsidered because it succeeds in addressing two democratic deficits diagnosed by contemporary democratic theorists. Of course, this argument is of limited force. There might be other solutions to the twofold democratic deficits. Or there could be strong independent reasons that speak against implementing council democracy. And even if council democracy as industrial autonomy turns out to be an all-things-considered desirable ideal, there are difficulties and open questions. What are the strategies and tactics of achieving industrial autonomy against the interest of current owners?

And what are the international preconditions under which council democracy could flourish? These are some of the questions that advocates of council democracy ought to address. In the meantime, a historically familiar slogan survives in a slightly modified form: (at least) some power to the councils!

Notes

1 For two prominent examples, see Robert A. Dahl, *A Preface to Economic Democracy*; Elizabeth Anderson, *Private Government*.
2 See, for example, Thomas Christiano, "The Uneasy Relationship between Capital and Democracy," 195. The arguments put forward by Wolfgang Streeck can be understood along similar lines. Wolfgang Streeck, *Buying Time*.
3 This proposal offers a slightly modified version of Kolodny's account in Niko Kolodny, "Rule Over None I: What Justifies Democracy?"; Niko Kolodny, "Rule Over None II: Social Equality and the Justification of Democracy."
4 For a recent discussion of authority and legitimacy, see Niko Kolodny, "Political Rule and Its Discontents," 35.
5 For accounts of democratic authority, see Thomas Christiano, *The Constitution of Equality*; Daniel Viehoff, "Democratic Equality and Political Authority."
6 Even though the notions of authority and legitimacy are closely linked, it is important to keep them conceptually distinct. There is a difference between possessing the normative power to generate reasons and having the right to treat others in particular ways. An institution may, for example, possess reason-giving power and still lack the right to use force.
7 For an emphasis on the difference between markets and firms, see Elizabeth Anderson, "Equality and Freedom in the Workplace."
8 For an emphasis on the similarity between firms and states, see Hélène Landemore and Isabelle Ferreras, "In Defense of Workplace Democracy."
9 For different versions of this claim, see Fred Block, "The Ruling Class Does Not Rule"; Christiano, "The Uneasy Relationship between Capital and Democracy."
10 The argument put forward in Christiano, "The Uneasy Relationship between Capital and Democracy."
11 See again ibid., 207ff.
12 For the notion of the "organising idea" of private property, see Jeremy Waldron, *The Right to Private Property*.
13 For the standard list of rights combined in a bundle of private property rights, see A. M. Honore, "Ownership," in *Oxford Essays in Jurisprudence*.
14 See Anderson, "Equality and Freedom in the Workplace."
15 See Peter Dietsch, *Catching Capital*.
16 One may think of this predicament as a particular moral variant of the socialisation dilemma discussed by Karl Kautsky and Karl Korsch: Karl Kautsky, *The Labour Revolution*; Karl Korsch, *Schriften Zur Sozialisierung*. See also the discussion by Vrousalis in Chapter 5, this volume.
17 In the democratic theory literature, these issues are discussed as the "boundary problem" or the problem of "constituting the demos." See, for example, Gustaf Arrhenius, "The Boundary Problem in Democratic Theory," in Folke Tersman (ed.), *Democracy Unbound*, 14–29; Robert E. Goodin, "Enfranchising All Affected Interests, and Its Alternatives."

18 For a recent contribution, see, for example, Tom Malleson, *After Occupy*.
19 For a similar typology, see Peter von Oertzen, *Betriebsräte in der Novemberrevolution*.
20 See the formulation "leer und nichtssagend" that Peter von Oertzen uses in his discussion of Korsch (Peter von Oertzen, *Betriebsräte in der Novemberrevolution*, 34).
21 Karl Marx, "Der Bürgerkrieg in Frankreich," in *Marx-Engels-Werke*, vol. 17, 342.
22 For anthologies discussing the history and ideal of council democracy, see Ernest Mandel, *Arbeiterselbstkontrolle, Arbeiterräte, Arbeiterselbstverwaltung*; Immanuel Ness and Dario Azzellini, *Ours to Master and to Own*.
23 For a discussion of these aspects of Anarcho-Syndicalism, see Daniel Guerin, *Anarchism*.
24 See G. D. H. Cole, *Guild Socialism*; Anton Pannekoek, *Workers Councils*; Korsch, *Schriften Zur Sozialisierung*.
25 See the discussion in Oertzen, *Betriebsräte in der Novemberrevolution*.
26 See, for example, Hans J. Degen and Augustin Souchy, "Die soziale Revolution in Spanien," in *Anarchistischer Sozialismus*, 136–84.
27 At least that is the ideal to be approximated. The historical realities of council democracy have often fallen short of fully realising it.
28 For a discussion of issues of vertical integration, see Vrousalis in Chapter 5, this volume.
29 Anton Pannekoek should in this sense count as a strong council democrat. See Anton Pannekoek, "Social Democracy and Communism."
30 For the view that economic councils should be combined with parliaments as institutions of political democracy, see the position of Karl Kautsky. For example, Kautsky, *The Labour Revolution*.
31 Korsch, *Schriften Zur Sozialisierung*, 34.
32 For a contemporary conception incorporating some of these aspects, see David Schweickart, *After Capitalism*.
33 Korsch, *Schriften Zur Sozialisierung*, 36.

References

Anderson, Elizabeth. "Equality and Freedom in the Workplace: Recovering Republican Insights." *Social Philosophy and Policy* 31, no. 2 (2015): 48–69. https://doi.org/10.1017/S0265052514000259.

———. *Private Government: How Employers Rule Our Lives*. Princeton, NJ: Princeton University Press, 2017.

Arrhenius, Gustaf. "The Boundary Problem in Democratic Theory." In *Democracy Unbound: Basic Explorations I*. Edited by Folke Tersman. 14–29. Stockholm: Filosofika Institutionen, Stockholms Universitet, 2005.

Block, Fred. "The Ruling Class Does Not Rule: Notes on the Marxist Theory of the State." *Socialist Revolution* 33 (1977): 6–28.

Christiano, Thomas. *The Constitution of Equality: Democratic Authority and its Limits*. Reprint. Oxford: Oxford University Press, 2010.

———. "The Uneasy Relationship between Capital and Democracy." *Social Philosophy and Policy* 27, no. 1 (January 2010): 195.

Cole, G. D. H. *Guild Socialism: A Plan for Economic Democracy*. London: Forgotten Books, 2012.

Dahl, Robert A. *A Preface to Economic Democracy*. Berkeley, CA: University of California Press, 1985.

Degen, Hans J. and Augustin Souchy. "Die soziale Revolution in Spanien: Vortrag und Diskussion." In *Anarchistischer Sozialismus*, 1st edn. 136–84. Münster: Unrast, 2010.

Dietsch, Peter. *Catching Capital: The Ethics of Tax Competition*. New York, NY: Oxford University Press Inc, 2015.

Goodin, Robert E. "Enfranchising All Affected Interests, and Its Alternatives." *Philosophy & Public Affairs* 35, no. 1 (2007): 40–68.

Guerin, Daniel. *Anarchism*. New edn. Translated by M. Klopper. New York: Monthly Review Press, U.S., 1971.

Honore, A. M. "Ownership." In *Oxford Essays in Jurisprudence*. 107–47. Oxford: Oxford University Press, 1961.

Kautsky, Karl. *The Labour Revolution*. Abingdon: Routledge, Taylor & Francis Group, 2012.

Kolodny, Niko. "Political Rule and Its Discontents." *Oxford Studies in Political Philosophy* 2 (2016): 35.

———. "Rule over None I: What Justifies Democracy?" *Philosophy & Public Affairs* 42, no. 3 (1 June 2014): 195–229. https://doi.org/10.1111/papa.12035.

———. "Rule over None II: Social Equality and the Justification of Democracy." *Philosophy & Public Affairs* 42, no. 4 (2014): 287–336.

Korsch, Karl. *Schriften Zur Sozialisierung*. Frankfurt am Main: EVA, 1969.

Landemore, Hélène and Isabelle Ferreras. "In Defense of Workplace Democracy: Towards a Justification of the Firm–State Analogy." *Political Theory* 44, no. 1 (2016): 53–81.

Malleson, Tom. *After Occupy: Economic Democracy for the 21st Century*. Oxford: Oxford University Press, 2014.

Mandel, Ernest. *Arbeiterselbstkontrolle, Arbeiterräte, Arbeiterselbstverwaltung: Eine Anthologie*. Frankfurt am Main: Europ. Vlg.-Anst., H., 1991.

Marx, Karl. "Der Bürgerkrieg in Frankreich." In *Marx-Engels-Werke*, vol. 17. 313–65. Berlin: Dietz Verlag, 1973.

Ness, Immanuel and Dario Azzellini. *Ours to Master and to Own: Workers' Control from the Commune to the Present*. Chicago: Haymarket Books, 2011.

Oertzen, Peter von. *Betriebsräte in der Novemberrevolution: Eine politikwissenschaftliche Untersuchung über Ideengehalt und Struktur der betrieblichen und wirtschaftlichen Arbeiterräte in der deutschen Revolution 1918/19*. Bonn-Bad Godesberg: Dietz Verlag J. H. W. Nachf, 1976.

Pannekoek, Anton. "Social Democracy and Communism." Accessed at www.marxists.org/archive/pannekoe/1927/sdc.htm.

———. *Workers' Councils*. Scottsdale, AZ: Prism Key Press, 2010.

Schweickart, David. *After Capitalism*. Lanham, MD: Rowman & Littlefield, 2011.

Streeck, Wolfgang. *Buying Time: The Delayed Crisis of Democratic Capitalism*. Brooklyn, NY: Verso, 2014.

Viehoff, Daniel. "Democratic Equality and Political Authority." *Philosophy & Public Affairs* 42, no. 4 (2014): 337–75.

Waldron, Jeremy. *The Right to Private Property*. Rev. edn. Oxford: Oxford University Press, 1991.

5 Council Democracy and the Socialisation Dilemma

Nicholas Vrousalis

Introduction

One of the main discoveries of nineteenth-century socialist thought is the idea that the state and the market are not the only forms of collective organisation of the economy. For the intellectual pioneers of socialism, the gestation of a co-operative movement within the womb of capitalist society implied the possibility of economic organisation mediated neither by coercion – the hallmark of the state – nor by commodification – the hallmark of the market. Instead, co-ordination between consumption and production is accomplished through the democratic association of the direct producers. This vision of an economy of workers' councils, federated along non-coercive, egalitarian lines, came into its own during the nineteenth- and twentieth-century struggles for democracy. Radical currents in these movements held that liberal capitalism, even the democratic capitalism of parliamentary Britain, were forms of dictatorship. What Marx called the "dictatorship of the bourgeoisie," for example, is the political content of the domination of workers – the proletariat – by capitalists – the bourgeoisie.[1] The remedy to this domination, Marx maintained, consists in the democratisation of production relations through the newly discovered institution of the workers' council.

Suppose you accept this Marxian story. You propose to retrieve the means of production from the capitalist mode of production, turning them from alien forces conspiring *against* freedom into an expression *of* freedom. How might you do *that*? Two answers pervade the discussion of socialisation since the Russian Revolution. The first answer, *statism*, associates socialisation with exclusive state ownership and control of the means of production. Such ownership can assume state capitalist and social democratic forms. The former was exemplified by the Soviet Union, the latter by the welfare state capitalism of the 1960s. The second view, *syndicalism*, associates socialisation with exclusive worker ownership and control. There are many variants of syndicalism: one is exemplified by the political theories of Daniel De Leon and by the political practice of the Wobblies, the Industrial Workers of the World union. The socialisation question therefore gives rise to a *socialisation dilemma*. Both horns of the dilemma have unpalatable consequences.

In this chapter, I first show that the socialisation dilemma pervades the writings of twentieth-century socialist thought. I then discuss a prominent way out, proposed by Karl Kautsky. After illustrating the Kautskian programme's importance to the socialisation debate – from Karl Korsch and Otto Bauer, through to Nicos Poulantzas and David Schweickart – I argue that the programme's principles are incongruous with its strategies. This incongruity issues from the subordinate role that Kautsky assigns to the workers' councils. I then conclude by proposing a Madisonian solution to the socialisation dilemma, based on the idea of a workers' parliament.

In what follows, I assume that socialisation is desirable if and only if it is democratic. For the purposes of this chapter, I assume that democracy requires some form of equality: each must count as one, and only as one. "Each must count as one": this is the *inclusion proviso*, which says that socialisation is democratic only if it is inclusive. That is, *each* must count for one: no adult and competent member of the polity can be permissibly excluded from having a say. "Only as one": this is the *equal-power proviso*, which says that socialisation is democratic only if no one can dominate others or use her power to abridge their right to an equal say.[2] I will show that most existing theories of socialisation fall foul of either of these necessary conditions for democratic socialisation, or both.

Origins

The term "socialisation" has its origins in debates taking place during and after the German Revolution of November 1918. Friedrich Ebert, the conservative social democrat heading the provisional government of 1918, appointed Karl Kautsky and Rudolf Hilferding, two stalwarts of social democracy, to a Socialisation Commission.[3] The Commission was a diversionary tactic; Ebert's real aim was to appease popular demands for council democracy, on the one hand, without making significant concessions to the German bourgeoisie, on the other. In his former aspiration, he found a willing ally in Kautsky, who had, since November 1917, turned his gaze against the Spartacist agitation for a council republic. The latter idea would, according to Kautsky, inevitably drift towards a "bureaucratic despotism" of sorts.[4] The German social democrats – the majority SPD, along with Kautsky's Independent Social Democratic Party (USPD) – therefore sought to create a blueprint for socialisation that at once realised popular demands and marginalised demands for Bolshevik-style minority rule.

Kautsky

The Socialisation Commission immediately found itself faced with a dilemma. Kautsky summarises it as follows:

> our duty will be to replace bureaucratic autocracy by a type of management which would accord a wide measure of self-government to the workers without losing sight of the consumers' interest or creating a Labour aristocracy of the municipal workers.[5]

The first horn of the socialisation dilemma is a Bolshevik-type "bureaucratic autocracy" that usurps power from the worker and gives it to the state. The Bolshevik system therefore violates both the inclusion proviso – non-producers have no say – and the equal-power proviso – bureaucrats have more power than non-bureaucrats. The second horn of the dilemma is a syndicalist-type ascription of ownership and control to individual firms, such that they can safely ignore the general requirements of the common good or the interests of the non-producers. The assumption here is that certain industries, if left unregulated, will work to the detriment of consumers and other non-producers, through a combination of price-gouging, monopoly/monopsony power and rent-seeking.[6] For example, capitalists may sell off inputs for a pittance, if they consider them likely to be socialised. Worker-owners might be inclined to do similar things.[7] So even if syndicalist socialisation satisfies the inclusion requirement – by making room for universal suffrage – it violates the equal-power proviso, giving some producers, a "Labour aristocracy," power over consumers. On the assumption that all consumers are also producers, this is tantamount to allowing some producers power over others.

Unlike many of his predecessors in the Second International, Kautsky was intensely interested in questions of industrial organisation. More precisely, he was interested in the relationship between socialisation and the organisation of production. In *The Labour Revolution*, Kautsky summarises some of the findings of the short-lived Socialisation Commission, from which he unceremoniously resigned in 1919. He kicks off the discussion by arguing, against Lenin, that the state is not the "appointed" instrument of socialisation. Rather, the state must only own the means of production, whereas the workers must possess residual rights over their workplace conditions of production. This possibility of separation between the rights of ownership and control shows, Kautsky thinks, that the socialisation dilemma is not exhaustive. His view is that there should be a separation of powers between state and industry, such that the state owns and regulates total production, while the workers work at their own initiative and in the absence of state interference on the shop floor. How exactly this separation plays out will vary by industry.

Borrowing from Marx's *Capital* discussion of the division of labour under capitalism – ranging from simple co-operation to large-scale industry – Kautsky broaches the different forms of socialisation which, he thinks, correspond to each mode of the division of labour. In the case of the building trade, for example, he argues that something like guild socialism would be appropriate. That is, guild socialism is an apposite form of social organisation for industries where fixed capital plays only a minor role. The idea is that local municipalities should own the building inputs and instruments of production, whereas builders' associations should provide labour inputs. Things are different with large-scale mechanised industry, says Kautsky. Here the democratic organisation of the workplace is more difficult. With machinery, the number and minuteness of tasks that need to be performed, in addition to the complexity of machine utilisation and maintenance, engender a complex set of power relations. These relations, arising spontaneously from the material conditions of production and the need for special managerial skills and knowledge, may produce a "Labour aristocracy." In addition, the existence of machinery leads to market power, and eventually monopoly power, which enable individual firms to raise prices and costs at the expense of consumers and other producers. These ramifications of mechanised industry underlie the syndicalist horn of the socialisation dilemma.

In light of these problems, Kautsky criticises G. D. H. Cole, the intellectual father of guild socialism, for proposing mere ad hoc remedies to the infirmities of syndicalism. Kautsky writes:

> It would be far more fitting and effectual if … institutions were set up, by virtue of which consumers and producers would be brought together in every branch of production at the very commencement of production, when the details of its organisation and its management were being settled, in order to reach unanimous decisions upon these matters. This would involve not two, but three factors: first the producers, then the consumers, who would be directly interested in the products, as for example the farmers in the matter of agricultural machinery, and finally the community, which would represent alike the whole of the producers and the whole of the consumers, that is to say, the State.[8]

The way out of the socialisation dilemma, according to Kautsky, consists in some form of centralised investment planning *in conjunction with* worker control at the level of the individual firm. *Who* should do this planning? Cole thinks that the basic building blocks of a "democracy of Labour" would be the worker-controlled workplaces. These would, in turn, unite in "Guild parliaments," exclusively comprising workers. Kautsky criticises Cole for thinking that these parliaments can perform planning operations without state involvement, specifically concerted state support for worker management and socialised investment planning. Indeed, Kautsky suggests that the central role Cole – and other syndicalists – assign to unions is incoherent. On the one hand, says Kautsky, the union-sponsored guilds would be expected to hire *more* workers during bouts of unemployment – at a time when they would have the least income – and *fewer* workers during periods of full employment – at a time when most workers would be paying their dues. This is incoherent. Instead, the state is indispensable in its role as guild-funder-of-last-resort, as legislator for worker control, and as defender of macroeconomic stability and full employment.

Korsch

Another prominent Marxist to have addressed the socialisation problem is Karl Korsch, in an essay response to Bernstein's "What Is Socialization?" of the same name.[9] Korsch begins his study by distinguishing between two strategies for socialisation. The first, due to Bernstein, involves a gradual process of co-optation through legal inroads into private property, together with voluntary expansion in "united associations" between employers and workers. The second strategy involves the complete expropriation of capitalist private property in the interest of producers and consumers. The problem, says Korsch, is that the latter socialisation programme will "either create a more or less complete community property in a true communal economy, or it will indeed eliminate private property, but only to replace it with some kind of *special property*."[10]

Korsch proceeds to discuss two ways in which socialisation might lead to "special property":

> Socialization, as nationalization ... of plants ... is indirect from the standpoint of the producing labourers, direct from the standpoint of the totality of consumers. In none of these ... cases does the producing labourer immediately achieve any share in the control and benefits of production, but rather remains as before a wage labourer. This is due to the replacement of the capitalist private owner with functionaries of the state, then community, or the consumer cooperative.[11]

This is the statism horn of the socialisation dilemma: to assign property rights to the state, in the way nationalisations normally do, is to endow the state with "special ownership." Crucially, nationalisation does not meaningfully provide workers with control over the residual, or indeed over their workplace conditions of production. The workplace becomes the "special property" of the "functionaries of the state" and, as such, falls foul of the equal-power proviso.

The second horn of the socialisation dilemma confers exclusive control over workplace conditions of production to their workers. Korsch writes:

> The form of socialization which is direct from the standpoint of labourers, and indirect from the standpoint of the totality of

> consumers, consists of the transfer of ownership of all means of production of a plant (branch of industry) to the labouring participants in that plant (branch industry participants). Through this transfer, the labouring participants in production achieve control over the entire process of production and over its yield. True community property can … no more be created through this process alone … The capitalism of the private capitalist would only be replaced by a producer-capitalism, a special ownership of certain groups of producers.[12]

This is the syndicalism horn of the dilemma: special property for the direct producers. Under the syndicalist arrangement, the "totality of consumers" are "placed at the mercy of the individual plant (the individual branch of industry)."[13] Syndicalism therefore also violates the equal-power proviso. Unlike Kautsky, Korsch does not explain how the individual firm, or even the individual branch of industry, comes to have that power. That is, Korsch's essay lacks a theory of industrial organisation. The missing premise seems to be that individual firms, or branches thereof, either possess considerable *market* power over consumers – by dint of monopolistic structure – or come to possess such power *through* competition – by dint of centralisation and concentration of capital. This additional premise justifies Korsch's emphasis on the syndicalist horn, but at the cost of making his discussion a trivial subset of Kautsky's.

What about the way out of the dilemma? Korsch's solution consists in arguing that it is not exhaustive; what we need is a form of socialisation that involves *neither* statism nor syndicalism. He writes:

> First, the means of production are transferred out of the power sphere of individual private owners into the power sphere of some sort of social functionaries and second, there is a public legal limitation of the power privileges of the present directors of social production in the interest of the totality.[14]

In this system, autonomous producers produce to the interest of the "totality," and not just for their self-interest. Korsch calls this system "industrial autonomy." There are three levels of socialisation here: state – region – workplace. The state owns the means of production *as a whole*, but regional representatives of workers have considerable autonomy over their allocation, subject to legal limitations constraining them to consider the interests of consumers. Similarly, plant representatives have considerable autonomy over the allocation of means of production to plants from regional representatives, subject to legal restrictions pertaining to the interests of consumers. Finally, *within* plants, workers' committees have considerable autonomy from each other, subject to similar restrictions. This is, again, Kautsky's theory, slightly amended.

Bauer and Adler

Otto Bauer and Max Adler, both leaders of Austrian social democracy, offer two of the most important post-First World War treatments of socialisation. Bauer was secretary of the Austrian Social Democratic Party (SDAPÖ) from 1907 to 1914 and one of its main theoreticians. He was also part of the first post-war Austrian coalition government; he chaired the Austrian Socialisation Commission from 1918 until its dissolution in 1920. Adler, also active in the SDAPÖ, published an important treatise on the relationship between the Austrian workers' and soldiers' councils and the parliament. I will briefly rehearse the arguments of both.

Bauer agreed with Kautsky that socialisation should be the outcome of a non-violent, non-revolutionary, gradual process of appropriation of the means of production. He campaigned for the insertion of a socialisation manifesto, along such lines, in the SDAPÖ's 1918 party programme. The socialisation manifesto broached the idea that the main Austrian industries – including the biggest factories, banks, land and forests – should be nationalised under worker control. Under pressure from both the Communist Party's socialisation programme and the National Congress of the Workers' and Soldiers' Councils of March 1919, the government took heed of Bauer as the helm of the Socialisation Commission. The Commission drew up a plan to nationalise steel, iron, coal and electricity. Some of the Commission's proposals made it into law: they included the extension of unemployment insurance, the eight-hour working day, and the creation of industrial councils for firms with 20 employees or more. These councils were, in theory, tasked with "controlling the implementation of social legislation, maintaining labour agreements, securing workers' participation in determining wages, protecting workers with unlawful dismissal ... monitoring the finances and wage statistics of the company."[15] In practice, only the regulatory aspect of the council law was fully implemented.

Like Kautsky and Korsch, Bauer was acutely aware of the socialisation dilemma. Statist socialisation, in his view, would sap domestic industries of productive power, alienate the Entente and precipitate civil strife. It would, moreover, violate basic democratic constraints – the equal-power proviso – by empowering state bureaucrats and disempowering workers. Syndicalist socialisation, on the other hand, entailed special privileges for the producers, specifically those with monopoly and monopsony power.

> As an alternative to both state socialism and syndicalism, [Bauer] proposed a 3/3 principle of socialized workplaces and production co-operatives – i.e. the creation of collective administration boards consisting of an equal number of delegates from three interest groups: producers, consumers and the state. Common economic interests and a comprehensive economic plan would guide them.[16]

The tripartite composition of the factory councils reflected Kautsky's proposals of early 1919. As in Kautsky's plan, moreover, Bauer did not envisage any long-term role for the workers' and soldiers' councils; only the "works committees" were enshrined in law.

Max Adler, by contrast, maintained that the councils should play a central role in the process of socialisation. The Austrian councils shared the pyramid-like federal structure of the German councils; they likewise enjoyed extensive popular support. Their National Council, the body on top of local and district councils, remained a powerful political agent from the autumn of 1918 to the spring of 1919. Adler maintained that it was possible to sustainably combine the existence of the National Council with the parliament, in a system of permanent constitutional dyarchy:

> Until ready to take over the whole power, [the Council] was to deal with all matters of economics, communications, and finance, with the right of bringing Bills before Parliament, or vetoing the decrees of that body, which was to be left with such political and cultural questions as did not touch on economics.[17]

Adler maintained that the councils, as grass-roots organisations for worker control, would have the final say on economic matters, such as investment planning. At the same time, the councils would agitate for a socialist majority in parliament. This would, in due course, produce a worker-led coalition in parliament and eventuate in rule of, by and for the people. All this, without recourse to violence or civil war. Adler wagered on all power to the soviets on the cheap.

Outcomes

Russia, Germany, Austria

The short-lived history of workers' control in Russia has been recounted innumerable times. The history is important, if only by way of juxtaposition to the German and Austrian cases. In November 1917, the Soviet government (*Sovnarkom*) published its Decree on Workers' Control. The decree conferred control rights on factory councils over their places of work. Factory councils had spread throughout Russia since 1905 and blossomed in 1917; they formed the core of popular power. In addition, the central body co-ordinating demobilisation plans for the factories – plans to switch production from military to consumer goods – was the Petrograd Central Council of Factory Committees, another spontaneously created, federated institution, with grass-roots membership. To complicate matters, *Sovnarkom* established a Supreme Economic Council (*Vesenkha*) to supervise production. The idea was that the state would appoint commissars to the largest Russian workplaces, where they would serve as managers. Within months, it became clear that, for *Sovnarkom*, "workers' control" meant "control by *Vesenkha*." As usual, Lenin was more candid than anyone else: he dubbed the emerging system "state capitalism," that is, a system of centralised production by a few large state-owned and state-*managed* firms. *Sovnarkom*'s plan, in other words, was to replace the despotism of capital by the despotism of the state.[18]

By June 1918, all Russian stock companies had been nationalised and were being operated through the *Vesenkha*. The emaciated body of worker autonomy survived, when it did, in the trade unions. Bukharin and Preobrazensky, the authors of the *ABC of Communism*, went as far as to suggest that "the whole of economic life ... shall constitute a unity which is effectively controlled by industrial (productive) unions."[19] By the end of 1918, however, the trade unions themselves were directly subordinated to the state through the Commissariat of Labour, headed by Trotsky.

Germany and Austria had to reckon with these facts, as they emerged from the Russian experiment in the East. The facts help explain the strictures of German and Austrian social democrats against revolutionary gymnastics, their reluctance vis-à-vis experimentation with new tactics, and their gradualism.

In Germany, the Kautskian programme hardly saw the light of day. At the end of 1918, the Socialisation Commission issued a preliminary statement, recommending the socialisation of highly monopolistic industries, such as coal and iron. Later that December, the first Congress of workers' and soldiers' councils issued a demand for socialisation of "appropriate" industries, with an emphasis on mining. At about the same time, the workers' council of Essen set up a board purported to take control of local mines. However, the Constituent Assembly election of January 1919 resulted in defeat for the social democrats. The SPD and the USPD together garnered less than 46 per cent of the vote; the SPD had to join a coalition with bourgeois parties. After a wave of strikes in early 1919 – and the repression of the Spartacist uprising – the German workers managed to force a watered-down system of co-determination for a limited number of industries. No part of Kautsky's plan was carried out, with the exception of the coal industry. Coal was nationalised under the aegis of a National Coal Council, which was jointly managed by state officials, employers, workers and consumers.

By contrast with Germany, the situation in 1918 in Austria appeared propitious for the Kautskian programme. In addition to unemployment insurance and the eight-hour working day, the workplace councils were permanently enshrined into law. Moreover, the Austrian social democrats wanted to use the councils as a "defence against communism," which lent the latter significant political clout during the febrile early months of 1919.[20] In addition, the first coalition government of 1918–19 entrusted the councils with managing the housing shortage, cracking down on profiteering and the black market, and managing the stock of munitions. By the end of 1919, however, most of these functions had been absorbed by state and parliament, now under "bourgeois restoration." And by the end of 1921, the industrial councils had merged with the unions, despite Max Adler's admonition that the councils be insulated from union and party bureaucracies. The Austrian revolution was over. Could it have been otherwise? Any affirmative answer has to reckon with the fact that parliament controlled the army from late 1918. To what extent the leadership of the SDAPÖ were responsible for this remains a subject of debate.[21]

Sweden

Before offering a critique of the Kautskian programme, I must briefly describe the closest social democracy ever came to its realisation. That near-realisation occurred in the capital of social democracy, Sweden, some 57 years later. In 1975, the Swedish Social Democrats were in their thirty-ninth consecutive year in government. Olof Palme, the prime minister, was faced with a booming economy under full employment. The boom led to inflation; this meant that capitalists were eating into productivity gains, accruing an increasing share of national income. With the blessing of the Social Democratic party, Rudolf Meidner, an economist at the Swedish Trade Union Federation, developed a socialisation model explicitly designed to deprive capitalists of their new-found power. Under the Meidner plan, profitable firms would issue stocks worth 0.2 krona for every 1 krona of profit. The stock would go into employee insurance funds and would be collectively owned and managed by trade unions, under the aegis of the Trade Union Federation.

Meidner predicted that the workers' representatives would eventually come to control – through their local, regional and national representatives – majority shares in all major Swedish traded companies, within about 35 years. That would also give them indirect control over management. The plan was never implemented, as Palme lost the 1976 election. The plan's main provisions were subsequently watered down and inscribed into law in 1983. The plan was criticised, among other things, for the centrality of unions to its functioning. One fear was that union officials would prioritise their own interests, and the interests of their members, over other producers and consumers. This form of opposition to the Meidner plan, in other words, grasped the syndicalism horn of the socialisation dilemma in inchoate form.[22]

Diagnoses

The broadly Kautskian socialisation programme was advocated, with minor variations, by Bernstein, Bauer, Hilferding and Korsch, among many others. It failed because its principles outran its strategy. This incongruity between principles and strategy issues, I think, from the subordinate role the Kautskian programme assigns to the workers' councils. The rest of this section elaborates on this thought. The next section sketches a Madisonian solution that avoids the incongruity problem.

Strategy

Kautsky's way out of the socialisation dilemma consisted in: (P1) avoiding statist socialisation, by assigning significant autonomy to regions and municipalities, in addition to legal measures guaranteeing industrial autonomy for individual firms; (P2) avoiding syndicalist socialisation, by supplementing the state regulation of industry with investment planning bodies comprising consumers and scientists, in addition to producers. The Kautskian programme envisaged, in addition to these principles, two *strategies*: (S1) a gradual socialisation of industry, beginning with coal, iron and steel, eventually expanding to the whole industrial sector; and (S2) a subordinate political role for the councils, their sole task being "to ensure that [parliament] constantly heard the voice of the workers in their class organisation."[23] Both strategies, S1 and S2, turned out to be incompatible with the conjunction of the overarching principles, P1 and P2.

Take, first, S1. For reasons originally explained by Oscar Lange and, more recently, by Adam Przeworski, the *gradualist* strategy of socialising production sector by sector – as opposed to complete socialisation at one fell swoop – is incompatible with economic growth. That is, as long as a substantial part of the economy is operated along capitalist lines, the moment a socialist candidate emerges as a likely ruler, production stops. The explanation is simple: growth under capitalism depends on private investment, which depends on profit, which depends on stable and secure private property. The prospect of a government set on significantly raising wages and/or socialising investment is therefore sufficient to precipitate a cutback of investment – a capital strike – engendering a deep and lasting recession. Recovery on the basis of economic democracy, even if forthcoming, is likely to take years or decades. Therefore some workers will be significantly worse off under socialism than they would have been under capitalism, under the gradualist strategy.[24] In other words, you can't have both gradual socialisation *and* economic growth; something has to give. In the case of Germany and Austria, what gave was socialisation. S1 turned out to be incompatible with socialisation subject to P1 and P2.

Now take S2. A solid, vibrant and self-confident workers' movement is necessary for the joint realisation of P1 and P2. But how can you hope to sustain this confidence without assigning a permanent role to those in whose name and interest socialisation is carried out? The German National Assembly of 1919 did not involve them, nor did it promise to; there is no reason to think *any* national parliament would. Yet even a gradualist socialisation programme requires systematic and *institutionalised* pressure from below.[25] Kautsky knew – or should have known – that this kind of pressure would issue from neither party nor union. Its main source was the councils. And yet the Kautskian programme assumed that the councils should acquiesce in their eventual self-abolition after the set of Kautskian transitional demands is met. S2, it turns out, is also incompatible with socialisation subject to P1 and P2.

Seen from 2018, Kautsky's 1918 strictures seem inapposite: when your strategy conflicts with your principles, you must change your strategy. This is a conceptual truth. So if socialisation requires revolution and one-fell-swoop socialisation, as opposed to reform and many-fell-swoops socialisation, then revolution and one-fell-swoop it is. If, moreover, socialisation requires institutionalisation of the councils, as opposed to treating them like poor relations, then institutionalisation it is. Salvadori argues, convincingly, that Kautsky wanted to forestall civil war in Germany by preserving the unity of social democracy.[26] Might this desire not have been better served by dropping the commitment to gradualism and endorsing the Executive Council of the workers' and soldiers' councils as the proper instrument for socialisation? Whatever the answer this question, dropping a commitment to S1 and S2 removes the incongruity problem.

Principles

The Kautskian programme runs into more problems. For it is likely to fall foul of the anti-statist horn of the dilemma, as such. It seems perfectly possible, after all, that there is such a thing as *social democratic* statism. Suppose you nationalise the means of production, vesting control over them in unelected state officials – as opposed to workers elected directly from below. This is roughly the nationalisation stratagem devised by European social democracy during the *Trente Glorieuses*. Under the auspicious economic circumstances of post-war reconstruction, high-ranking trade union officials colluded with high-ranking politicians and state officials to keep industrial democracy at bay. In return, workers were provided with better welfare, wages and work conditions. This stratagem violates the equal-power proviso; it implies that state officials, not capitalists, abridge democratic equality. So if one grants – with Kautsky – that public ownership without worker control is undemocratic, then it follows that the social democratic stratagem violates the equal-power proviso. This is why the democratic socialisation of production may *require* an independently elected labour parliament, that is, a federation of workers' councils, elected from individual workplaces, and endowed with control rights over socialised production.

To summarise the argument so far: if control over the means of production is vested exclusively in state officials, even those serving democratic parliaments, then the best we can hope for is a parliamentary system served by an unaccountable and undemocratic state bureaucracy. If control over the means of production is vested exclusively in workers' councils, on the other hand, then the likely outcome is the undemocratic rule of producers, managers and experts. Poulantzas formulated this version of the socialisation dilemma starkly, some 40 years after Kautsky:

> The basic dilemma from which we must extricate ourselves is the following: *either* maintain the existing state and stick exclusively to a modified form of representative democracy – a road that ends up in social-democratic statism and so-called liberal parliamentarianism; *or* base everything on direct, rank-and-file democracy or the movement for self-management – a path which, sooner or later, inevitably leads to statist despotism or the dictatorship of experts.[27]

What Poulantzas calls "social-democratic statism" reflects the statist horn of the socialisation dilemma. What he calls a "dictatorship of experts" reflects the syndicalist horn of the dilemma.

Poulantzas's version is not a mere curiosity. It is ubiquitous in post-war socialist theory. Consider, for example, the socialism of David Schweickart. Out of many contemporary models of worker control, Schweickart's stands out for its perspicacity and clarity of vision. Schweickart's solution to the socialisation dilemma follows Kautsky, in that it presupposes a separation between ownership – ascribed to the state – and control – assigned to the workers. In this model, workers operate and manage profit-seeking firms, where the means of production are state-owned. Aggregate investment is funded by a tax on worker-controlled firms. It is, moreover, socially controlled.

In the Schweickart model, social control of the "national investment fund" is assigned to state-owned banks and to "national" or "regional legislatures" controlling these banks.[28] But therein lies the rub. Schweickart's state-administered national investment fund is liable to replacing capitalist oligarchies by state oligarchies. His model, in other words, is likely to confer too much power on bureaucrats, even if they are parliament-appointed. Of course, Schweickartian socialisation – unlike Soviet-style statism – is compatible with parliamentary institutions. It therefore satisfies the inclusion proviso. But it is still likely to fall foul of the equal-power proviso. Indeed, it is liable to disintegrating into what Ralph Miliband disparagingly called "Labourism." Like Kautsky, Schweickart's principles seem to outrun his strategies.

So what is the solution to the socialisation dilemma? The answer, I think, must begin where Poulantzas left off. And it must have something to do with the separation of powers; what we need is a kind of Madisonianism for communists. As Poulantzas's own formulation suggests, the socialisation dilemma is not exhaustive.[29] That is, one can have a federated system of workers' councils – a workers' congress – *in conjunction with* parliaments. The former would durably uphold the equal-power proviso, while the latter would uphold inclusion. This is, effectively, a variant on Adler's dyarchy model.

Solutions

The idea behind council democracy is simple: workers own and manage their workplace conditions of production through democratically elected workplace councils. Each council then elects representatives to a regional workers' council. Regional councils elect national councils, which are, in turn, entrusted with control over aggregate investment in the economy. In this model, workplace councils are the building blocks of economy-wide councils, which exercise direct control over economy-wide conditions of production.

Now suppose, plausibly, that the desirability of parliaments and councils depends on whether they promote democracy and the values that justify it – the inclusion and equal-power proviso. Communists agree that both unchecked state and capitalist power undermine these values. Suppose, further, that there is a system of dual power, in which parliaments and independently constituted workers' councils share control over the means of production in the economy as a whole. Suppose that, as a result, the power of capitalist, manager or bureaucrat does not hold sway; everyone gets an equal say. Then the envisaged transfer of power from state institutions to workers' councils is not inapposite to democratic values. Indeed, it is *required* by these values. In light of the strategic and moral incongruities plaguing the Kautskian programme, I think the Madisonian solution offers a better way out of the socialisation dilemma. The rest of this section discusses the principles behind the Madisonian programme and responds to some objections.

Advantages

Unlike Kautsky and Bauer, Max Adler recognised the emancipatory potential of the councils. He assigned them a central role in aggregate investment planning, and, by implication, in any democratic socialisation programme. Adler's model envisages a dyarchy between parliament and councils, so I will call it the *Madisonian programme*. Unlike the Kautsksian programme, the Madisonian programme is coherent: it affirms P1 and P2, without committing to S1 or S2. Indeed, Madisonianism retains a healthy scepticism vis-à-vis S1, while explicitly repudiating S2. Unlike the Kautskian programme, it also has the potential to do away with trade union and party bureaucracies, promising genuinely democratic management of the economy from below.

Madisonian socialisation has a further elegant implication: whenever workers' parties obtain majorities in both council and parliament, the agenda of freedom is on. Economic power flows directly from the self-administration of "the democratically elected assemblies of the municipalities, districts and provinces."[30] So when freedom is on, parliament acts as a mere enforcer of democratic decision-making from below. When the workers' parties lack majorities in parliament, by contrast, freedom is on standby. The councils then assume a prophylactic role: they function as a shield against the onslaught of capitalist power, vetoing labour-unfriendly legislation and defending the socialisation of production. Crucially, the Madisonian solution disarms a common anti-communist argument, to the effect that communism violates the inclusion and/or the equal-power proviso. Under the Madisonian programme, anyone running for anti-communist parties or voting for anti-communist policy would be able to do so. In addition, the programme preserves the separation between legislative and executive, thereby preserving the democratic role and value of legitimate opposition.

What would a Madisonian dyarchy look like, exactly? What prerogatives would fall under the purview of the councils and what prerogatives under parliament? Who would control the police and the army? Who would appoint the government and the bureaucracy? The whole intellectual itinerary of political thought since Montesquieu reappears, this time in communist garb. Adler made some progress answering these questions,[31] but his account remains sketchy on crucial details. I will not attempt to respond to any of these questions here. I will, instead, spend the rest of this chapter rebutting objections to the *principles* enunciated by the Madisonian programme.

Objections

Two central questions that immediately arise are: (a) Is there a transitional political strategy that satisfies the Madisonian programme? Call this the *existence* problem. (b) Suppose there is such a transition. Does it lead to a stable political equilibrium? Call this the *stability* problem.

Consider the existence problem first. There is no reason to think there are no transitional strategies satisfying the Madisonian programme. Historically, there have been transitional strategies eventuating in the separation of upper and lower houses – in bicameral systems – and in the separation between executive, legislative and judiciary – in all democratic systems. The communist problem of institutional design is akin to that faced by the English Levellers, to wit, who rules once the throne has been abolished. But a first step towards the dethronement of capital consists in building economy-wide workers' and citizens' assemblies, with a substantial degree of independence from the state, that assume control of their local conditions of production. In this connection, independence from the state suffices to keep statism at bay. The threat of syndicalism can equally be attenuated if the councils are sufficiently inclusive.

In respect of the internal composition of the councils: suppose it were decided, along Kautskian lines, that consumers and experts should be represented in the workers' councils and their federal congress. The question arises of how the diverse interests of these groups might be reconciled. Workers, for example, will want to raise wages and improve work conditions. Consumers, on the other hand, will want to reduce prices and improve the quality of goods. These desires conflict. If broad agreement is beyond reach, and if simple majoritarianism is infeasible or undesirable, scientific panels might need to be consulted. These possibilities raise further difficult questions of institutional design. But democratic practice has developed interesting answers in dealing with them (citizen conferences, expert testimonies, deliberative assemblies, etc.).

The dangers of syndicalism might also be attenuated by the fact that the managers of individual firms have the same control rights as everyone else; they also lack ownership rights. Their incentives can therefore be steered against the kind of abuse that comes with market power or rent-seeking.[32] Moreover, as Kautsky realised, the regulation of individual industries depends on complex issues in industrial organisation. If the machine plays a marginal role in an industry, such that its hierarchies are relatively horizontal – think of universities, law firms, etc. – then competition between firms might attenuate *inter*-firm power differentials, while simultaneously reducing *intra*-firm managerial power. In these industries, industrial democracy is best served by allowing the councils to regulate themselves. If, on the other hand, the machine has a central role to play in an industry, such that its hierarchies are relatively vertical – think of factories, technology firms – then state regulation is likely to be necessary. State regulation is necessary to attenuate both *inter*-firm power differentials, because competition will tend to be weaker in these industries, and *intra*-firm managerial power, as horizontal hierarchies provide ample opportunities for abuse of power. In these industries, industrial democracy is best served by allowing state and councils to regulate the workplace together. The Madisonian solution facilitates and encourages long-term co-operation of this variety.

Now consider the stability problem. A token Leninist objection to Madisonianism charges that the latter is both undesirable and infeasible. Undesirable, because the separation of powers between councils and parliaments is merely the result of class forces: in the case of the councils, the power of the proletariat, and in the case of liberal parliaments, the power of the bourgeoisie. Sooner or later, power will tilt in the direction of one or the other. In the case of Russia, power fell into the hands of the councils soon after the revolution of February 1917, a revolution establishing a de facto dyarchy. In the case of Germany in 1918–19 and Spain in 1936–7, power fell into the hands of social democrats and nationalists, respectively. It follows that proletarian rule, or "proletarian dictatorship," must do away with parliaments sooner rather than later. The dual-power arrangement is, moreover, infeasible, because inherently unstable: eventually power must fall into the hands of one class. Therefore the only sustainable expression of proletarian rule does away with parliaments.

The Leninist objection is multiply confused. There is no reason why parliaments cannot be instruments of proletarian rule. Indeed, proletarian rule *presupposes* liberal parliaments, for it presupposes the basic liberties that will bring revolutionaries to power. These liberties include equal suffrage and freedom of the press, association and assembly. Rosa Luxemburg is therefore right that banning parliaments is not an expression of a "higher form of democracy," as Lenin argued in December 1917, but rather a "remedy worse than the disease it is supposed to cure."[33] The Leninist instability argument, moreover, is irrelevant: it took decades for the separation of powers between legislative, executive and judiciary to find stable expression within *bourgeois* democracies. Why should things be any different in socialist democracies?

The Leninist objection also confuses revolutionary strategy with revolutionary principles. In revolutionary situations, control over guns is intimately connected with control over factories. In 1917, the Bolsheviks ended up controlling the factories because they controlled the guns. In 1918, by contrast, the Executive of the German councils lost control over the factories because it never managed to create a Red Army. Now suppose it did have an army. There is no reason why the Executive should not reconstitute the parliamentary assembly *after* a successful seizure of power.[34] To be sure, such reconstitution involves voluntary transfer of power. But no revolution unwilling to make a power concession can achieve its emancipatory goal: unwillingness to concede means willingness to subject. This willingness can lead to statism, or worse.

Notes

1 See, for example, Karl Marx and Friedrich Engels, *Collected Works*, 76.
2 On inclusion, see Iris Marion Young, *Inclusion and Democracy*; on equality, see Robert Dahl, *A Preface to Democratic Theory*; Thomas Christiano, *The Constitution of Equality*.
3 See Emil Frankel, "The Status of 'Socialization' in Germany"; Massimo Salvadori, *Karl Kautsky and the Socialist Revolution 1880–1938*.
4 Salvadori, *Karl Kautsky*, 231.
5 Karl Kautsky, *The Labour Revolution*, 183.
6 Ibid., 205.
7 In respect of the more egregious cases: there is evidence that workers in medium-sized enterprises in Russia performed firesales of factory equipment and tools, or sold them for scraps. See Thomas Remington, *Building Socialism in Bolshevik Russia*, 54.
8 Kautsky, *The Labour Revolution*, 204.
9 Korsch's pamphlet on socialisation, like Kautsky's early essay, appeared in January 1919 (Kautsky, "Richtlinien fur eine sozialistisches Aktionsprogramm"). Korsch was invited to be an assistant to the first Socialisation Commission in early 1919 (Karl Korsch, *Revolutionary Theory*, 9). Moreover, he refers explicitly to Kautsky's essay (Karl Korsch, "What Is Socialization?," 66).
10 Korsch, "What Is Socialization?", 67–8.
11 Ibid., 69.
12 Ibid., 69.
13 Ibid., 72.
14 Ibid., 75.

15 Ewa Czerwinska-Schupp, *Otto Bauer 1881–1938*, 214.
16 Ibid., 211.
17 Carlile Aylmer Macartney, *The Social Revolution in Austria*, 130.
18 Cf. Maurice Brinton, *The Bolsheviks and Workers' Control*; Oskar Anweiler, *The Soviets*.
19 Bukharin and Preobrazensky, cited in Remington, *Building Socialism*, 99.
20 Otto Bauer, cited in Raimund Loew, "The Politics of Austro-Marxism," 32.
21 Ibid., 35.
22 For a summary of the proceedings around and after the Meidner plan, see Leif Lewin, *Ideology and Strategy*.
23 Salvadori, *Karl Kautsky*, 238.
24 Adam Przeworski, *Capitalism and Social Democracy*.
25 Assuming such a programme is coherent, an assumption disputed in the previous paragraph.
26 Salvadori, *Karl Kautsky*, 245–50.
27 Nicos Poulantzas, *The Poulantzas Reader*, 366, emphases added.
28 David Schweickart, *After Capitalism*, 51–5.
29 Note the "stick *exclusively* to…" and "base *everything* on…" [se tenir à la seul] clauses. Poulantzas clearly has something like the separation of powers in mind (*The Poulantzas Reader*, 366).
30 Kautsky, "Richtlinien," cited in Salvadori, *Karl Kautsky*, 233.
31 In addition to Adler, the dyarchy solution was addressed by Sidney and Beatrice Webb in England and by Martov and the "heavenly twins" Zinoviev and Kamenev in revolutionary Russia. See Sidney Webb and Beatrice Webb, *A Constitution for the Socialist Commonwealth of Great Britain*; Anweiler, *The Soviets*, 187; and more recently John Medhurst, *No Less than Mystic*, 568–9, for discussion.
32 *How* might these incentives be affected? One influential answer is provided by John Roemer, *A Future for Socialism*, who defends a model of publicly owned consortia, similar to the Japanese *keiretsu* system, in which banks monitor and reward managerial performance.
33 Rosa Luxemburg, *The Rosa Luxemburg Reader*, 302.
34 Cf. Luxemburg's admonition to Lenin *à propos* of the Russian Constituent Assembly. Ibid., 302.

References

Anweiler, Oskar. *The Soviets*. London: Pantheon Books, 1974.

Brinton, Maurice. *The Bolsheviks and Workers' Control*. London: Black Rose Books, 1970.

Christiano, Thomas. *The Constitution of Equality*. Oxford: Oxford University Press, 2008.

Czerwinska-Schupp, Ewa. *Otto Bauer 1881–1938*. Rotterdam: Brill, 2016.

Dahl, Robert. *A Preface to Democratic Theory*. Chicago: University of Chicago Press, 1956.

Frankel, Emil. "The Status of 'Socialization' in Germany." *Journal of Political Economy* 32 (1924): 68–85.

Kautsky, Karl. *The Labour Revolution*. London: Routledge, 2013.

Korsch, Karl. *Revolutionary Theory*. Edited by Douglas Kellner. Austin, TX: University of Texas Press, 1977.

———. "What Is Socialization?" Translated by Frankie Denton and Douglas Kellner. *New German Critique* 6 (1975): 60–81.

Lewin, Leif. *Ideology and Strategy: A Century of Swedish Politics*. Cambridge: Cambridge University Press, 1988.

Loew, Raimund. "The Politics of Austro-Marxism." *New Left Review* 118 (1979): 15–51.

Luxemburg, Rosa. *The Rosa Luxemburg Reader*. Edited by Peter Hudis and Kevin B. Anderson. London: Monthly Review Press, 2004.

Macartney, Carlile Aylmer. *The Social Revolution in Austria*. Cambridge: Cambridge University Press, 2014 [1926].

Marx, Karl and Friedrich Engels. *Collected Works*, vol. 10. London: Lawrence & Wishart, 2010.

Medhurst, John. *No Less than Mystic: A History of Lenin and the Russian Revolution for a 21st Century Left*. London: Repeater Books, 2017.

Pannekoek, Anton. *Workers' Councils*. London: AK Press, 1947.

Poulantzas, Nicos. *The Poulantzas Reader*. Edited by James Martin. London: Verso, 2008.

Przeworski, Adam. *Capitalism and Social Democracy*. Cambridge: Cambridge University Press, 1985.

Remington, Thomas. *Building Socialism in Bolshevik Russia*. Pittsburgh, PA: University of Pittsburgh Press, 1984.

Roemer, John. *A Future for Socialism*. Cambridge, MA: Harvard University Press, 1994.

Salvadori, Massimo. *Karl Kautsky and the Socialist Revolution 1880–1938*. London: New Left Books, 1979.

Schweickart, David. *After Capitalism*. London: Rowman & Littlefield, 2011.

Young, Iris Marion. *Inclusion and Democracy*. Oxford: Oxford University Press, 2002.

Webb, Beatrice and Sidney Webb. *A Constitution for the Socialist Commonwealth of Great Britain*. London: Longman, 1920.

6 A Theory of Council Republicanism

Michael J. Thompson

"*If* democracy is justified in governing the state, then it must *also* be justified in governing economic enterprises."

– Robert Dahl

Introduction

The problem of economic power is one of the most durable and potent forms of domination in modern societies. The expansion of economic divisions that continue to plague capitalist society seems to be morphing into an entrenched oligarchy where the political sphere is increasingly fused to economic power. In addition to this, democratic culture seems also to be withering. By most accounts, political activity of all kinds has been decreasing as economic inequality widens and embeds itself into the structure and lifeworld of modern society, fostering anti-democratic attitudes towards authority and a relative quiescence of organising and critical attitudes against oligarchic policies.[1] What these realities demonstrate is that the economic sphere in capitalist societies is a central source of hierarchical and non-democratic forms of life. Extending democracy into economic life is therefore a question of considerable importance. The surge in economic inequality, the increasing dominance of technocratic elites and the rise of cultural alienation from political concerns and activity have ground Western democracies down.

As a result, political theorists search in earnest for forms of democratic practice and institutions that can serve to counter the strong, integrating trends rooted in capitalist economic life. One trend that has re-emerged in recent left political theory is the concern with workers' councils: a form of self-management and self-rule by workers over their respective firms. This has not been the sole purview of socialist thinkers and theorists. Liberal thinkers, such as John Stuart Mill in the nineteenth century and Robert Dahl in the late twentieth, have been drawn to the idea of economic democracy and co-operative ownership of firms.[2] Nevertheless, workers' councils find their most historically robust formulation in the post-First World War era when countries such as Germany, Austria and

Italy, among others, saw the emergence of workers' councils as a reaction to hierarchical and non-democratic social relations, both in the workplace and the military. But the exact role that these councils should play has been an open question.

What I want to suggest in this chapter is a theory of council democracy informed by the republican tradition. In this sense, the purpose of the council system is to deepen democratic life, to counter domination in social relations and to make economic institutions accountable to and oriented towards the common interest and common purposes of the community as a whole. As I see it, this is the important contribution of merging the council tradition with an account of republicanism: first, it retains a layer of political realism by holding on to institutions such as the state, constitutionalism and the rule of law. But second, it also places emphasis on the common good, or common interest of the community as a whole, and makes all institutions – especially economic ones – accountable to as well as oriented towards the res publica. Councils therefore play a crucial role in the enhancement of a democratic republic and should be seen not as autonomous institutions that will bear the weight of all political affairs, but rather as embedded within the institutions of the modern constitutional, republican state in order to serve as an institutional framework for economic democracy.

Unfortunately, many theoretical reflections on the theory of council democracy evince what I think we can view as a romantic conception of radical politics, one that places emphasis on expressivist ideas about human agency and under-theorises the concerns that democratic theorists have tried to grapple with since the dawn of the Enlightenment. Specific among these is the idea of democratic accountability and democratic direction of social institutions that affect citizens' common lives together. The evolution of the modern state has taken on many of these functions, particularly during the social democratic and welfare state interventionist periods in capitalist society. But these institutional forms are themselves being undermined by neoliberal policies that are re-creating an oligarchic social order. As I see it, a mature form of democratic socialism will require not the abolition of the state, but rather its democratic *expansion*. I want to defend a different conception of the ways that workers' councils can function within the structure of the modern state and to elaborate the ways that democratic life can be deepened without giving in to what I think we should see as the utopian interpretation of workers' councils: the idea of a form of political life constituted purely by self-governing, spontaneous, direct participatory forms which will explode all forms of the modern state and legal institutions. What I suggest is that aspects of the councilist tradition can be intertwined with progressive aspects of the modern state to produce a more democratic conception of the state, which includes the democratisation of the economy. I also claim that a "councilist" paradigm that focuses exclusively on a vision of a pure, participatory, anti-statist society is not only unable to produce political stability, but would also fail to achieve the kind of democratic society that it intends.

But this should not mean that the theory of workers' councils should be abandoned. Indeed, the deepening of democratic life requires the widening of democratic institutions. I maintain that this can be best achieved through a push towards institutionalising workers' councils as an integral part of the modern state, expanding the radical republican impulse that can be found at the root of all valid expressions of radical democracy. This radicalness, however, should be found not in the elimination of representative institutions, an abolition of the state, or other ideas that can best be described, after Georg Lukács, as "romantic anti-capitalism." Rather, it must be based on the principle of depriving

> people of the power to use other people as means to an end, however worthy the increase of productivity or the national welfare ... The aim then is to check the command powers through the countervailing powers of labour and other organisations.[3]

The council system, when properly constructed, can indeed fulfil this basic principle. It can be accomplished through expanding the democratising powers of the modern state and be secured through the legal protections of the modern constitutional order. To put this more fundamentally, it can only be achieved through the transformation of the modern state into a *modern social republic*, or what German socialist legal theorists appropriately called a *sozialer Rechtsstaat*.[4]

Indeed, my thesis here will therefore be that we require a theory of councils that can be integrated into the representative institutions of the modern state. The purpose of workers' councils cannot be to achieve sole political dominance over the community, which I see as a romantic conception championed by some contemporary theorists, but rather to add a layer of democratisation to those institutions and social settings where hierarchy and domination are fundamentally embedded. In addition to this, the council system must be understood as weaving itself with the structure of the modern state rather than being in ontological opposition to it. What I propose is a theory of what I will call *council republicanism* that makes the state and the council system interdependent structures of a more enhanced expression of democracy. As I see it, this is a paradigm of democracy that can be sought after by social movements to deepen the democratisation of society and secure these gains through constitutional reforms and the creation of new state institutions.

The Utopian Theory of Council Democracy

The theory of council republicanism is in stark contrast to the prevailing theory of workers' councils that has emerged in theoretical writings on left politics since the late 1960s. Characteristic of this approach is the tendency to see the councils as displacing the modern state. In its place is envisaged a transformative human praxis that would provide a shift in "being" due to the creative praxis unleashed by the councils as a new form of organisation. I see this as a chimerical interpretation of workers' councils, which is essentially anti-political. It is anti-political because it ignores the complex checks and balances, the competition of interests and the "dirty hands" reality of how politics is accomplished. For Hannah Arendt, the political is not about such concerns, it is about the co-operative sharing of opinion that she saw as the essence of politics. In this view, workers' councils are a political formation that allows for the participatory control of workers in governing not only their workplace, but also the society as a whole. At the heart of councilism is the thesis that workers' councils are mechanisms of direct, participatory control by working people over their community as a whole. Although one can point to a host of different interpretations of workers' councils, the main thrust of councilist theories was to overcome the state; its intention was to supplant it with a direct form of participatory activity that would serve as a framework for self-governance and self-expression. Anton Pannekoek, for instance, makes the case clearly when he writes:

> Council organization is a real democracy, the democracy of labour, making the working people master of their work. Under council organization political democracy has disappeared, because politics itself disappeared and gave way to social economy. The activity of the councils, put in action by the workers as the organs of collaboration, guided by perpetual study and strained attention to circumstances and needs, covers the entire field of society. All measures are taken in constant intercourse, by deliberation in the councils and discussion in the groups and the shops, by actions in the shops and decisions in the councils. What is done under such conditions could never be commanded from above and proclaimed by the will of a government. It proceeds from the common will of all concerned; because it is founded on the labour experience and knowledge of all, and because it deeply influences the life of all.[5]

The underlying justification for almost the entire workers' council tradition can be found here. Its essential thesis lies in its emphasis on direct, participatory activity that will serve to transform its members into a self-governing society of producers. For Pannekoek, the utopian aspect of the workers' council lies in the idea that "politics disappears" and gives way to a new social formation that has more akin with the fantasies of anarchism rather than the actual needs of real politics.

Another claim of the councilist tradition that has gained influence is the thesis, most notably put forward by Arendt, that the councils were an institutionalised space for creative expression and self-disclosure. According to this thesis, the workers' councils enabled what she saw as the essence of political life, that which is genuinely "political" in her terms. Arendt's discussion of the workers' councils is a strong expression of this thesis when she writes:

> the councils have always been primarily political, with social and economic claims playing a very minor role, and it was precisely this lack of interest in social and economic questions which, in the view of the revolutionary party, was a sure sign of their "lower-middle-class, abstract, liberalistic" mentality. In fact, it was a sign of their political maturity, whereas the workers' wish to run the factories themselves was a sign of the understandable, but politically irrelevant desire of individuals to rise into positions which up to then had been open only to the middle class.[6]

For Arendt, the true aim and purpose of the councils was to embody her conception of the "political," or the capacity of individuals to come together and share their opinions about the world and enlarge one another's mentality in order to deliberate and act on matters of common concern. Although, historically, the councils were set up to combat hierarchical and subordinating relations within the workplace as well as the military, Arendt dismisses these concerns and instead sees them as being created as spaces of political freedom. What the councils are supposed to achieve is a renewed sense of public activity and public-spiritedness – free from any concrete economic concerns, they are to serve to open its participants up to what Durkheim called the "collective effervescence" of being-with-others. In her utopian vision of citizenship, her naive understanding of real politics, her narrow view of the modern state and her phenomenological theory of consciousness, she presses a theory of the councils that has resonated among many contemporary theorists: as one with transformative powers over the self and society, rather than their actual historic aim which was the confrontation with economic power, hierarchy and domination.[7]

The emphasis is therefore once again on what we can call the trans-political: philosophically utopian and romantic ideas about self and social transformation that will emerge once people are able to get together and share their work or their opinions with one another and create a spontaneous, creative community transcending all forms of bureaucracy and alienation.[8] As Pannekoek argues, the councils will lead to self-government which will lead to a new form of reality: "When life and work in community are natural habit, when mankind entirely controls its own life, necessity gives way to freedom and the strict rules of justice established before dissolve into spontaneous behaviour."[9]

Such theses are deeply mistaken and delusional; they are also non-historical and simply non-political in any serious sense. There is no argument given of how social co-ordination problems will be handled by these councils; there is no argument given about the defects of direct democracy; no sense of how non-economic political matters are to be adjudicated without constitutional principles or institutions of law; there is no real sense given about how this system is to be secured and how executive power is to be exercised; and there is no real attention paid to the problem of how and if the common interest can be kept in view with such decentralised forms of political action. Indeed, both Pannekoek and Arendt stress problematic ideas about the concept of the workers' councils. They both claim for the councils an anti-bureaucratic and spontaneous element that would unleash a direct democratic potential and lead to the withering away of the modern state. They also misunderstand the nature of decentralising politics: it does not lead to furthering democracy, but expands the opportunities for elite control and domination by loosening the powers of oversight over particular interests.[10] The state is therefore a crucial ingredient to any system of economic democracy, as I will explain below. This has led many contemporary theorists to see this more anarchist model of the workers' councils as overcoming alienation and transforming our "being." But, as Henry Pachter has convincingly argued:

> Ultraleft utopians have given it an even sharper, or perhaps more ludicrous form. It seems to them that under socialism people will undergo a fundamental change of character; not being alienated, they will have neither different interests nor different opinions, but will gladly cooperate in any reasonable assignment that the government [or councils] decides upon.[11]

But why should we view this as romantic, utopian and impractical? One reason is that the emphasis on direct forms of democracy are assumed to express a more pure and genuine form of democracy. But why should we accept such a claim? Indeed, direct forms of democratic life have generally been more unstable, more prone to conflict and less inclined towards consensus than its advocates claim. Immediate forms of democracy – whether direct or immediate recall of representatives – diminishes the capacity of democracy to embody and express the general interest. Governability is still a crucial issue, and the capacity of political forms to be able to both express interests and concerns as well as serve as a stable framework for political and legal procedures and processes is dependent on some degree of that governability. Representative institutions ought not to be equated with an alienation of power. Rather, they encourage democratic will-formation and secure legitimacy to governing institutions. Democratic theorists in the modern period learned much from the failures of the Athenian polis: namely that the more direct the democratic system was as a whole, the more anarchic it became, the less it became a vehicle for expressing the common interest, and the more it encouraged factionalisation and segmentation of particular interests. As Pierre Rosanvallon has argued on this point: "the problem is that such immediacy would paradoxically lead to its destruction: it would end by dissolving itself through its segmentation, existing only in perpetual variation."[12] We can cultivate the general interest not through immediate democratic forms, but via institutional spaces where democratic participation leads to a response by the institutions of governance.[13] The key is to maintain a complex of layers of representative bodies that can serve to check and control one another.[14]

The model of direct or immediate forms of democracy are therefore impracticable. There is no way that citizens can regulate and decide on all issues within a large-scale modern polity. The key to a radical politics, it seems to me, is to shape the constitutional structure of the polity so as to secure the democratisation of all spheres of life. The more this is achieved, the less individuals become alienated from political life as a whole. Councils therefore can play this role without the illusions of direct democracy or the practice of direct mandates and immediate recall of representatives, which causes a similar problem to concerns of governability and tends towards volatility. As Mark Shipway correctly points out:

> If this emphasis on working-class autonomy and spontaneity is taken to an absurd extreme, however, it can lead to two dangers: first, the denial of all necessity or reason for any political organisation distinct from the majority of the working class, and, second, the fetishisation of any organisational form created spontaneously and autonomously by the working class.[15]

The attempt to either see the workers' councils as the central political institution or practice of socialist democracy should therefore be seen as problematic. An alternative is to see them as institutional forms that can broaden the capacities of democratic life and, more importantly, extend democracy into economic institutions and decision-making. This can have the effect of changing representative institutional forms as well, injecting them with more vigour and reducing their susceptibility to capture by oligarchic and technocratic elites.[16]

The idea that workers' councils will have some transformative effect on human agency and human "being" simply misses the real political point that is truly at stake: workers' councils are political organisations that seek to extend democratic accountability and exert countervailing powers against the decisions and imperatives of private command over capital which is, in its basic essence, a social product. These institutions will only emerge as a result of struggles *within* the structures of the modern state. The struggles of working people and the organisations that they will require in order to carve out these spheres of power must be directed towards the expansion and transformation of the powers of the modern state over economic concerns and the powers of elites to control capital and economic processes and policies.[17] The political form that this might take is, of course, impossible to predict, but we can seek to theorise how workers' councils can integrate with the powers of the modern state via the model of council republicanism. Before this, I would like to defend what I see as the basic principles that are to be maximised by this institutional scheme.

Council Republicanism and Social Justice

I would now like to suggest how the council system can be employed to deepen and widen democratic life. My thesis here is that this can only be accomplished by embedding councils within the legitimate structure of a constitutional state. I call this model *council republicanism* and argue that one of its defining characteristics is not simply the democratisation of the economic sphere of society through self-management, but also the embedding of these institutions into the architecture of the state via constitutional-legal structures that secure their powers not only for self-management at the local firm level, but also higher structures of institutional power that enable a more democratic shape of national economic and social policy more generally. One of the primary deficits of contemporary "left" political theory is a sizeable cynicism about the institution of the modern state instead of appreciating its capacities to shape the power of society as a whole and to administer complex social affairs for the common interest.[18] As Jürgen Habermas suggests, replying to Arendt:

> A state relieved of the administrative handling of social affairs, a politics cleansed of all questions of social politics, an institutionalizing of public liberty that is independent of the organization of welfare, a radically democratic formation of consensus that puts a stop to social repression – this is not a conceivable path for any modern society.[19]

Council republicanism is a model distinct from the more immature, ultra-left ideas about workers' councils outlined above and the unfortunate influence they still wield in left political theory. It consists of an embedding of workers' councils – seen as sites of economic democratisation and self-control – on the one hand within the structures of the modern state where they will be able to advance and protect policies that concern economic life and working concerns on a more general, national scale. But it also places emphasis on the concept of a common, public good towards which legal structures, state institutions and political decisions must be oriented. Workers' councils must also be absorbed into this structure and not simply be premised on a contestatory model but a constitutive model as well. This means that the workers' councils themselves will not only require their own local sphere of influence over working conditions and decisions, but also reach up into higher institutional levels in national political decision-making. Before outlining what this will look like institutionally and what kind of roles this will play politically, I want to defend the thesis, first, that workers' councils are necessary for any deeper conception of democracy, and, second, that the councils can play a role not in militating *against* the state, but rather in *enhancing* the democratic character of the representative or parliamentary state.

Any theory of social justice must consider the ways in which modern forms of economic life create social structures that affect the institutions, norms and culture of democratic life. One of the core arguments that bring economic affairs into the political realm is what we can call the basic principle of a radical, social republic. A socialist theory of justice would therefore require that we posit principles distinct from liberal principles of social justice which are based more on equality of opportunity or a fair distribution of initial starting points for individuals within society. A socialist principle of social justice will emphasise equal relations in all spheres of society, or a condition of *non-domination* in social and economic relations, and also emphasise *common ends* for social-economic activities, decisions and institutions.[20] We can express this more simply as two interdependent principles that must be maximised in order for any polity to achieve the status of a social republic:

(I) *the principle of non-domination;*
(II) *the principle of common or public utility.*

These two principles are, as I see it, fundamental to a socialist theory of democracy and should be the basic criteria of judgement for all social institutions – economic and non-economic. The theory of council republicanism is therefore meant to embody these twin principles that can express and realise a more compelling theory of social justice.[21]

If we consider (I), we can say that domination is the capacity to extract some form of surplus benefit from another. Domination relations are those that consist of any agent's capacity to sustain a relationship with another agent that results in the surplus benefit of the dominator at the expense of the subordinate. It need not be a zero-sum form of unequal exchange, but can be expressed as the capacity of an agent to gain in some way at the expense of the agent that is dominated.[22] It is a capacity that any agent possesses over another agent by means of the structure of social relations sanctioned by specific legal structures as well as cultural norms and practices. This principle of non-domination as anti-extractive power also informs (II), since the kind of domination that (I) exhibits also affects the form and content of the common fund of resources and economic life as a whole. Principle (II) maintains that all economic activities, institutions and decisions must maximise public ends rather than private, particular ends. The accountability of capital – private or public – must be a central concern of workers' councils and the higher institutions of a social republican state. In a society dominated by private property over economic resources, production decisions are made generally without social utility or common purposes being taken into account. Rather, the production and investment decisions are made with an eye towards maximising surplus under private control.

Hence, both (I) and (II) are shaped by such decisions since maximising extractive power over people also affects the purposes and ends of community as a whole. The key idea here is the more overall principle that merges (I) and (II): that the common good of any community lies in the maximisation of its social wealth, i.e. the quality of and egalitarian access to the produce of the co-operative work of the community as a whole for each individual. Relations of extraction, exploitation, inequality of access based on income, wealth or status, as well as the orientation of this production (i.e. whether a production decision is meant to benefit common or private purposes) therefore constitute a basic feature of a just social order. This theory of social justice is therefore distinct from a liberal theory of social justice since its emphasis is not on a "fair" sense of distribution (whether of opportunities, desert or whatever) but rather on the democratic transformation of both economic relations and the common ends or purposes towards which economic firms and production are oriented.

These twin principles help shape the structure of social wealth within the society. The reason is that unequal relations of power in economic life are largely, if not wholly, derived from the powers of some to control the labour of others. The core problem with this kind of power is that decisions are made based on the particular interests of generating surplus and not on social needs. These may coincide, at times, but the power to orient the ends of economic production remains in the hands of this particular class of ownership of capital. This shapes the kind of wealth that society as a whole possesses. As I have argued elsewhere,[23] social wealth can be defined as the total of economic surplus produced by society as a whole. It consists of the totality of the products, services and so on that any society produces and maintains for itself. But social wealth also comes in two distinct forms. Oligarchic wealth is a kind of wealth that grants any given agent *the power to command, control and direct the labour of any other for the purpose of generating some surplus benefit*. Democratic wealth, on the contrary, is *a form of social wealth to which all have access and which is also produced by common decision for common ends and purposes*. A theory of economic democracy must therefore extend the institution of councils beyond the shop-floor or the firm level and reach into higher levels of co-ordination and steering.

It is this problem that council republicanism seeks to address, and it can be seen in a whole family of theories of council socialism from Karl Kautsky, Beatrice and Sidney Webb and Karl Renner, among many others. Both principles (I) and (II) require more than a decentralised system of workers' councils. They require for their concretisation an institutional architecture that can democratise the hierarchical nature of the economic sphere but also steer economic activities, ends and purposes towards the common utility. As such, I will now turn my attention to the elaboration of a theory of council republicanism as an institutional proposal for expanding the power of democratic life into the economic sphere.

Socialist Democracy: Radical Constitutionalism and Council Republicanism

Let me now turn to the question of institutional structure and the relation between the council system and the national political system of the state. I take as a starting point the legal architecture put forth by Hugo Sinzheimer in the Weimar Constitution, whose radicalism should be recognised in the present context. Indeed, much of contemporary left theory on the question of workers' councils takes more from the anarchist and council communism tradition than from what I am calling here the council republican tradition. This is a mistake. For one thing, in Germany and in Austria in 1918 and 1919 – where the most vibrant and mature workers' councils were being formed – there was in fact limited opposition to republican government and parliamentary institutions.[24] What I want to do here is draw on this basic architecture and elaborate its radical implications and suggest that this is a more politically viable and desirable path to follow than the anti-statist iteration of workers' councils in contemporary theory.

Indeed, the maturity and radicalness of the German and Austrian workers' councils found expression in the idea that the national state possesses powers that were complementary to the interests of working people and to a socialist form of democracy. We can perhaps outline what these powers are and why the modern state and councils are in fact complementary. The reason for this is that the liberal traditions of private law have sustained a structure of power where private persons have control over what is otherwise an intrinsically social institution: economic firms and capital. The problem emerges with the extension of private property over capital. Since capital is conceived of as a private thing, *res*, rather a social institution involving people, *personae*, the power of private property over capital violates the basic principles of the social republic because it allows the legal owner of a thing to extend itself into a power over people. The power over things, *res*, has transformed into power over persons, *personae*, and "the owner of a *res* imposes his will upon *personae*, autonomy is converted into heteronomy of will."[25] The move from a *power over things* to a *power over people* is what is essentially at the base of capitalist society. The concern of council republicanism should therefore be to rework the political and legal structures of society so that this polarity between public and private control is overcome.

The move from power over people via power over things, i.e. the link between *res* and *personae*, must now be mediated by the concept of the common, public accountability of economic life, of the *publicum*. Indeed, this is not totally foreign to modern liberal conceptions of law. But in council democracy and council republicanism, this will be carried further, at least to the extent that all forms of social-economic activity must be accountable to the *publicum* instead of being the right of control as the *res* of the private person. The key importance of this shift is that the preconditions of law and state now become based not on the protection of private property over capital, but rather on the protection and maintenance of public concerns and goods. The transformation of the basic constitutional principles concerning private property is therefore one of the core shifts required in order to change the boundary between the economic and political spheres. Control over those institutions that involve and affect society must be fundamentally accountable to – and ideally controlled by – democratic will. This grants to council republicanism a more secure foundation for its legal and political powers. Private ownership over capital – which must be re-conceptualised as a *social institution* – is now accountable to the public as a whole. The truly radical moment here is in the capacity of democratic worker movements to erase this distinction through the mechanisms of law and the state. A private-acquisitive system now becomes a democratic-social one.

I assume that the council system can be articulated through a series of levels, each with different capacities and roles. *First*, a local level that will have control over decisions within firms and/or to accumulate demands within industries – over wages, working conditions and the distribution of surplus, for example, as well as self-management and self-administration of the workplace. One can also see this in a non-industrial setting such as service workers and restaurants, where workers from multiple small sites accumulate demands in a council that communicates demands across a sector or industry as a whole. Representatives on this council can be elected on short-term bases, such as six-month terms to avoid isolation from worker demands. A *second* layer would serve to co-ordinate local councils with one another and accumulate demands across larger institutional structures, deal with local economic and political issues, as well as send representatives to the *final* level which would serve at the national level and be made of representatives from the council system as a whole. The role of the national level will be to have veto power over legislation on economic policy, industrial policy, tax policy and other policies of economic concern. As such, we can see the roots of this layer of the council system as interweaving with the state and as having its roots in the Roman republican system of the *tribuni plebis* which was created to protect the common people (*plebs*) from the dominance of the patrician senate. Taken together, these three levels of the council system exercise not only a countervailing power to capital, but also a capacity to transform the private control over capital into a democratic one. It seeks to reverse the most basic legal and political power in all society, that of capital as property and its power to possess, in Karl Renner's words, "control over strangers."[26]

The purpose of this system of councils is therefore meant to extend democratic practices and accountability, and also to create an institutional framework for steering economic activities towards common, public purposes and interests. The three levels of what we can call this branch of politics extending into the modern state therefore possess different purposes and capacities. Local workers' councils are organised at the level of the firm and their central purposes is the organisation of self-management and self-administration of workers within that particular firm. These can be organised in numerous ways, but the basic aim of this self-administration is to make decisions on the working structure of different levels of the firm, on how it is run, and even, in its more radical manifestation, on how to distribute and utilise surplus and even make investment decisions. The district level would be populated by representatives from the firm-level councils. It would operate on higher levels in order to co-ordinate and mediate the local and higher state levels of economic policy and interests. In the US system, for instance, this might mean having district councils at a county or state level, or in other systems at a provincial level, and so on. The basic purpose of these councils would again be addressed to the problem of co-ordination: the organisation of more local workers' councils into broader coalitions, the filtering of information and interests to the Tribune Council, and so on.

At the national level, or what we can call the Tribune Council, the council will be composed of representatives voted on by all members at the firm level and serve the purpose of making decisions about national economic policy. In this sense, the power of the Tribune Council is stronger than what we see in the US National Labor Relations Board but not as elaborate as the Social Parliament proposed by Beatrice and Sidney Webb, the latter acting as a parallel parliament to the political parliament.[27] Karl Renner also saw the possibility of councils reaching into higher institutional structures such as a "Congress of Councils" that would "assume the functions of a parliament."[28] The purpose of the Tribune Council would still be essentially political in the sense that its purview is to approve and propose legislation in the sphere of economic policy and its social implications. Its aim is not to accumulate total power, but to serve as an organ of economic democracy within a parliamentary system. Indeed, it cannot be ignored that non-economic concerns still would require their own voice.[29] Concerns about environmental issues, race, gender and international issues will also have to be balanced with the concerns of economic democracy, and there is no reason to simply assume that the Tribune Council will always take such concerns into account. Politics is more complex than class concerns alone; but it is also true that class concerns require their own political sphere. It would also break down the division between the economic and the public in terms of democratic accountability as well as open up possibilities for democratic steering of national economic policy.

As such, we can see two crucial powers that this Tribune Council must possess. Taking after the *tribuni plebis* of the Roman republic, it will have the power to veto national legislation coming from parliamentary institutions of the state as well as possess the capacity to propose legislation to that body. Roman tribunes possessed both powers, that of *ius intercessionis* or the power to intercede in legislation coming from the senate, and to convene a *concilium plebis* or a council of plebeians that would be able to propose legislation to the senate. These correspond to the two powers of veto and proposing legislation in the council republic. The Tribune Council will therefore ideally possess both *veto power* (intercessional capacity) and the power to *propose legislation* (propositional capacity). Hence, the powers of the Tribune Council would be tethered to the firm level via frequent representative elections and would be able to steer macro-level policy issues and economic decisions based on its constituency: of working people who do not control capital.

It may be objected that this proposal in fact negates the "spirit" of what council democracy was always meant to achieve: direct, participatory powers over economic firms and local life.[30] But this is largely a fiction of a small subset of the council tradition. The real aim of council republicanism is to socialise democracy by applying democratic principles to the economic sphere. It is simply wrong to assert that direct democratic procedures are somehow a more authentic expression of democracy. In truth, representative forms foster more democracy, not less.[31] Council republicanism seeks to concretise democratic aspects of economic life and to socialise private power over what should be publicly accountable. But it is also meant to extend democratic *steering powers* over economic decisions into the structure of the state as a whole. The interaction of the Tribune Council with the regular political branch of the state – of parliament or congress – is therefore meant to break down fundamentally the barrier in bourgeois law and political science between the public and private spheres and extend democratic participation, control and accountability to economic structures and activities. The apocalyptic hope for revolution, for some kind of total breakdown of the system and the construction of a new society without capitalism or the apparatus of the state, is a deeply misguided as well as historically and sociologically deluded vision. As I argued above, I find this aspiration utopian as well as non-viable, at least within the confines of modern historical experience. The model I have sketched above is therefore one that can be built gradually through struggles to transform the powers of the state, and which would have to be enlarged and expanded over time through political struggles. But more importantly, we should be clear that council republicanism allows for the extension of democratic life into the workplace, thereby providing a countervailing power to dominating and exploitive relations within economic life and, second, it allows for an institutional architecture that has steering powers over macro decisions in the economy as a whole. Hence, there is a connection between the local and the national and in such a way both can shape economic life with different levels of consideration and information.

Conclusion

In the end, I hope that my thesis goes in no small way to changing hegemonic ideas in Marxist theory about the nature of economic democracy and the role that workers' councils and the state can play in the advancement of socialist democracy. There is little question that the ideas I have sketched here require for their realisation a degree of democratic agency that is nowhere present in post-industrial societies. Decades of material affluence, pressures of de-politicisation in all spheres of life, commodified forms of culture and consciousness, the breakdown of social, not to mention worker, solidarity, no less than increasingly successful legislative attempts to roll back the power of organising labour and secure corporate power, and more, all conspire to undermine democratic agency and class consciousness. Even more – and this is no doubt due to the withering of the centrality of the labour movement in Western politics – contemporary left theory advocates an increasing autonomy of movements from and against the state. But this is a mistake: the real concern should in fact be to make the institutions of the state *accountable and subservient to the common interest of the community as a whole*.[32]

It has also been one of my central intentions here to counter what I see as a politically immature position on the concept of the state in Marxist and other brands of left theory.[33] Whereas many today advocate for an anti-state position with respect to social movements,[34] my thesis here opens for us again the possibility of envisioning a more mature and more democratically rich conception of political reality: one where movements have been able to establish their interests within the constitutional structure of the state and where economic democracy can achieve an objective institutional referent within political reality. A radical theory of constitutionalism and the modern state will see that the real emphasis should be placed not on utopian and irrational schemes for a withering of the state, nor on cynical ideas of the state's inherently anti-democratic powers. Rather, as Otto Kirchheimer notes:

> If the state is founded on the will or the needs of men, then men can determine with their will and their needs the direction of state activity. At the moment at which the working class becomes class-conscious, and has constituted itself into a real class, capitalism is confronted with the danger that the will of the working class will determine the contents and direction of state activity.[35]

Marxian ideas should therefore be seen as compatible with modern ideas about constitutionalism, the rule of law and the parliamentary systems of the modern state.[36] Thinking in more concrete terms about the kinds of social institutions and state institutions that can be erected to expand democratic life and democratise the economy requires a renewed theoretical maturity about the aims of socialist democracy and the realistic ways that workers' movements can transform the composition of the bourgeois state. My own proposition here is only a means to the end of inspiring that kind of thinking. But, to be sure, the real issue of concern must be on the fostering of class consciousness and the cultivation of critical reflection that can merge principles and interests. Only when this first step is taken can the long struggle towards a new form of democratic life be pursued.

Notes

1 Frederick Solt, "Economic Inequality and Democratic Political Engagement"; Frederick Solt, "The Social Origins of Authoritarianism"; Frederick Solt, "Economic Inequality and Nonviolent Protest."; Frederick Solt *et al.*, "Economic Inequality and Class Consciousness"; Michael J. Thompson, *The Politics of Inequality*; Jeffrey Winters, *Oligarchy*.

2 John Stuart Mill, *Principles of Political Economy*; Robert Dahl, *A Preface to Economic Democracy*.

3 Henry Pachter, *Socialism in History*, 328.

4 See Franz Neumann, "The Social Significance of the Basic Laws in the Weimar Constitution," in Keith Tribe (ed.), *Social Democracy and the Rule of Law*; Otto Kirchheimer, *Politik und Verfassung*, 9ff, Otto Kirchheimer, "Constitutional Reform and Social Democracy," in Tribe (ed.), *Social Democracy and the Rule of Law*.

5 Anton Pannekoek, *Workers' Councils*, 48.

6 Hannah Arendt, *On Revolution*, 274.

7 John Medearis points out against Arendt's reading of the council movement that "her tendency to misread the experience of the councils was reinforced by the occasional appearance of a rather naïve sociology, a resistance to analysing the social and economic power relations and structures to which the councils responded." John Medearis, "Lost or Obscured?," 470.

8 See Greg Smulewicz-Zucker, "Illusory Alternatives," in Greg Smulewicz-Zucker and Michael J. Thompson (eds), *Radical Intellectuals and the Subversion of Progressive Politics*.

9 Pannekoek, *Workers' Councils*, 44; cf. Anton Pannekoek, *Anthropogenesis*, 88ff; and Herman Gorter, "Die Klassenkampf-Organisation des Proletariats," in Hans Manfred Bock (ed.), *Organisation und Taktik der proletarischen Revolution*.

10 Grant McConnell puts this thesis well when he argues that "The cult of decentralization is based upon a desire to abolish power. Nevertheless, the local elites are readily brought together on a federal basis and their differences are easily reconciled, since these differences are usually only that and not conflicts. Within each sphere of policy, power is not abolished but rather enhanced by decentralization. At the same time, decentralization means weakness of public officers in contests with private organizations and the elites these represent." Grant McConnell, *Private Power and American Democracy*, 245.

11 Pachter, *Socialism in History*, 46.

12 Pierre Rosanvallon, *Democracy Past and Future*, 205.
13 See the discussion by Nadia Urbinati, *Mill on Democracy*, 42ff.
14 See Rosanvallon, *Democracy Past and Future*, 202ff.
15 Mark Shipway, "Council Communism," in Maximilien Rubel and John Crump (eds), *Non-Market Socialism in the Nineteenth and Twentieth Centuries*, 123.
16 Indeed, this is a salient point worth mentioning: workers' councils should perhaps be seen as having the potential to enhance representative political bodies rather than dismiss them as ineffective and alienating. Their primary role is to break down hierarchical structural relations that are rooted in economic processes and economic power. As Clarissa Rile Hayward points out: "Why do structural inequalities pose a problem for the conventional normative view of representation? The principal reason is that those whom they disadvantage often cannot, by virtue of their positions in the hierarchies structural inequalities define, authorize representatives and/or hold them account." Clarissa Rile Hayward, "Making Interest," in Ian Shapiro *et al.* (eds), *Political Representation*, 113.
17 Milton Fisk, *The State and Social Justice*, 301ff.
18 See Simon Critchley, *Infinitely Demanding*; Miguel Abensour, *Democracy against the State*.
19 Jürgen Habermas, *Philosophical-Political Profiles*, 180–1.
20 Thompson, *The Politics of Inequality*.
21 Cf. ibid.
22 I should stress my difference on this point with the work of Philip Pettit. See my paper on differentiating my theory of domination from his in Thompson, "The Two Faces of Domination in Republican Political Theory." I cannot develop this point with any significance here.
23 Thompson, *The Politics of Inequality*.
24 Eberhard Kolb, *Die Arbeiterräte in der deutschen Innenpolitik, 1918–1919*; Wolfgang Elben, *Das Problem der Kontinuität in der deutschen Revolution*; Knut Wolfgang Nörr, "'Economic Constitution'"; Otto Bauer, *The Austrian Revolution*; Eric Weitz, *Weimar Germany*.
25 Karl Renner, *The Institutions of Private Law and Their Social Functions*, 106.
26 As Renner states the relation between the institution of private property and economic capital: "The right of the capitalist is delegated public authority, conferred indiscriminately upon the person who will use it for his own benefit. The employment relationship is an indirect power relationship, a public obligation to service, like the serfdom of feudal times. It differs from serfdom only in this respect, that is based on contract, not upon inheritance"; ibid., 115. Also cf. David Ciepley, "Beyond Public and Private," for more on the political origins of the corporation and its powers.
27 Beatrice Webb and Sidney Webb, *A Constitution for the Socialist Commonwealth of Great Britain*.
28 Karl Renner, "Demokratie und Rätesystem," 55.
29 In this sense, the council republicanism model I am advocating here departs from the model proposed by Rosa Luxemburg. For her, the Executive Council would come to possess sole legislative and executive power. She argues that there would similarly be a three-tier system where "workers' councils would be elected all over Germany, as well as soldiers' councils; and the Central Council would elect the Executive Council as the highest organ of legislative

and executive power." Ralph Miliband, *Marxism and Politics*, 177. This seems to me to be unrealistic and not politically viable for a modern society and that the council republican model is a better vehicle for socialist democracy.

30 See Brian Peterson, "Workers' Councils in Germany, 1918–1919."

31 See David Plotke, "Representation is Democracy."

32 I find it important to quote Pachter on this point: "It is a mistake to reject [parliamentary institutions] because they give access to the levers of power all too impartially to the rich and to the poor; the answer is to find means of making the system work for the majority." Pachter, *Socialism in History*, 45–6.

33 See Rafael Khachaturian, "On Thinking With and Against the State."

34 Critchley, *Infinitely Demanding*; Abensour, *Democracy against the State*.

35 Otto Kirchheimer, "On the Marxist Theory of the State," in Tribe (ed.), *Social Democracy and the Rule of Law*, 83.

36 David MacGregor, "Marxism's Hegelian Blind Spot"; David MacGregor, *Hegel, Marx and the English State*; Miliband, *Marxism and Politics*, 154ff; Norman Arthur Fischer, *Marxist Ethics within Western Political Theory*.

References

Abensour, Miguel. *Democracy against the State: Marx and the Machiavellian Moment*. Cambridge: Polity, 2011.

Arendt, Hannah. *On Revolution*. New York: Penguin Books, 1963.

Bauer, Otto. *The Austrian Revolution*. New York: Burt Franklin, 1970 [1925].

Ciepley, David. "Beyond Public and Private: Toward a Political Theory of the Corporation." *American Political Science Review* 107, no. 1 (2013): 139–58.

Critchley, Simon. *Infinitely Demanding: Ethics of Commitment, Politics of Resistance*. London: Verso, 2007.

Dahl, Robert. *A Preface to Economic Democracy*. Berkeley, CA: University of California Press, 1985.

Elben, Wolfgang. *Das Problem der Kontinuität in der deutschen Revolution*. Dusseldorf: Droste Verlag, 1965.

Fischer, Norman Arthur. *Marxist Ethics within Western Political Theory*. New York: Palgrave Macmillan, 2015.

Fisk, Milton. *The State and Social Justice: An Essay in Political Theory*. Cambridge: Cambridge University Press, 1989.

Gorter, Herman. "Die Klassenkampf-Organisation des Proletariats." In *Organisation und Taktik der proletarischen Revolution*. Edited by Hans Manfred Bock. 228–46. Frankfurt: Neue Kritik Verlag, 1969 [1921].

Habermas, Jürgen. *Philosophical-Political Profiles*. Cambridge, MA: MIT Press, 1983.

Hayward, Clarissa Rile. "Making Interest: On Representation and Democratic Legitimacy." In *Political Representation*. Edited by Ian Shapiro, Susan C. Stokes, Elisabeth Jean Wood and Alexander S. Kirshner. 111–38. Cambridge: Cambridge University Press, 2009.

Khachaturian, Rafael. "On Thinking with and against the State." *Logos: A Journal of Modern Society and Culture* 17, nos. 1–2 (2016).

Kirchheimer, Otto. "Constitutional Reform and Social Democracy." In *Social Democracy and the Rule of Law*. Edited by Keith Tribe.

———. "On the Marxist Theory of the State." In *Social Democracy and the Rule of Law*. Edited by Keith Tribe.

———. *Politik und Verfassung*. Frankfurt: Suhrkamp, 1964.

Kolb, Eberhard. *Die Arbeiterräte in der deutschen Innenpolitik, 1918–1919*. Dusseldorf: Droste Verlag, 1962.

McConnell, Grant. *Private Power and American Democracy*. New York: Vintage, 1966.

MacGregor, David. *Hegel, Marx and the English State*. Toronto: University of Toronto Press, 1996.

———. "Marxism's Hegelian Blind Spot: The Theory of the State in Hegel and Marx." *Current Perspectives in Social Theory* 9 (1989): 143–75.

Medearis, John. "Lost or Obscured? How V. I. Lenin, Joseph Schumpeter, and Hannah Arendt Misunderstood the Council Movement." *Polity* 36, no. 3 (2004): 447–76.

Miliband, Ralph. *Marxism and Politics*. Oxford: Oxford University Press, 1977.

Mill, John Stuart. *Principles of Political Economy*, 2 vols. New York: The Colonial Press, 1899.

Neumann, Franz. "The Social Significance of the Basic Laws in the Weimar Constitution." In *Social Democracy and the Rule of Law*. Edited by Keith Tribe.

Nörr, Knut Wolfgang. "'Economic Constitution': On the Roots of a Legal Concept." *Journal of Law and Religion* 11, no. 1 (1994): 343–54.

Pachter, Henry. *Socialism in History: Political Essays*. New York: Columbia University Press, 1984.

Pannekoek, Anton. *Anthropogenesis: A Study of the Origin of Man*. Amsterdam: North-Holland Publishing Co., 1953.

———. *Workers' Councils*. London: AK Press, 2003 [1941].

Peterson, Brian. "Workers' Councils in Germany, 1918–1919: Recent Literature on the *Rätebewegung*." *New German Critique* 4 (1975): 113–24.

Plotke, David. "Representation Is Democracy." *Constellations* 4, no. 1 (1997): 19–34.

Renner, Karl. "Demokratie und Rätesystem." *Der Kampf* 14 (1921): 54–67.

———. *The Institutions of Private Law and Their Social Functions*. London: Routledge & Kegan Paul, 1949.

Rosanvallon, Pierre. *Democracy Past and Future*. New York: Columbia University Press, 2006.

Shipway, Mark. "Council Communism." In *Non-Market Socialism in the Nineteenth and Twentieth Centuries*. Edited by Maximilien Rubel and John Crump. 104–26. New York: St. Martin's Press, 1987.

Smulewicz-Zucker, Greg. "Illusory Alternatives: Neo-Anarchism's Disengaged and Reactionary Leftism." In *Radical Intellectuals and the Subversion of Progressive Politics*. Edited by Greg Smulewicz-Zucker and Michael J. Thompson. 121–48. New York: Palgrave Macmillan, 2015.

Solt, Frederick. "Economic Inequality and Democratic Political Engagement." *American Journal of Political Science* 52, no. 1 (2008): 48–60.

———. "Economic Inequality and Nonviolent Protest." *Social Science Quarterly* 96, no. 5 (2015): 1314–27.

———. "The Social Origins of Authoritarianism." *Political Research Quarterly* 65, no. 4 (2010): 703–13.

Solt, Frederick, Yue Hu, Kevan Hudson, Jungmin Song and Dong "Erico" Yu. "Economic Inequality and Class Consciousness." *Journal of Politics* 79, no. 3 (2018): 1079–83.

Thompson, Michael J. "The Limits of Liberalism: A Republican Theory of Social Justice." *International Journal of Ethics* 7, nos. 3–4 (2011): 1–21.

———. *The Politics of Inequality: A Political History of the Idea of Economic Inequality in America*. New York: Columbia University Press, 2007.

———. "The Two Faces of Domination in Republican Political Theory." *European Journal of Political Theory* 14, no. 1 (2018): 44–64.

Tribe, Keith (ed.). *Social Democracy and the Rule of Law*. London: Allen & Unwin, 1987.

Urbinati, Nadia. *Mill on Democracy: From the Athenian Polis to Representative Government*. Chicago: University of Chicago Press, 2002.

Webb, Beatrice and Sidney Webb. *A Constitution for the Socialist Commonwealth of Great Britain*. London: Longman, 1920.

Weitz, Eric. *Weimar Germany: Promise and Tragedy*. Princeton, NJ: Princeton University Press, 2007.

Winters, Jeffrey. *Oligarchy*. Cambridge: Cambridge University Press, 2011.

Part III

The Councils and Radical Democratic Theory

7 The Councils as Ontological Form

Cornelius Castoriadis and the Autonomous Potential of Council Democracy

Christopher Holman

Introduction

Despite being the most notable theorist of workers' councils within the influential French political group *Socialisme ou Barbarie* (*SouB*), Cornelius Castoriadis is generally not included in standard lists of those figures who are most important for the development of councilist theory. Nor do readers of Castoriadis typically attempt to specify the place of his engagement with the council tradition within his thought. This fact is almost certainly related to the unique personal trajectory of Castoriadis' intellectual development. Castoriadis' writings on the councils were developed in the context of his early critique of bureaucratic management as it manifested itself in both the so-called private capitalist countries and the so-called Eastern socialist ones. After these early analyses, however, the councils seemingly disappear as an object of study for Castoriadis. His thought undertakes something of a substantive shift, a shift usually associated with his self-identified break with the Marxist tradition. Some commentators go so far as to write that his earlier Marxist and *SouB* period constitutes only a "pre-history" within his oeuvre, his genuine political and theoretical commitments being revealed later.[1] In this later period we observe the philosophical elaboration of Castoriadis' ontology of the social-historical, and his location of the potential for democratic autonomy in the chaotic flux of the human psyche and being. However, rather than see in this transition an abandonment of a concern with the council tradition, I will instead demonstrate the extent to which it reveals a new method for interpreting the significance of this tradition.

Closer study of Castoriadis' engagement with the council tradition has the effect of not only more sharply clarifying the trajectory of the former's own intellectual development, but advancing more generally our understanding of council democracy and its possible ethical foundations. I argue in this chapter that Castoriadis' defence of the positive political potential of council institutionalisation is ultimately grounded in a philosophical-anthropological principle of human beingness. Theorising the latter in terms of the radical imagination, the specifically human generation of a perpetual flux of forms and figures of meaning, social-historical creation at the collective level is considered in terms of the sublimation of this psychic energy. Castoriadis' political project is to think the possibility of the institution of a form of society in which the capacity to reflectively institute the community is generalised, such that all citizens have the opportunity to autonomously affirm their essential creative orientation through participation in politics. The democratic council as an institutional form, therefore, can be read as a concrete field for the expression of that non-determinate creative desire that for Castoriadis constitutes the essence of the human. Contrary to all forms of representative and liberal government, the councils are an institutional order that have the potential to collectively affirm human autonomy and creativity through sublimating psychic desire. In the final instance the normative defence of council democracy is grounded in the perception of a certain ontological content contained within it, the intuition that council structures are capable of functioning as an institutional media for the explicit and lucid affirmation of a fundamental human creativity. Castoriadis' conception reveals itself to be distinct from many others within the councilist tradition as a result of this emphasis on creativity, as it forecloses theorising council democracy in terms of the technical application of a fixed political schema, driven by the rational demands of social or economic necessity.

The Critique of Bureaucracy and the Positive Content of Socialism

Castoriadis' relation to certain established currents within the councilist tradition is best characterised as ambivalent. On the one hand, he was an admirer of the work of Anton Pannekoek, engaging in a productive exchange with the latter[2] and, in his most significant elaboration of his ideas regarding the political potential of council organisation, noting the proximity of his thought to the analysis developed by Pannekoek in the first chapter of *Workers' Councils*.[3] Nevertheless, Castoriadis in one of his earliest writings contended that existing council communist groups, although having generally avoided the bureaucratisation that has characterised most working-class revolutionary movements, were at the present moment characterised by "political and ideological bankruptcy."[4] More specifically, he would retrospectively identify what he had taken to be a deep contradiction between certain council communists' affirmation of popular creativity and spontaneity, and their continued belief that capitalism is inherently moved by scientifically determinable economic laws.[5] Far too shackled to determinate philosophical models formulated in different historical circumstances, they have not demonstrated a willingness to adapt their theoretical and practical commitments in light of changing realities.

The key social reality that revolutionary theory must grapple with is the emergence and intensification of bureaucratic political forms, a political phenomenon unexplainable through traditional historical materialist thought. Although at this point still self-identifying as a Marxist, for Castoriadis the essential core of Marxism is not the logical positing of objectively necessary historical laws, but is rather found in the critique of alienation and the correlative affirmation of human creativity. The bureaucratic experience must be understood and critiqued in light of this latter content. Castoriadis writes that "[b]y bureaucratization we mean a type of social structure in which the direction of collective activities is in the hands of an impersonal, hierarchically organized apparatus."[6] What defines bureaucratic modes of activity is the instauration of a form of social relation in which the trajectory of the activity is determined by a director who assumes sole responsibility for decision-making, while the determination formulated is carried out by a mere executant without a substantive role to play in said determination. In capitalist society we see the logic of bureaucratisation at play not only in the organisation of production and of the administrative apparatus of the state, but also within the trade union variants of the labour movements. The tendency towards bureaucratisation is eventually generalised so as to engulf all aspects and spheres of social life, including consumption, leisure, culture and science.

It is in light of the bureaucratic division between directors and executants that Castoriadis pronounces what he takes to be the "fundamental contradiction of capitalism," the fact that the latter, if it is to reproduce itself, must simultaneously effect both the participation and the exclusion of workers from the process of production:

> [t]he capitalist system can only maintain itself by continually trying to reduce wage earners to the level of pure *executants* – and it functions only to the extent that it never succeeds in so reducing them. Capitalism is constantly obliged to solicit the *participation* of wage earners in the production process and yet it also tends to render this participation impossible.[7]

Even hierarchically directed work processes – or at least capitalist ones: the USSR did tend to be successful at effacing all worker initiative, although precisely at the cost of perpetual economic disorganisation and inefficiency – depend upon the exercise of the spontaneity and creativity of labourers:

> [n]o modern factory could function for twenty-four hours without this spontaneous organization of work that groups of workers, independent of the official business management, carry out by filling in the gaps of official production directives, by preparing for unforeseen and

> for regular breakdowns of equipment, by compensating for management mistakes, etc.[8]

The functioning of the capitalist system thus depends upon individuals' active exercise of their critical rationality and their capacity for self-organisation. In Castoriadis' view, this essential contradiction between the simultaneous demands for passivity and activity in labour can only be surmounted through the institution of democratic self-management within the productive process, and indeed society as a whole. Socialism must thus aim at the abolition of the bureaucratic relation and the complete affirmation of the human capacity for creative innovation that workers constantly demonstrate, but which they are unable to fully realise as a result of deliberative hierarchy within the labour process.

Although the overcoming of the contradiction of capitalism remains the task of revolutionary practice, for Castoriadis the Bolshevik experience demonstrates that revolution cannot succeed if the direction of social life is entrusted to one part of society separated from the rest, that is, if it continues to maintain a distinction between directors and executants. Genuine socialism must be self-management in all human spheres, most especially but not exclusively that of production. Castoriadis was always adamant that revolutionary struggle must be total, that is to say, a struggle for autonomy in all aspects of life as opposed "to a few transformations in the economic system."[9] Indeed, socialism is defined precisely in terms of autonomy, a concept that, as we will see, will take on an additional significance in Castoriadis' later work. He writes, "[s]ocialism is autonomy, people's conscious direction of their own lives."[10] It thus implies a general abolition of that division between directors and executants that characterises both private capitalist and bureaucratic-socialist modes of organisation, and the explicit and non-contradictory recognition and affirmation of human creativity. This affirmation involves a reconfiguration of the relation between the subjective and the objective: "[t]he subjective exists only inasmuch as it modifies the objective, and the objective has no other signification than what the actions of the subjective confer upon it in a given context and condition."[11] Socialism is the form of society which allows for the subjective creation of the objective in a specifically autonomous form, by all individuals themselves as opposed to a separate part of society endowed with a special legislative capacity.

Even after his break with Marxism Castoriadis would continue to identify the essential element of the content of socialism as "the free deployment of the creative forces of individuals and groups."[12] Such a deployment can only be achieved, however, if there exist positive institutional forms that are capable of providing spaces of deliberation in which subjects can articulate their will. Ultimately Castoriadis suggests that it should be the councils that perform this institutional role. He thus links together the ideas of socialism, creativity and councilism, sharpening the definition of the former by describing it as "nothing other than *workers' management*. Workers' management of power, i.e., the power of the masses' autonomous organizations (soviets or councils) … the unleashing of the free creative activity of the oppressed masses."[13] Socialism is thus worker autonomy, and worker autonomy is identified with creative self-expression, the councils being that organisational form facilitating or mediating this creative self-expression, from the local level of the workplace up to the general level of society as a whole:

> Workers' councils, based on one's place of work, are the *form* of workers' management and the institution capable of fostering its growth. Workers' management means the power of the local workers' councils and ultimately, at the level of society as a whole, the power of the *central assembly of workers' councils* and the *government of the councils*.[14]

Crucially, however, Castoriadis is clear that precisely to the extent that socialist society is defined in terms of the expression of the creative desire of individuals themselves, there is no possibility for constructing in advance a formula or model for its realisation.[15] Nevertheless, he will provide some speculative thoughts on what a concrete distribution of offices structured according to councilist principles might look like.

Council Democracy and the Political Form of Socialist Society

As we have seen, it is within the context of his critique of bureaucracy and redefinition of socialism that Castoriadis undertakes an investigation into the political potential of council organisation. His most detailed examination of this potential occurs in the important essay, "On the Content of Socialism, II." Like Hannah Arendt, Castoriadis makes the historical observation that the councils "have come to the forefront every time the question of power has been posed in modern society."[16] Indeed, we see the emergence of such positive political forms in 1871, 1905, 1917–18, 1918–19 and 1956. These examples

> have shown the possibility of a centralized social organization that, instead of politically expropriating the population for the benefit of its "representatives," on the contrary places these representatives under the permanent control of their electors and for the first time in modern history achieves democracy on the scale of society as a whole.[17]

Castoriadis' writings on the councils, however, are generally concerned less with tracing the historical contours of past council experiences, and more with theoretically elaborating the potential for a new council system capable of affirming his redefined vision of socialism. In particular, he asks how it is possible to think about a form of council institutionalisation that "will unite the functions of deliberation, decision, and execution" in an explicitly democratic form.[18]

Castoriadis assumes that in this future society workers' councils will function as the primary unit of political organisation for society as a whole. This is because the place of work is the space in modern society where most cultural socialisation occurs. In this context, worker self-management of the economy thus takes on a decisive importance. This self-management must be co-ordinated by representatives of particular councils who aim to harmonise and standardise processes of production within particular branches of industry. These councils should be interrelated through the construction of a federal system of democratic organisation in which delegates arrange production at national, sub-national and local levels. This democratic federalisation of local work-based political units is achieved via the creation of a central assembly and a federal government of councils. Such federalisation, though, must not be thought of in terms of a unidirectional delegation of power, but rather in terms of a two-way transmission of information between base and summit that functions to express the very power of the former:

> [o]ne of the essential tasks of central bodies, including the central government, will be to collect, transmit, and disseminate information conveyed to them by the local groups. In all essential fields decisions will be made at the grass-roots and will be sent back up to the "summit", whose responsibility it will be to ensure their execution or to carry them out itself. A two-way flow of information and decisions thus will be instaurated and this will not only apply to relations between the government and the councils but will be a model for relations between all institutions and those who participate in them.[19]

Castoriadis theorises potential institutional mechanics at both the local and national levels. Managerial functions at the level of the workplace would be administered by two institutional forms: the factory council, composed of immediately revocable delegates who rotate into and out of office and are elected by workers; and the general assembly, a body composed of all workers and the highest decision-making authority within the workplace. On Castoriadis' account,

> [t]his general assembly will embody the restoration of direct democracy into what should, in modern society, be its basic unit: the place of work. The assembly will ratify all but routine decisions of the factory council. It will be empowered to question, challenge, amend, reject, or endorse any decision made by the council.[20]

It is essential that such spaces for discussion and deliberation exist, for there are no technical or objective formulae whose application might determine rational decisions regarding the organisation of social production or distribution:

> [t]here is no "objective" rationality allowing one to decide, by means of mathematical formulas, about the future of society, work, consumption, and accumulation. The only rationality in these realms is the living reason of mankind, the decisions of ordinary people concerning their own fate.[21]

As Castoriadis would later elaborate, after his turn to psychoanalysis, human desire is not an object that can be thematised via the application of a psychological science, a science presuming that the observation of patterns of behaviour may serve as a ground to regularise the latter as fixed rules.

Castoriadis speculates on what decision-making within the council body might look like. Initial policy proposals would be formulated by the councils, with these proposals discussed at the general assembly. The plan factory – that office charged with the technical evaluation of the feasibility of the multiplicity of potential plans – would evaluate the proposals and, on the basis of various factors (such as their potential effects on and compatibility with others sectors and society as a whole), attempt to project the consequences of the implementation of the plans. Further discussion of the proposals would take place at the level of the general assembly and the council, with a final discussion and decision being made via assembly majority vote. Any plan ultimately instituted, however, must always be seen as a starting point rather than an end point, there being no possibility for a finally fixed form or policy. Interrogation and potential modification of policy is perpetually needed in light of shifting historical realities. In Castoriadis' words, "[n]ew products, new means of production, new methods, new problems, new difficulties, and new solutions will constantly be emerging."[22] Indeed, it was precisely Castoriadis' recognition of the role of worker creativity in negotiating the emergence of such contingencies that structured his identification of the central contradiction of capitalist social production and the need to transcend it.

Self-management, however, is not restricted to the sphere of production. Despite Castoriadis' privileging of the point of production at this stage, he is nevertheless clear that the councils represent the general form of human self-organisation, and are not limited to an application in workplace life: "[t]he basic units of social organization, as we have envisaged them so far, will not merely manage *production*, they will, at the same time and primarily, be organs for popular self-management *in all its aspects*."[23] Castoriadis points out the extent to which Pannekoek errs, for example, in asserting that *SouB* would restrict council institutionalisation to economic self-management in the sphere of labour:

> [w]e believe that the activity of these soviet organisms – or workers' councils – will extend to the total organization of social life after the taking of power, that is to say, as long as there be a need for an organism of power, its role will be filled by the workers' councils.[24]

Society as a whole thus requires direction via an assembly of delegates that will co-ordinate activities in spheres that are not immediately related to work. These delegates will be drawn from local assemblies and will elect a central council, known as the government. Despite the terminology,

> [t]his network of general assemblies and councils is all that is left of the *State* or of *power* in a socialist society. It is the *whole* state and the *only* embodiment of power. There are no other institutions that could manage, direct, or make binding decisions about people's lives.[25]

The councils will thus also absorb the so-called municipal functions of public life, including policing, education, judicial occupation and so on. Indeed, the various offices of the political state, to the extent that they perform tasks that will remain necessary in the new society, must all be restructured according to the logic of the councils, becoming firms like any other. Tasks will be managed by the councils, with functions limited to the execution of duties assigned to them via popular determination.

Castoriadis highlights how a council government's form of delegation differs fundamentally from typical modes of political representation:

> [c]ertainly, the designation of representatives, or of delegates by different collectivities, as well as the existence of organs – committees or councils – formed by such delegates will be, in a host of cases, indispensible. Such a procedure, however, will not be comparable with self-management unless those delegates genuinely represent the collectivity from which they emanate, and that implies they remain subject to its power. That, in its turn, signifies that this collectivity not only elects them but also can revoke them each time it deems it necessary.[26]

Indeed, political representation, as it is traditionally conceived in the history of political thought, is a form of political alienation: "[p]olitical power is expropriated from the 'represented,' and appropriated by the 'representatives.' To decide is to decide oneself. It is *not* to 'decide' who is going to decide."[27] Such a conception of representation perpetuates the myth that there is a specifically political knowledge that belongs only to some, who through their possession of it acquire a unique title to govern.[28] Castoriadis' vision of council delegation, by contrast, represents a recuperation of the expropriated political power of individuals, and its redeployment in a democratic context that looks to affirm these individuals' fundamental human creativity. It abolishes the division between directors and executants through providing institutional spaces for all citizens to articulate their political will and contribute to the formulation of policies that orient the historical direction of their community.

Being and Social-Historical Creation

After Castoriadis' much-discussed break with the Marxist tradition, the political phenomenon of council democracy seemingly disappears as an object of sustained consideration.[29] Many commentators identify a necessary connection between these two intellectual developments. Andrew Arato, for example, maintains that Castoriadis' concern with council organisation in his early work is not only a part of a specifically Marxist heritage, but a manifestation of his commitment to an "evolutionary philosophy of history."[30] Such a characterisation, however, misses what was always, for Castoriadis, Marx's most penetrating observation: the human potential for radical creation. Indeed, what could no longer be sustained was the co-existence of the Marxian emphasis on human creativity with the counter-stream in Marx's thought emphasising deterministic historical development.[31] What Castoriadis makes clear is that his project was always one of divesting the potential for self-determination from all remnants of teleological impulsion, including those located within a Marxist philosophy of history. Hence, in his introduction to the 10/18 re-edition of the *SouB* writings, he articulates the relation between his early and late works in terms of the consistent affirmation of this autonomous self-determination.[32] Castoriadis' turn to primarily philosophical reflection was stimulated by his recognition of the incapacity of inherited thought to *comprehend* the being of politics, including revolutionary working-class politics, as creation. An entirely new conception of society and history was needed in order to fully grasp the project of autonomous action, from ancient Athens to the workers' councils. It is thus not that concern with the latter was abandoned, but rather that Castoriadis attempted to elucidate a philosophical conception capable precisely of making sense of the latter's underlying ontological ground. In this sense, then, not only does Castoriadis' post-Marxist work not amount to an abandonment of his concern with council democracy, but in fact it further contextualises it so as to reveal within it a more primary ontological significance.

A detailed examination of the main outlines of Castoriadis' ontological reflections on the nature of being are beyond the scope of this chapter. A few very general observations must be noted, however. Most simply, being is not system, but chaos. What is most significant about being as chaos is its openness, not just to the reorganisation of its elements, but rather to genuine, ontological creation: the creation of new forms. The world as chaos is not "absolute and complete indetermination," but rather the positing of other determinations.[33] Chaos is organised into cosmos through the creation of orders and forms. There is not, however, any fundamental substratum of being that would determine the various orders and forms that emerge: creation is thus *ex nihilo*. Indeed, time itself is precisely this creation. Inherited ontology – including traditional Marxist thought – has attempted to cover up this relation between being, time and creation through positing being as being determined, and time thereby as the logical unfolding of determinacy. But "what is given in and through history is not the determined sequence of the determined but the emergence of radical otherness, immanent creation, non-trivial novelty."[34] History is thus nothing other than the creative self-deployment of society in time.

This conception of being and creation depends upon the existence of the radical imaginary. The radical imaginary has two aspects, manifesting itself at the level of the psyche and the level of society. For Castoriadis the fundamental defining characteristic of the human being relative to all other living beings, discovered by psychoanalysis, is its existence as a psyche insofar as it is radical imagination.[35] The radical imagination is defined in terms of perpetual alteration, the spontaneous and non-determined emergence of new psychic forms and figures of meaning. It is the "constantly creative imagination, the uninterrupted surging forth, in the (unconscious as well as conscious) psychical world, of a spontaneous and unmasterable flux of representations, affects, and desires."[36] The human being is capable of physically surviving, however, only to the extent that this radical imagination is pacified. This occurs through socialisation, where the psyche is transformed into an individual through being compelled to absorb and internalise the institution of society and its significations. This socialisation does not abolish the creativity of the psyche, but rather sublimates it. By means of socialisation the radical imagination of the psyche can become the source of an anonymous-collective creation at the level of society. Radical imagination thus serves as the "psychic *sap*" to social-historical creation.[37] Social-historical creation – the creation of society's forms, institutions, values, social imaginary significations and so on – is not the result of the activity of particular individuals, but of the anonymous-collective, the instituting power of the social imaginary. Although it is the social imaginary as opposed to the imagination that creates the social institution, this social-historical creation is only possible to the extent that individuals are psyches. Although neither psychic nor social-historical being are possible without the other, neither one is reducible to the other.

For Castoriadis, then, the essence of the human being lay in the capacity for creation, for instituting new modes of individual and collective life. Creation at the psychic level is deployed via the imagination, while at the social-historical level via the imaginary. The question is not whether society participates in its own self-deployment, for all societies do, but rather whether this self-deployment is recognised by society for what it is. Most societies are cognitively closed, that is, they do not possess mechanisms for the self-questioning of the inherited world of meaning produced by the generation of social imaginary significations and the institutions embodying them. This self-questioning cannot be undertaken if the origin of the institution of society is not attributed to society itself, but rather to an extra-social source exterior to the instituting community, be it God, nature, laws of history and so on. Such societies are heteronomous. An autonomous society, by contrast, is one "that not only knows explicitly that it has created its own laws but has instituted itself so as to free its radical imaginary and enable itself to alter its institutions through collective, self-reflective, and deliberate activity."[38] Although Castoriadis contends that this is a new concept of autonomy, one that has philosophical and ontological as opposed to merely political substance, he nevertheless affirms that the term autonomy is nothing more than what he had earlier taken to be the essential content of socialism: "[w]hat was intended by the term 'socialist society' we henceforth call autonomous society."[39] Only the *term* socialism must be discarded, and this is because traditional socialist theory, including certain variants of council communism, participates in the mystification characteristic of heteronomy when it interprets the realisation of self-management in terms of the application of an intrinsically rational technique, or according to intrinsically rational demands of social production. Autonomy requires placing *all* modes of social life into question, recognising that there is nothing that can escape society's instituting power. The just society is not that which has discovered a just organisation of things, but rather a society in which the question of justice is perpetually open: "[i]n other words, a society in which there is always the socially effective possibility of questioning the law and its foundation. This is another way of saying that it is constantly in the movement of explicit self-institution."[40] The question then becomes: How might such a form of society be institutionally structured? It is at this point that we can reconsider the potential of council democracy anew, although now from the standpoint of the ontological claims regarding creation and autonomous being.

Council Democracy as Autonomous Self-Institution

Castoriadis thus redefines the concept of autonomy to refer not only to collective self-management primarily within the sphere of work, but rather the "*ongoing explicit self-institution of society*."[41] It is within the context of this redefinition of autonomy that I re-evaluate council institutionalisation. In particular, and against those readers who suggest that the councils are irrelevant to Castoriadis' later project, I argue that the council form as a general organisational mode must be understood as a primary organ for the facilitation of explicit ontological self-creation. Not only is the defence of council democracy related to the philosophy of the social-historical and the project of autonomy, but it is that institutional form which, at least in the present historical circumstances, is most appropriate for facilitating autonomous ontological creation. How is this the case? We can begin by noting that any such form must first of all be broadly democratic, each member of the community participating in the instituting power. Democracy as genuine self-government is the rendering explicit of self-institution by a community that collectively deploys the social imaginary to perpetually interrogate existing modes and forms of beings, in a conscious and reflective way. To participate in power is to be an equal member of a community that autonomously self-institutes itself. Freedom and equality are thus mutually co-constitutive, the actualisation of the one necessitating the actualisation of the other. The equality of participation in public affairs – that is, the equal capacity to contribute to the autonomous institution of society – is the only real form of equality there is. To realise such equality, individuals require access to specific types of institutions that allow them to participate in discussions regarding the direction of their instituting activity. It is precisely this type of mediation that council democracy is able to provide.

Although the fact has generally been overlooked by commentators, Castoriadis himself continued to suggest in his later work that council organisation may play precisely such a role in democratic society.[42] For example, in a 1976 interview after the discovery of the imaginary as "the source of all life and social-historical creation," Castoriadis continues to speak of the council system as the key institutional form characterising a potential post-revolutionary society.[43] Indeed, even within *The Imaginary Institution of Society*, his major philosophical work, council organisation is still identified as a relevant form for autonomous self-management, and Castoriadis speculates that it may become even more relevant given the recent historical trajectory: considering the nature of "economic knowledge and the existing techniques of information, communication and computation," we can envision "the 'cybernation' of the global economy in the service of the collective self-management of human beings," beings "organised into councils of producers."[44] Although never systematically elaborating this point, Castoriadis' sporadic reaffirmations of the political potential of the council form are undertaken precisely to the extent that he considers it a form that is able to facilitate the expression of that inherent creative human power, the recognition of which motivated the philosophical theorisation of the radical imaginary. That the councils are now reinterpreted in this way, with a new ontological or philosophical-anthropological content, is suggested most clearly in Castoriadis' later reflections on the continuing significance of the events of the Hungarian revolution.

Castoriadis maintains that the greatest legacy of the Hungarian revolution lay in its creation of institutions of self-organisation that could function as positive spaces of collective deliberation and decision-making. This significance continues to be germane in the present time, despite the apparent waning of the revolutionary project: "[d]espite current trends and the present state of opinion, this alternative [to 'representative democracy'] has not lost its relevance."[45] The general mobilisation of all strata of the population during the revolution, who broke with existing political forms in order to institute entirely new political relations and organs, produced a creative opening up of history, one that facilitated the universal expulsion of creative energy. Through instituting councils the participants established "a new structure of power and a new institution of society," a positive regime of institutionalisation embodying the principle of autonomous social-historical creation.[46] Inherited social significations regarding politics and work were radically rejected, and in their place was posited "the germ of a new institution of society."[47] What characterised this institution was a general affirmation of human creativity, one that was realised through the generation of spaces allowing for the continued political participation of citizens. Hence the ultimate significance of the Hungarian events: "[d]espite its short life span, the Hungarian revolution has posited organizational forms and social significations that represent a social-historical institutional *creation*."[48] The type of social organisation instituted was not a state of being, but rather a mode of being, the institutional structures perpetually facilitating the ongoing creative activity of the participants:

> [i]t is not that people have finally found "the" appropriate form of social organization, but rather that they realized that this "form" *is* their activity of organizing themselves, in accordance with their understanding of the situation and of the ends they set for themselves.[49]

This latter point is particularly important, and it is a point that was not necessarily stressed in Castoriadis' earlier writings on the councils. Indeed, in these writings the councils were interpreted as the *necessary* form of socialist organisation, whose instauration would "realize democracy for the first time in human history."[50] The positing of such a principle of historical necessity, however, clearly violates the conception of being and history affirmed after the discovery of the radical imaginary. The Hungarian experience and council democracy are now interpreted to be a *continuation* of the project of autonomy that was initiated in Greece and rearticulated in early modern Europe: "[t]he democracy of the councils has its roots in the Greco-Western tradition of struggle for the self-government of the people – in the project of collective and individual autonomy."[51] Workers' councils are institutional inventions that realise the principles of autonomous social-historical creation, although in a specifically modern context. They are "a creation that embodies the principles of authentic self-government, that is to say, direct democracy in the conditions of the modern world."[52] This historical contextualisation of the council phenomenon suggests that the institutional form does not hold a universal applicability, as shifting realities and experiences may, at some point, render it inadequate as a concrete mode of organisation. The council is thus not "a *miraculous institution*" whose legitimacy adheres in all contexts, but rather "an *adequate* form of organization."[53] It does not guarantee the development of a will to autonomous activity, but it makes such a development possible, as opposed to other political forms – such as representative democracy – which render this impossible.

There is thus no finally found form that would be capable of permanently regulating human relations, precisely to the extent that the fundamental characteristic defining human being is its impulse towards the creative reinstitution of form, itself grounded in the chaotic flux of always non-identical psyches. In his dialogue with Anton Pannekoek, therefore, Castoriadis makes sure to note that the councils are not envisaged as perfectly neutral institutional spaces that would facilitate mutual understanding and the harmonisation of interests. On the contrary, they will be necessarily, given the non-identity of human desire, sites of disputation and contestation between conflicting forces and tendencies.[54] They would seem, therefore, to be specifically agonistic democratic institutions, there being no possibility of creating an internally harmonious society in which all individual interests are reconciled.[55] Contrary to what he sees as the procedural account of democracy characteristic of writers such as Habermas, for Castoriadis we must resist the impulse to theorise democracy in terms of the instauration of institutional orders considered as fixed schemata that may be technically applied to societies independent of detailed consideration of social-historical context, the direction of popular will and determination, and so on.[56] The essential thing is not the exact structure of the offices that comprise the democratic system, but the positive investment of a people who can express its creativity autonomously through institutional means. The precise form, however, will vary depending upon the historical articulation of popular desire and objective conditions within society. Hence, "we obviously should condemn any fetishism for the 'soviet' or 'council' type of organization."[57] The content of both socialism and the autonomous society is the free exercise of the creativity of individuals who constitute this society, yet the exact form of the activity that mediates this expression cannot be anticipated in advance. This is precisely because creative activity perpetually alters existing arrangements and realities through its very mode of being.

Because history is creation and society is always instituting at the same time as it is instituted, it is impossible to produce a final institutional form that would be capable of indefinitely ordering human affairs. Castoriadis theorises council democracy as a political form that expresses human self-activity, not a form that terminates the need for such self-activity through producing an administrative apparatus capable of independently formulating policy determinations: "the form of the revolution and of post-revolutionary society is not an institution or an organisation given once and for all, but the *activity* of self-organisation, or self-institution."[58] It represents not a terminal historical point, but only a potential field for the expression of the creative power of individuals, a field which, even if we continue to invest with a political potential today, might at some point in the future, like the polis before it, cease to have direct relevance to our lived political experiences. Nevertheless, even in that case it would remain a potentially fruitful germ, as opposed to a model, stimulating and inspiring us to consider various creative solutions to the question of autonomous self-institution. The key political question for us today is not how to literally recuperate prior forms, but rather to consider what forms we might create ourselves, given the existing state of privatisation and the accelerating dissolution of collectives spaces: how might we theorise the possibility of formalising the instituting power of society through the creation of specific institutions that render participation in this power explicit and general? In Castoriadis' words, "[w]hat in these conditions can stimulate new forms of socialization or could ground a direct democracy, and in what concrete form – this is an open question, to which only the creative historical activity of populations can provide an answer."[59] In modern times experiments in council political organisation have certainly provided us with the most concrete evidence regarding the possibility of breaking historical closure and freeing the imaginary, of explicit power being exercised through reflective democratic self-activity.

Notes

1 Brian Singer, "Cornelius Castoriadis," 141. For rejections of this type of periodisation of Castoriadis' work, see Yohan Dubigeon, "Le conseillisme ou l'étroit sentier de l'auto-émancipation," 284; Arnaud Tomès and Philippe Caumières, *Cornelius Castoriadis*, 263; Arnaud Tomès, *Castoriadis*, 113–14; Nicolas Poirier, *L'ontologie politique de Castoriadis*, 21.

2 Cornelius Castoriadis, "Réponse au comrade Pannekoek," in *La question du mouvement ouvrier, tome 1*, 101–7; Cornelius Castoriadis, "Postface à la 'Réponse au comrade Pannekoek'," in *La question du mouvement ouvrier, tome 1*, 109–19.

3 Cornelius Castoriadis, "The Question of the History of the Workers' Movement," in *Political and Social Writings*, vol. 3, 158.

4 Cornelius Castoriadis, "Socialism or Barbarism," in *Political and Social Writings*, vol. 1, 77.

5 Castoriadis, "The Question of the History of the Workers' Movement," 158.

6 Cornelius Castoriadis, "Modern Capitalism and Revolution," in *Political and Social Writings*, vol. 2, 271.

7 Ibid., 228, 259.

8 Cornelius Castoriadis, "The Proletarian Revolution against the Bureaucracy," in *Political and Social Writings*, vol. 2, 68.

9 Cornelius Castoriadis, "For a New Orientation," in *Political and Social Writings*, vol. 3, 11.

10 Cornelius Castoriadis, "On the Content of Socialism, II," in *Political and Social Writings*, vol. 2, 93.

11 Castoriadis, "Modern Capitalism and Revolution," 301.

12 Cornelius Castoriadis, "Recommencing the Revolution," in *Political and Social Writings*, vol. 3, 48. On the key element of Castoriadis' concept of socialism being self-management as self-creation, see Ferenec Fehér, "Castoriadis and the Redefinition of Socialism," 397.
13 Cornelius Castoriadis, "On the Content of Socialism, I," in *Political and Social Writings*, vol. 1, 297.
14 Castoriadis, "On the Content of Socialism, II," 5.
15 Castoriadis, "On the Content of Socialism, I," 301.
16 Castoriadis, "On the Content of Socialism, II," 95. For comparison of Arendt and Castoriadis on the councils, see Ingerid S. Straume, "A Common World?," 369; Christos Memos, *Castoriadis and Critical Theory*, 47–55.
17 Cornelius Castoriadis, "Proletariat and Organization, I," in *Political and Social Writings*, vol. 2, 198.
18 Castoriadis, "On the Content of Socialism, II," 95.
19 Ibid., 101.
20 Ibid., 128.
21 Ibid., 118.
22 Ibid., 131.
23 Ibid., 136.
24 Castoriadis, "Réponse au comrade Pannekoek," 101.
25 Castoriadis, "On the Content of Socialism, II," 132.
26 Cornelius Castoriadis, "Self-Management and Hierarchy," in *Political and Social Writings*, vol. 3, 218.
27 Cornelius Castoriadis, "The Hungarian Source," in *Political and Social Writings*, vol. 3, 261.
28 For a defence of the democratic potential of representative government in the face of Castoriadis' critique, see Jean Cohen, "The Self-Institution of Society and Representative Government," 9–37; Dick Howard and Diane Pacom, "Autonomy," 97–9; Christophe Premat, "Castoriadis and the Modern Political Imaginary," 251–75.
29 On Castoriadis' break with Marxism, see Castoriadis, "Recommencing the Revolution"; Cornelius Castoriadis, "Why I Am No Longer a Marxist," in *A Society Adrift*, 28–39; Cornelius Castoriadis, *The Imaginary Institution of Society*, 10–70.
30 Andrew Arato, "Facing Russia," 280. See also Andreas Kalyvas, "Norm and Critique in Castoriadis's Theory of Autonomy," 162–3.
31 For discussions of this Marxian antinomy with respect to Castoriadis, see Axel Honneth, "Une sauvegarde ontologique de la révolution," 193; Romain Karsenty, "De Marx à Castoriadis et au-delà," 53–71; Philippe Caumières, "Au-delà du marxisme," 36–9.
32 Cornelius Castoriadis, "General Introduction," in *Political and Social Writings*, vol. 1, 18.
33 Cornelius Castoriadis, "Done and to Be Done," in *The Castoriadis Reader*, 369.
34 Castoriadis, *The Imaginary Institution of Society*, 184.
35 Cornelius Castoriadis, "Psychoanalysis and Politics," in *World in Fragments*, 127–8.
36 Cornelius Castoriadis, "Psychoanalysis and Politics," in *The Castoriadis Reader*, 356.

37 Cornelius Castoriadis, "Psychoanalysis: Project and Elucidation," in *Crossroads in the Labyrinth*, 95.
38 Castoriadis, "Psychoanalysis and Politics," 132.
39 Cornelius Castoriadis, "Socialism and the Autonomous Society," in *Political and Social Writings*, vol. 3, 317. See also Jeff Klooger, "The Meanings of Autonomy," 94.
40 Castoriadis, "Socialism and the Autonomous Society," 329.
41 Castoriadis, "Why I Am No Longer a Marxist," 41.
42 This fact has been noticed by Manuel Cervera-Marzal, who writes that Castoriadis "never ceased to defend the idea that a true democracy should function like a system of councils." Manuel Cervera-Marzal, "Miguel Abensour, Cornelius Castoriadis," 317.
43 Cornelius Castoriadis, "The Revolutionary Exigency," in *Political and Social Writings*, vol. 3, 244, 238.
44 Castoriadis, *The Imaginary Institution of Society*, 86.
45 Cornelius Castoriadis, "Les problèmes d'une démocratie des donseils," in *Quelle démocratie? Tome 2*, 390.
46 Castoriadis, "The Hungarian Source," 253.
47 Ibid., 260.
48 Ibid., 254.
49 Ibid., 257.
50 Castoriadis, "On the Content of Socialism, II," 98.
51 Castoriadis, "Les problèmes d'une démocratie des conseils," 390.
52 Ibid.
53 Castoriadis, "On the Content of Socialism, II," 95.
54 Castoriadis, "Réponse au comrade Pannekoek," 102.
55 On the agonistic dimensions of Castoriadis' thought, see Alexandros Kioupkiolis, *Freedom after the Critique of Foundations*.
56 See, for example, Cornelius Castoriadis, "Democracy as Procedure and Democracy as Regime," in *The Rising Tide of Insignificancy (The Big Sleep)*, 329–59; Andreas Kalyvas, "The Politics of Autonomy and the Challenge of Deliberation," 1–19.
57 Castoriadis, "On the Content of Socialism, II," 95.
58 Castoriadis, "The Revolutionary Exigency," 238.
59 Castoriadis, "Les problèmes d'une démocratie des conseils," 393.

References

Arato, Andrew. "Facing Russia: Castoriadis and the Problem of Soviet Society." In *Autonomie et autotransformation de la société: la philosophie militante de Cornelius Castoriadis*. Edited by Giovanni Busino. 269–91. Geneva: Librairie Droz, 1989.

Castoriadis, Cornelius. *The Castoriadis Reader*. Edited and translated by David Ames Curtis. Oxford: Blackwell Publishers, 1997.

———. *Crossroads in the Labyrinth*. Translated by Kate Soper and Martin H. Ryle. Cambridge, MA: The MIT Press, 1984.

———. *The Imaginary Institution of Society*. Translated by Kathleen Blamey. Cambridge: Polity Press, 1997.

———. *Political and Social Writings, Vol. 1, 1946–1955: From the Critique of Bureaucracy to the Positive Content of Socialism*. Edited and translated by David Ames Curtis. Minneapolis, MN: University of Minnesota Press, 1988.

———. *Political and Social Writings, Vol. 2, 1955–1960: From the Workers' Struggle against Bureaucracy to Revolution in the Age of Modern Capitalism*. Edited and translated by David Ames Curtis. Minneapolis, MN: University of Minnesota Press, 1988.

———. *Political and Social Writings, Vol. 3, 1961–1979: Recommencing the Revolution: From Socialism to the Autonomous Society*. Edited and translated by David Ames Curtis. Minneapolis, MN: University of Minnesota Press, 1993.

———. *Quelle démocratie? Tome 2: écrits politiques, 1945–1997, IV*. Edited by Enrique Escobar, Myrto Gondicas and Pascal Vernay. Paris: Éditions du Sandre, 2013.

———. *La question du mouvement ouvrier, tome 1: écrits politiques, 1945–1997 I*. Edited by Enrique Escobar, Myrto Gondicas and Pascal Vernay. Paris: Éditions du Sandre, 2012.

———. *The Rising Tide of Insignificancy (The Big Sleep)*. Edited and translated by Anonymous. 2003. Accessed at www.notbored.org/RTI.pdf.

———. *A Society Adrift: Interviews and Debates, 1974–1997*. Edited by Enrique Escobar, Myrto Gondicas and Pascal Vernay, translated by Helen Arnold. New York: Fordham University Press, 2010.

———. *World in Fragments: Writings on Politics, Society, Psychoanalysis, and the Imagination*. Edited and translated by David Ames Curtis. Stanford, CA: Stanford University Press, 1997.

Caumières, Philippe. "Au-delà du marxisme: l'apport de la critique castoriadienne du marxisme." In *Imaginer avec Castoriadis*. Edited by Aurélien Liarte and Philippe Georges. 19–40. Nice: Les Éditions Ovadia, 2013.

Cervera-Marzal, Manuel. "Miguel Abensour, Cornelius Castoriadis: un conseillisme français?" *Revue du MAUSS* 40 (2012): 300–20.

Cohen, Jean. "The Self-Institution of Society and Representative Government: Can the Circle Be Squared?" *Thesis Eleven* 80 (2005): 9–37.

Dubigeon, Yohan. "Le conseillisme ou l'étroit sentier de l'auto-émancipation." In *Autonomie et barbarie: la démocratie radicale de Cornelius Castoriadis et ses défis contemporains*. Edited by Manuel Cervera-Marzal. 283–301. Neuvy-en-Champagne: Éditions le passager clandestin, 2015.

Fehér, Ferenc. "Castoriadis and the Redefinition of Socialism." In *Autonomie et autotransformation de la société: la philosophie militante de Cornelius Castoriadis*. Edited by Giovanni Busino. 393–404. Geneve: Librairie Droz, 1989.

Honneth, Axel. "Une sauvegarde ontologique de la révolution: sur la théorie sociale de Cornelius Castoriadis." In *Autonomie et autotransformation de la société: la philosophie militante de Cornelius Castoriadis*. Edited by Giovanni Busino. 191–207. Geneve: Librairie Droz, 1989.

Howard, Dick and Diane Pacom. "Autonomy: The Legacy of the Enlightenment – A Dialogue with Castoriadis." *Thesis Eleven* 52 (1998): 83–101.

Kalyvas, Andreas. "Norm and Critique in Castoriadis's Theory of Autonomy." *Constellations* 15, no. 2 (1998): 161–82.

———. "The Politics of Autonomy and the Challenge of Deliberation: Castoriadis Contra Habermas." *Thesis Eleven* 64 (2001): 1–19.

Karsenty, Romain. "De Marx à Castoriadis et au-delà: dépasser l'antinomie théorie/pratique." In *Autonomie et barbarie: la démocratie radicale de Cornelius Castoriadis et ses défis contemporains*. Edited by Manuel Cervera-Marzal and Éric Fabri. 53–71. Neuvy-en-Champagne: Éditions le passager clandestin, 2015.

Kioupkiolis, Alexandros. *Freedom after the Critique of Foundations: Marx, Liberalism, Castoriadis and Agonistic Autonomy*. Basingstoke: Palgrave Macmillan, 2012.

Klooger, Jeff. "The Meanings of Autonomy: Project, Self-Limitation, Democracy, and Socialism." *Thesis Eleven* 108 (2012): 84–98.

Memos, Christos. *Castoriadis and Critical Theory: Crisis, Critique and Radical Alternatives*. Basingstoke: Palgrave Macmillan, 2014.

Poirier, Nicolas. *L'ontologie politique de Castoriadis: création et institution*. Paris: Payot, 2011.

Premat, Christophe. "Castoriadis and the Modern Political Imaginary: Oligarchy, Representation, Democracy." *Critical Horizons* 7, no. 1 (2006): 251–75.

Singer, Brian. "Cornelius Castoriadis: Auto-Institution and Radical Democracy." In *Thinking Radical Democracy: The Return to Politics in Post-War France*. Edited by Martin Breaugh, Christopher Holman, Rachel Magnusson, Paul Mazzocchi and Devin Penner. 141–60. Toronto: University of Toronto Press, 2015.

Straume, Ingerid S. "A Common World? Arendt, Castoriadis and Political Creation." *European Journal of Social Theory* 15, no. 3 (2012): 367–83.

Tomès, Arnaud. *Castoriadis: L'imaginaire, le rationnel, et le réel*. Paris: Éditions Demopolis, 2015.

Tomès, Arnaud and Philippe Caumières. *Cornelius Castoriadis: réinventer la politique après Marx*. Paris: Presses Universitaires de France, 2011.

8 Hannah Arendt, the Council System and Contemporary Political Theory

Shmuel Lederman

Introduction

Hannah Arendt was a strange bedfellow to the council tradition. One of the few prominent thinkers of the twentieth century to advocate a council democracy, her reflections on the councils met with bafflement on the part of many of her interpreters, as well as with harsh criticism from those more familiar with the history of the councils. In this chapter, I seek to show that while much of this critique is well founded, we should not miss the genuine contribution Arendt made to the council tradition. It is precisely her controversial historical and theoretical distinctions and categories, I argue, that allowed Arendt to add a new and important dimension to the meaning of the councils as participatory institutions, one that should be considered more seriously than it has been so far.

Arendt and the Councils

In May 1963, after reading *On Revolution*, Karl Jaspers wrote to Arendt:

> Your comparison and identification of the meaning of the "workers" and "soldiers" councils, the "small republics", the beginnings and the truth of all revolutions since the American one, were familiar to me from your Hungary essay. That essay left me hesitant; but now I am convinced of the parallels of meaning and of the opportunity you see in them, though that opportunity has so far always been lost.[1]

Arendt then responded:

> I can't tell you how much your approval of the revolution book pleased me. Not only because I was afraid you mightn't like it, but because every word you wrote strikes at the very heart of what I meant to say. A tragedy that warms and lightens the heart because such great and simple things were at stake. Heinrich's experience, of course, and the experience of America.[2]

"Heinrich's experience" was Arendt's husband, Heinrich Blücher's participation in the workers' and soldiers' councils in Germany in 1918–19.[3] The "tragedy that warms and lightens the heart" was the appearance and demise of the councils and, more broadly, the modern revolutionary spirit of association and action by ordinary citizens in an attempt to found and secure political freedom. Blücher's participation in the councils in Germany, we can see, proved enormously significant to Arendt's political thought, including the way she interpreted the American Revolution (discussed further below). It was not, however, the only source for Arendt's support for a council democracy. Rosa Luxemburg, a figure Arendt greatly admired and one of the few to whom she dedicated an essay in her *Men in Dark Times*,[4] had an important influence on Arendt's support for the councils as well, although, as we shall see, she interpreted the councils significantly differently than Luxemburg or other observers of the councils.[5]

Arendt's first explicit reference to the councils occurred in 1948, as she observed the ongoing fighting between Jews and Arabs in Palestine. The only alternative to war, Arendt stated, is a federalist structure in Palestine that would "have to rest on Jewish-Arab community councils, which would mean that the Jewish-Arab conflict would be resolved on the lowest and most promising level of proximity and neighborliness."[6] These councils would be local, at the city and village level, and as numerous as possible. For Arendt, these suggestions were not utopian, as one might think, but "the only realistic political measures that can eventually lead to the political emancipation of Palestine."[7]

Arendt did not elaborate on this suggestion in this context. It is important to note, however, that Arendt seemed to have the councils in mind as an alternative form of government to that of the centralised nation-state already in 1945, and in a more significant context. In the essay "Approaches to the 'German Problem'," she noted approvingly the insistence of the French resistance not only on the federalisation of Europe, but also on the federalisation of each of the European states:

> The cardinal principle of French resistance was *libérer et fédérer*; and by federation was meant a federated structure of the Fourth Republic … integrated in a European Federation. It is in almost identical terms that the French, Czech, Italian, Norwegian, and Dutch undergrounds' papers insist on this as the primary condition of a lasting peace – although … only the French underground has gone as far as to state that a federative structure of Europe must be based on *similarly federated structures in the constituent states*.[8]

While this remark by Arendt, little noted by commentators, is rather obscure, it is almost certain that she was thinking about the councils or similar institutions. Indeed, as she explained, it was no coincidence that it was the French resistance that insisted on the decentralisation of the state itself. In France,

> the repudiation of old centralized forms of government, which left very little responsibility to the individual citizen, is gaining ground; the search for some new form, giving the citizen more of the duties as well as the rights and honors of public life, is characteristic of all factions.[9]

The state had to be decentralised to the point where each citizen could feel she shared in the responsibility, duties, rights and honours of public life.

This early, implicit reference to the councils or to the need for similar institutions, considered together with Arendt's later reflections on the possible solution for the situation in Palestine, shows to what extent many of the problems Arendt identified at this point with the structure of the nation-state were to be addressed by a council democracy: not only in the "periphery" of Palestine, but in the European "centre" as well. It speaks to the importance of the councils in understanding Arendt's political thought, which is hardly recognised, as we shall see, in the scholarly literature. Another important point to note is that in the contexts of both Palestine and Europe the most important thing Arendt found in the potential council democracy was not a form of government that would resist class domination, as in the council tradition, but rather one that would address what for Arendt was a distinctly *political* question: the spaces the citizen had for participation, public appearance, public responsibility and public honour. This, as we shall see, is a crucial point, which distinguishes Arendt from other thinkers who have tried to conceptualise the meaning and goals of the councils, and allowed her to consider institutions like the American town-hall meetings, which historically had nothing to do with the councils, as part of the promise embedded in the council tradition.

The fact remains that we can find only cursory remarks on the councils by Arendt until the 1956 Hungarian uprising. Arendt was enormously impressed by the spontaneous reappearance of the institution of the councils, which

> for more than a hundred years now has emerged whenever the people have been permitted for a few days, or a few weeks or months, to follow their own political devices without a government (or a party program) imposed from above.[10]

She added her essay to the second edition of *The Origins of Totalitarianism* – a significant decision. Arendt analysed totalitarianism as a new form of government, radically different from any other kind of government. She attributed to a potential council democracy the same differentiation from traditionally known forms of government:

> Just as the modern masses and their leaders succeeded … in bringing forth in totalitarianism an authentic, albeit all-destructive, new form of government, thus the people's revolutions, for more than a hundred years now, have come forth, albeit never successfully, with another new form of government: the system of people's councils to take the place of the Continental party system.[11]

Totalitarian government has shown the radical possibilities of the destruction of human beings. The rise of totalitarian movements to power was to a large extent possible, according to Arendt, because of the atomisation and alienation from the world which citizens in modern societies experience. A council democracy, she held, marked the promise of creating a form of government that would constantly bring people together not as masses, but as individuals who through speech and action in the public sphere could take responsibility for their political communities, and would experience the sense of belonging, freedom and power that comes with this experience.

Arendt's renewed enthusiasm for the councils was reflected also in her 1958 book, *The Human Condition*. She described how, from the revolutions of 1848 to the Hungarian revolution of 1956, the European working class, "by virtue of being the only organised and hence the leading section of the people, has written one of the most glorious and probably the most promising chapter of recent history."[12] In those "rare and yet decisive moments," it turned out that the workers had their own ideas about the "possibilities of democratic government under modern conditions": the establishment of a council democracy.[13]

It was in the last part of her book, *On Revolution*, that Arendt offered her most extensive discussion of the councils. Arendt argued in this study that to the extent that the real end of revolution is the "foundation of freedom," the French Revolution failed whereas the American Revolution succeeded. At the same time, the French Revolution did introduce, through the Parisian Commune, "the germs, the first feeble beginnings, of a new system which would permit the people to become Jefferson's 'participators in government'."[14] The popular societies that emerged during the revolution formed pressure groups of the poor, but the people who participated in them found that they experienced something which was more than an instrument to make their demands: "An enormous appetite for debate, for instruction, for mutual enlightenment and exchange of opinion."[15] In Arendt's terms, they discovered the experience of political freedom and public happiness, the need for federalisation and decentralisation of the country to experience these human potentialities, and the communal council system as a suitable organ for this new form of government.

In a similar spirit, the American Revolution actually succeeded only in a limited way. It failed to preserve the revolutionary spirit that brought American citizens to convene in the town halls throughout America, discuss the questions of the day and act as best they could to shape together the fate of the republic. Another American "precursor" to the councils, in Arendt's narrative, was Jefferson's vision, late in his life and in private letters, to divide the American republic into wards that would constitute "elementary republics," allowing each citizen to directly participate in public affairs.[16] Arendt went as far as to suggest that if the ultimate end of revolution was freedom, then

> the elementary republics of the wards, the only tangible place where everyone could be free, actually were the end of the great republic whose chief purpose was to provide the people with such places of freedom and to protect them.[17]

The great failure of the American republic was that it did not establish for its citizens the public spaces in which they could associate, debate and act politically, and thereby cheated them of "their proudest possession."[18] The councils were similarly crushed or ignored during the 1871 Parisian Commune; the 1905 and 1917 Russian Revolutions; in Germany, Austria and elsewhere in Europe between 1918 and 1921; and in 1956 in Hungary. They remained for Arendt, however, the "hidden treasure" of modern revolutions.

Contrary to the arguments of some commentators,[19] Arendt did not waiver from her support for the councils after *On Revolution*. For example, she lauded the calls for participatory democracy by the protest movements of the late 1960s in the United States and elsewhere, writing to Jaspers:

> The student movement represents a real danger to the status quo precisely because it strikes at the heart of genuine political life. I can only say with Jefferson: *Ceterum censeo* [furthermore] ... – the ward or council system of small republics where everyone has a voice in public affairs.[20]

Most importantly, in an interview late in her life, she argued that a council democracy remained the most promising form of government: a new concept of state, which, together with complementary federalised structures between states, also has the most prospects of eliminating war from international affairs (!).[21] One may see, then, that the councils repeatedly appear in Arendt's writings, and seem to play an important role in her political thought. One may also note, however, that her treatment of them was significantly different than the way they have been commonly discussed by participants, observers and historians.

Arendt's Misrepresentation of the Council Movement

"There is thus practically no point," wrote historian Eric Hobsbawm in his review of *On Revolution*, "at which Miss Arendt's discussion of what she regards as the crucial institution of the revolutionary tradition touches the actual historical phenomena she purports to describe [the councils]."[22] Arendt presented herself as following other accounts of the councils, particularly Oskar Anweiler's. However, as Hobsbawm and other commentators have observed, Arendt's historical account of the councils often stands in sharp contrast to the accounts she relied on, as well as to accepted historical facts regarding the councils.[23]

Arendt's most salient distortion of the actual history of councils is her insistence that socio-economic matters were much less important to those who established and participated in the councils than political freedom. The councils, she declared, "were infinitely more interested in the political than in the social aspect of revolution," and this in contrast to the revolutionary parties as well as the trade unions.[24] This is patently false to anyone familiar with the history of the councils. As Cohen and Arato state bluntly:

> [h]er argument is entirely fictitious ... since the movements from 1848 to 1956 to which she refers cannot be represented as having no social and economic interests and demands, and even less as not playing a major part in the economic reproduction of society.[25]

Arendt's "distortion" of the actual history of the councils is not, of course, coincidental. It is directly related to her highly controversial distinction between "the social" and "the political," and her exclusion of socio-economic problems from "genuine" political action and debate in the public sphere. Society, for Arendt, is "the form in which the fact of mutual dependence for the sake of life and nothing else assumes public significance and where the activities connected with sheer survival are permitted to appear in public."[26] Accordingly, socio-economic problems have to do with the life-process of society, its need to preserve itself, to promote the private welfare of its members and to provide for the interests of the different groups within it. All these, argued Arendt, are matters for administration, rather than for politics. Politics concerns higher capacities and concerns, first and foremost the foundation, preservation and promotion of political freedom.[27]

To illustrate this point, consider the way Arendt interpreted Lenin's characterisation of the October Revolution as "electrification plus *soviets*." What is particularly surprising in this statement, Arendt told us, is that we are given an "entirely un-Marxist separation of economics and politics, a differentiation between electrification as the solution of Russia's social question, and the *soviet* system as her new body politic that had emerged during the revolution outside all parties."[28] It is doubtful that this is what Lenin actually meant. Arendt's interpretation of this statement, however, is revealing as to the way she saw the distinction between the social and the political. Social problems, particularly poverty, are to be solved by technical means such as economic development, technological innovation, etc. – there is no genuine political discussion there. *Political* questions emerge when liberty and freedom are at stake. Accordingly, the councils' essential end was not to achieve social justice and freedom from want, nor to provide for the needs of each citizen so she could fully develop her individual creative capacities; but rather to give expression to the "rise of freedom," to freedom as participation in government.

In much of her account of the council movement, then, Arendt seemed to have forced it into the straitjacket of her own, idiosyncratic political theory, with the price of various historical and theoretical flaws. However, I would argue that the criticisms that have been raised against Arendt's account of the councils, while certainly valid, miss a crucial point. As in other topics in her writings, in her discussion of the councils Arendt did not merely recount their historical appearance, but attempted to shed light on meanings and experiences that common ways of thinking about politics fail to capture. The challenging and interesting question when addressing Arendt's narrative of the councils is whether something important was gained in the "interpretive violence" she performed when retelling the story of the councils.

Arendt's Contribution to the Council Tradition

In order to understand Arendt's contribution to the council tradition, we have to consider the role the councils played in her thought differently from how it has been perceived by most commentators. The discrepancy between the vast amount of literature that has been written on Arendt's political thought and the relatively few studies that have been dedicated to her support for the council system is revealing.[29] To a large extent, this aspect of Arendt's thought seems to strike most commentators the same way it struck one of her first and most important commentators, Margaret Canovan. "Arendt's repeated references to the 'council' system," wrote Canovan, "make unambiguously clear that the idea was important to her."[30] Yet for "most of Arendt's readers," she adds in the next page, "her views in this area are something of an embarrassment, a curiously unrealistic commitment in someone who laid particular stress on realism in politics."[31] One should also note Canovan's remark in an earlier essay: "If she [Arendt] did indeed intend this system of direct popular participation in politics to be taken seriously as an alternative to party politics, she ought to have made a much more serious case for it."[32]

As I alluded to before, I suggest that we should understand Arendt's support for the councils as closely linked to her political philosophy as a whole; indeed, to use Sitton's words, as the "concentrated expression of her political philosophy."[33] In fact, I would argue that Arendt's political theory should be understood, to a large extent, as an attempt to lay the theoretical foundation for a participatory form of government in the form and spirit of the councils; or, in other words, that her political theory *is* her "case" for council democracy. I cannot defend this suggestion here, but once we at least keep in mind this possibility, we realise that the way Arendt diverged from common accounts of the councils reflects not only a historical distortion, but also a genuine and fruitful reinterpretation.

I believe it is largely correct to say that in the council tradition (to the extent that one may speak of such a tradition despite the different strands that existed within it), politics is for the most part understood as a means to an end. Whether the end is reforms for the benefit of workers or a revolutionary transformation of society, politics is perceived as a sphere of strategic action aimed at achieving an exterior goal. Accordingly, the councils are conceptualised as institutions that serve other goals, such as organising workers in their struggles and achieving workers' control over the workplace, or as an organ of a new society where workers will be in control over the means of production and the general affairs of their community. Shipway nicely renders this point as follows: "Council communism is a theory of working-class struggle and revolution which holds that the *means* that workers will use to fight capitalism, overthrow it, and establish and administer communist society, will be the workers' councils."[34]

For Arendt, in contrast, politics was an activity that held an intrinsic meaning, rather than being (only) a means to some other end.[35] While Arendt did not deny that strategic action plays an important role in politics and that political actors always strive to achieve specific goals,[36] she saw more than that in politics. Politics consists of action and speech in the public sphere, understood as a space of appearances where each discloses "who" one is, namely the unique identity that distinguishes one from every other person.[37] For Arendt, the public sphere was a privileged site for this disclosure of individuality. At the same time, it is a space in which we connect to others in a unique way through the exchange of opinions and joint action. When we deliberate with our fellow citizens in the public sphere, we learn to see the world from their point of view, and so arrive at a fuller sense of human reality itself, which is always intersubjective:

> For though the common world is the common meeting ground of all, those who are present have different locations in it … Being seen and being heard by others derive their significance from the fact that everybody sees and hears from a different position. This is the meaning of public life … Only where things can be seen by many in a variety of aspects without changing their identity, so that those who are gathered around them know they see sameness in utter diversity, can worldly reality truly and reliably appear.[38]

The problem, for Arendt, is that in contemporary society the spaces for appearance and action have shrunk almost to the point of non-existence, and without such spaces "neither the reality of one's self, of one's identity, nor the reality of the surrounding world can be established beyond doubt."[39] Furthermore, Arendt identified acting and speaking in the public sphere with political freedom. Freedom for Arendt was not something individuals have, but rather an activity shared with others in the public sphere.[40] Freedom, in this sense, is identical with political action itself: "Men are free … as long as they act, neither before nor after; for to be free and to act are the same."[41] This is why "[p]olitical freedom, generally speaking, means the right 'to be a participator in government,' or it means nothing."[42]

The opposite of being free is to be ruled by others, which is identical with not having the opportunity and the space to actively participate in decision-making in the public sphere, or, in other words, not to be able to engage with one's peers in the manner of speech and action. This conception of what it means to be ruled by others explains why, for Arendt, relations of rule exist not only in authoritarian forms of governments, but also in modern democracies: "[t]he relationship between a ruling elite and the people, between the few, who among themselves constitute a public space, and the many, who spend their life in obscurity, has remained unchanged."[43]

Note how Arendt added here the lack, in modern democracies, of "spaces of appearances" where citizens can enjoy the light of the public sphere, rather than remaining in the "obscurity" of strictly private lives, and its inherent connection to the lack of freedom and equality in this form of government. I stress this point since for Arendt there was a genuine, unique joy in the experience of "the political." It is public happiness in the literal sense of the word, namely a kind of happiness that can be experienced only through action and speech in the public sphere. This is another sense in which modern democracy is, for Arendt, inherently oligarchic:

> What we today call democracy is a form of government where the few rule, at least supposedly, in the interest of the many. This government is democratic in that popular welfare and private happiness are its chief goals; but it can be called oligarchic in the sense that public happiness and public freedom have again become the privilege of the few.[44]

Finally, modern democracies suffer, in Arendt's view, not only from social inequality, but first and foremost from deep political inequality, since political equality means that "all have the same claim to political activity."[45] Arendt recovered this understanding of equality from the Greek polis, which, since it allowed every citizen to actively participate in government, formed an *isonomy*, namely "a form of political organization in which citizens lived together under conditions of no-rule, without a division between rulers and ruled."[46] Political equality and political freedom, then, are possible only in a form of government where all have the right and *the space* to participate.

From this perspective, the best modern democracies can achieve, even when they function well, is

> a certain control of the rulers by those who are ruled ... The most the citizen can hope for is to be "represented," whereby it is obvious that the only thing which can be represented and delegated is interest, or the welfare of the constituents, but neither their actions nor their opinions.[47]

Opinions cannot be represented because the process of forming and expressing one's opinions, for Arendt, means the kind of exchange described above, where each presents the way the common world is seen from her standpoint, and is exposed to the way it is seen from the standpoints of others. It is neither mere self-expression, nor simply offering one's input into a process of decision-making; rather, it is a privileged way of experiencing the world and deepening our "sense of the real," to use Kimberley Curtis' apt term.[48]

The meanings Arendt attached to political participation, then, are significantly different from the way it is understood in the council tradition (and arguably in the history of political theory in general). The problem for Arendt was not control over the means of production, social inequality, etc.; rather, it was the lack of spaces where citizens could experience speech, action and freedom; where they could disclose their unique individuality and deepen their sense of reality. Accordingly, the councils were for Arendt not means to other ends or institutions of strategic action, but *political spaces*. They formed privileged sites where every citizen who chose to do so could experience "the political."

Arendt's different conceptualisation of politics stemmed from different ontological and epistemological assumptions, which she derived from Heidegger and then used to "recover" the experience of the Greek polis. A discussion of Arendt's "ontology of appearance" is beyond the scope of this chapter, but I mention this because, ultimately, Arendt's contribution to the council tradition reflects her broader, unique contribution to political theory, which is an important part of what made her one of the most important political theorists of the twentieth century. In this sense, while I agree with Muldoon that Arendt's support for the councils originated from twentieth-century movements and struggles rather than from a romantic penchant for the Greek polis as is sometimes argued,[49] I would contend that Arendt turned to the way "the political" was understood by the Greeks to reinterpret the councils along a conception of politics that was ultimately foreign to most observers and theoreticians of the councils.

It is in this sense that "no tradition" has preserved the meaning of the councils, to Arendt's mind. There have certainly been accounts of the councils, but no account has captured the deeper, political-existential meanings that Arendt believed lay in them. This, for Arendt, was no accident: our focus on social, economic and political-strategic aspects of the councils obscure these meanings, and this is part of the more general tendency of Western political thought on the one hand, and modern society and thought on the other, to deprive politics of its intrinsic dignity and ignore the distinct human experience that action and speech in the public sphere allow. There is no doubt that in attempting to recover this experience, Arendt suggested distinctions and historical narratives that are dubious at best. But this should not obscure the fact that Arendt suggested what might be a genuinely important contribution to the council tradition – and to the normative foundations of participatory democracy in general –understanding them (also) as political spaces that can allow citizens a unique "existential" experience, one that is doomed to be lost, practically and conceptually, as long as participatory democracy remains a utopian vision.

Arendt's Councils and Contemporary Political Theory

As I have noted, Arendt's support for the councils has received little systematic investigation, and for the most part has been treated as a romantic utopianism on her part. This, I would argue, is but a reflection of the more general way the vision and practice of participatory democracy remains in the margins of political theory, as an "unrealistic commitment" supplanted, as Hilmer puts it, by "liberal minimalist, deliberative, and agonistic theories of democracy,"[50] and, one may add, republican theory.

Arendt is often assimilated, with certain reservations, to the republican tradition of political thought. Already Canovan, in the first book-length study of Arendt, argued that "if any label at all were to be pinned on her, it could only be 'republican' ... in the old eighteenth century sense of a partisan of public freedom, a companion of men like de Tocqueville, Jefferson and Machiavelli."[51] Most commentators have accepted this interpretation of Arendt. As Winham has noted, "a consensus has emerged in the scholarly literature that she [Arendt] came to formulate her own distinctive vision of freedom primarily by way of the classical republican tradition of political thought in which freedom is identical with political action."[52]

There is no doubt that Arendt was influenced by the republican tradition and drew on it extensively. Yet there is a reason, I think, that Canovan felt uncomfortable with Arendt's support for a council democracy.[53] Freedom in the republican tradition means non-domination; namely, being secured against the arbitrary interference of the government in our private affairs by a form of government that is committed to the principle of citizens' representation, and to private and public liberties entrenched in law.[54] The republican notion of freedom is essentially a negative one, and citizens' participation in the decision-making process is not an essential part of it.[55] At least to the extent that this is how we understand the republican tradition,[56] Arendt's political theory in general, and her advocacy of the councils in particular, amount to quite a radical critique of this tradition. For Arendt, as we have seen, political freedom cannot be experienced outside of actual participation in government. As far as ordinary citizens are concerned, their political freedom depends on the constant opportunity and *spaces* for direct participation in government.[57] Settling for a kind of council republicanism that Arendt was advocating,[58] while a valuable interpretive direction, still obscures the actual sources of Arendt's political thought. It turns attention away from the fact that it is from the labour movement and socialist thought that the councils emerged, and despite the distance Arendt kept from these sources, it is still the left-critique of representative democracy rather than the republican tradition that first informed Arendt's advocacy of a council democracy.

Similarly, the theory of deliberative democracy, which has developed since the early 1990s, has often invoked Arendt as an inspiration due to her emphasis on the importance of the exchange of opinions in the public sphere. Yet to the extent that deliberative democracy is about political reasoning and legitimacy rather than the breadth and depth of political participation,[59] and that it aims to elucidate and strengthen certain aspects of existing democracy rather than replace it, Arendt's analysis amounts to a harsh critique of it as well.[60] As long as citizens are not part of the actual decision-making process, and as long as their admission to the public sphere in the manner of speech and action is dependent on the goodwill or self-interest of representatives, we remain in the same kind of political oligarchy Arendt wrote about.

Yet, I would argue, one can find that much of the hope Arendt invested in the councils resonates in the various experiments in participatory local government, particularly participatory budgeting, that have been conducted in the last three decades in places like Porto Alegre and elsewhere around the world, at least originally with the council tradition in mind.[61] Indeed, the explosion of experiments with and calls for the direct participation of citizens in decision-making, particularly in the Global South,[62] stands in sharp contrast to the relative absence of discussion of participatory democracy in mainstream political theory. Hilmer's observation, that "[i]ronically, some of the finest empirical work on participatory democratic practice has appeared while the theory of participatory democracy languishes,"[63] remains largely true today as well.

My suggestion that experiments such as in Porto Alegre express much of the hope Arendt saw in the councils is likely to sound peculiar: isn't such focus on participatory *budgeting* and economic redistribution what Arendt *excluded* from "genuine" political discussion and action? Perhaps so, but first, whatever her reservations about this aspect of such experiments in participatory democracy might have been, Arendt would have probably seen it as another manifestation of the legacy of the council tradition, or more broadly the "revolutionary spirit" of association, participation and freedom. She would have recognised, one may conjecture, the way the hopes embedded in such experiments have travelled across the world through activist organisations such as the World Social Forum, with the call for participatory democracy high on its agenda; to movements such as Black

Lives Matter, who on their platform demand participatory budgeting and community control of

> issues that directly affect their lives, land and security. Implicit in this definition is the clear statement that Black people must determine and control the pace, shape, and manner of change and decision-making at local, regional, state and national levels.[64]

Granted, Arendt would have probably argued that a focus on social and economic justice obscures the more crucial desire for political freedom and the resistance to *political* oligarchies (in the Arendtian sense). She would have then distorted the actual motivations and struggles that have put the vision of participatory democracy back on the agenda. At the same time, by highlighting these less conscious and less articulated grievances, she might have shed light on important, real experiences that accompany these struggles, and which tend to get much less attention than the more "urgent" social and economic demands.

Concluding Remarks

Paul Ricoeur has put it well: "Arendt would not be the first thinker to invoke a form of forgetting unrelated to the past."[65] In her narrative of the council movement, Arendt indeed invoked a certain kind of forgetfulness that, at least in a certain sense, was unrelated to the past. At the same time, however, it was a bold attempt to reconnect with the past in an original way. As I have suggested, despite the criticisms one may justly offer against her account, she does add an original new dimension to the council tradition, one that should be considered and investigated further.

In broader terms, it is not only the council tradition that is at stake here, but participatory democracy as a vision and practice. Arendt challenges us to think about radical democratic politics not only in terms of the various exterior objectives participatory democrats usually have in mind, but also as an attempt at creating spaces of political action and speech as "ends in themselves," namely as human activities that have an intrinsic meaning and dignity. By this, I believe, Arendt adds an important normative argument for the project of participatory democracy, and helps us conceptualise it in more creative and imaginative ways.

Notes

1 Jaspers to Arendt, 16 May 1963, in Lotte Kohler and Hans Saner (eds), *Hannah Arendt, Karl Jaspers*, 504–5.
2 Arendt to Jaspers, 29 May 1963, in Kohler and Saner (eds), *Hannah Arendt, Karl Jaspers*, 507.
3 Elisabeth Young-Bruehl, *Hannah Arendt*, 125.

4 Hannah Arendt, *Men in Dark Times*.
5 James Muldoon, "The Origins of Hannah Arendt's Council System."
6 Hannah Arendt, "To Save the Jewish Homeland," in *The Jewish Writings*, 400.
7 Ibid., 401.
8 Hannah Arendt, "Approaches to the 'German Problem'," in *Essays in Understanding, 1930–1954*, 114, my emphasis.
9 Ibid.
10 Hannah Arendt, "Totalitarian Imperialism," 28.
11 Hannah Arendt, *The Human Condition*, 216.
12 Ibid., 215.
13 Ibid., 216.
14 Hannah Arendt, *On Revolution*, 247.
15 Ibid., 249.
16 Ibid., 252–3.
17 Ibid., 258.
18 Ibid., 242.
19 J. M. Bernstein, "Political Modernism," in *Arendt and Adorno*.
20 Arendt to Jaspers, 19 February 1965, in Kohler and Saner (eds), *Hannah Arendt, Karl Jaspers*, 583.
21 Hannah Arendt, "Thoughts on Politics and Revolution," in *Crises of the Republic*, 201–33.
22 E. J. Hobsbawm, "Hannah Arendt on Revolution," in Garrath Williams (ed.), *Hannah Arendt*, vol. 2, 178.
23 Mike McConkey, "On Arendt's Vision of the European Council Phenomenon"; John Medearis, "Lost or Obscured?"; Muldoon, "The Origins of Hannah Arendt's Council System."
24 Arendt, *On Revolution*, 269; see also ibid., 278; Arendt, *The Human Condition*, 215–16.
25 Jean L. Cohen and Andrew Arato, *Civil Society and Political Theory*, 199.
26 Arendt, *The Human Condition*, 46.
27 This is a much-discussed topic in the scholarly literature on Arendt. Hannah F. Pitkin's *The Attack of the Blob: Hannah Arendt's Concept of the Social* is still the most extensive study of Arendt's understanding of "the social."
28 Arendt, *On Revolution*, 60.
29 See, in particular, John F. Sitton, "Hannah Arendt's Argument for Council Democracy," in Lewis P. Hinchman and Sandra K. Hinchman (eds), *Hannah Arendt*; Jeffery C. Isaac, "Oases in the Desert"; Richard J. Bernstein, *Hannah Arendt and the Jewish Question*, ch. 6; Mark Reinhardt, *The Art of Being Free*, ch. 5; Andreas Kalyvas, *Democracy and the Politics of the Extraordinary*, ch. 9; James Muldoon, "The Lost Treasure of Arendt's Council System"; Muldoon, "The Origins of Hannah Arendt's Council System."
30 Margaret Canovan, *Hannah Arendt*, 236.
31 Ibid., 237.
32 Margaret Canovan, "The Contradictions of Hannah Arendt's Political Thought," 8.
33 Sitton, "Hannah Arendt's Argument," 325.
34 Mark Shipway, "Council Communism," in Maximilien Rubel and John Crump (eds), *Non-Market Socialism in the Nineteenth and Twentieth Centuries*, 104, my emphasis.

35 Arendt, *The Human Condition*, 206.
36 Ibid., 182.
37 Ibid., 179.
38 Ibid., 57.
39 Ibid.
40 Arendt, *On Revolution*, 24.
41 Hannah Arendt, "What Is Freedom," in *Between Past and Future*, 151.
42 Arendt, *On Revolution*, 221.
43 Ibid., 281.
44 Ibid., 273.
45 Hannah Arendt, "Introduction into Politics," in *The Promise of Politics*, 118.
46 Arendt, *On Revolution*, 22.
47 Ibid., 272.
48 Kimberley Curtis, *Our Sense of the Real.*
49 Muldoon, "The Origins of Hannah Arendt's Council System."
50 Jeffrey D. Hilmer, "The State of Participatory Democracy Today," 6.
51 Margaret Canovan, *The Political Thought of Hannah Arendt*, 15.
52 Ilya Winham, "Rereading Hannah Arendt's 'What Is Freedom?'," 87.
53 See also Muldoon, "The Origins of Hannah Arendt's Council System."
54 Philip Pettit, *Republicanism*, 22; Quentin Skinner, "Freedom as the Absence of Arbitrary Power," in Cecile Laborde and John Maynor (eds), *Republicanism and Political Theory*, 85.
55 Republicanism, stresses Pettit, is "not the sort of tradition … that hails the democratic participation of the people as one of the highest forms of good" (Pettit, *Republicanism*, 8). In fact, as Skinner notes, among republican writers "few exhibit any enthusiasm for giving what Nedham calls 'the confused promiscuous body of the people' any direct share in government" (Quentin Skinner, *Liberty before Liberalism*, 31–2). The solution for most republican thinkers was, therefore, that the masses should be represented by the virtuous citizens (op. cit., 32).
56 Arendt's political thought has more complicated relations to J. G. A. Pocock's reading of the republican tradition, which emphasises much more the intrinsic meaning of political participation, as he himself was influenced by Arendt in his reading of this tradition. Unfortunately, I cannot address this problem here. See J. G. A. Pocock, *The Machiavellian Moment*.
57 See also Shmuel Lederman, "Agonism and Deliberation in Arendt."
58 See, for example, Lisa Disch, "How Could Hannah Arendt Glorify the American Revolution and Revile the French?," 352.
59 Joshua Cohen, *Philosophy, Politics, Democracy*, 341.
60 Seyla Benhabib, "Toward a Deliberative Model of Democratic Legitimacy," 84.
61 Rebecca Abers, *Inventing Local Democracy*, 49–50. See also Shmuel Lederman, "Councils and Revolution."
62 The literature on these experiments is quite large. Notable examples are Boaventura de Sousa Santos (ed.), *Democratizing Democracy*; Marion Gret and Yves Sintomer, *The Porto Alegre Experiment*; Jenny Pearce (ed.), *Participation and Democracy in the Twenty-First Century City*; Manoranjan Mohanty *et al.* (eds), *Grass-roots Democracy in India and China*; Richard Stahler-Sholk *et al.* (eds), *Latin American Social Movements in the Twenty-First Century*; Leonardo Avritzer, *Participatory Institutions in Democratic Brazil*; Brian Wampler and

Leonardo Avritzer, "Participatory Publics"; Leonardo Avritzer, "Living under a Democracy."

63 Hilmer, "The State of Participatory Democracy Today," 22.

64 See The Movement for Black Lives: *Platform*. Available at https://policy.m4bl.org/platform/.

65 Paul Ricoeur, "Power and Violence," in Garrath Williams (ed.), *Hannah Arendt*, vol. 3, 396.

References

Abers, Rebecca. *Inventing Local Democracy: Grassroots Politics in Brazil*. Boulder, CO: Lynne Rienner, 2000.

Arendt, Hannah. *Between Past and Future: Eight Exercises in Political Thought*. New York: Penguin Books, 2006.

———. *Crises of the Republic*. New York: Harcourt Brace Jovanovich, Inc., 1972.

———. *Essays in Understanding, 1930–1954: Formation, Exile, and Totalitarianism*. Edited by Jerome Kohn. New York: Schocken Books, 1994.

———. *The Human Condition*. Chicago and London: The University of Chicago Press, 1998.

———. *The Jewish Writings*. Edited by Jerome Kohn and Ron H. Feldman. New York: Schocken Books, 2007.

———. *Men in Dark Times*. New York: A Harvest Book, 1968.

———. *The Promise of Politics*. Edited by Jerome Kohn. New York: Schocken Books, 2005.

———. *On Revolution*. New York: The Viking Press, 1965.

———. "Totalitarian Imperialism: Reflections on the Hungarian Revolution." *The Journal of Politics* 20 (1958): 5–43.

Avritzer, Leonardo. *Participatory Institutions in Democratic Brazil*. Washington, DC and Baltimore, MD: Woodrow Wilson Center Press, 2009.

———. "Living under a Democracy: Participation and Its Impact on the Living Conditions of the Poor." *Latin American Research Review* 45 (2010): 166–85.

Benhabib, Seyla. "Toward a Deliberative Model of Democratic Legitimacy." In *Democracy and Difference: Contesting the Boundaries of the Political*. Edited by Seyla Benhabib. 67–94. Princeton, NJ: Princeton University Press, 1996.

Bernstein, J. M. "Political Modernism: The New, Revolution, and Civil Disobedience in Arendt and Adorno." In *Arendt and Adorno: Political and Philosophical Investigations*. Edited by Lars Rensmann and Samir Gandesha. 57–77. Stanford, CA: Stanford University Press, 2012.

Bernstein, Richard J. *Hannah Arendt and the Jewish Question*. Cambridge, MA: The MIT Press, 1996.

Canovan, Margaret. "The Contradictions of Hannah Arendt's Political Thought." *Political Theory* 6, no. 1 (1978): 5–26.

———. *Hannah Arendt: A Reinterpretation of Her Political Thought*. Cambridge: Cambridge University Press, 1992.

———. *The Political Thought of Hannah Arendt*. London: Aldine Press, 1974.

Cohen, Jean L. and Andrew Arato. *Civil Society and Political Theory*. Cambridge, MA and London: The MIT Press, 1995.

Cohen, Joshua. *Philosophy, Politics, Democracy: Selected Essays*. Cambridge, MA: Harvard University Press, 2009.

Curtis, Kimberley. *Our Sense of the Real: Aesthetic Experience and Arendtian Politics*. Ithaca, NY and London: Cornell University Press, 1999.

Disch, Lisa. "How Could Hannah Arendt Glorify the American Revolution and Revile the French? Placing On Revolution in the Historiography of the French and American Revolutions." *European Journal of Political Theory* 10, no. 3 (2011): 350–71.

Gret, Marion and Yves Sintomer. *The Porto Alegre Experiment: Learning Lessons for Better Democracy*. Translated by Stephen Wright. London and New York: Zed Books, 2005.

Hilmer, Jeffrey D. "The State of Participatory Democracy Today." Paper presented at the 66th annual meeting of the Midwest Political Science Association, Chicago, IL, 3–6 April 2008.

Hobsbawm, E. J. "Hannah Arendt on Revolution." In *Hannah Arendt: Critical Assessments of Leading Philosophers*, vol. 2: *Arendt and Philosophy*. Edited by Garrath Williams. 201–8. London and New York: Routledge, 2006.

Isaac, Jeffery C. "Oases in the Desert: Hannah Arendt on Democratic Politics." *American Political Science Review* 88, no. 1 (1994): 156–68.

Kalyvas, Andreas. *Democracy and the Politics of the Extraordinary: Max Weber, Carl Schmitt and Hannah Arendt*. Cambridge: Cambridge University Press, 2008.

Kohler, Lotte and Hans Saner (eds). *Hannah Arendt, Karl Jaspers: Correspondence, 1926–1969*. Translated by Robert and Rita Kimber. New York: Harcourt Brace & Company, 1992.

Lederman, Shmuel. "Agonism and Deliberation in Arendt." *Constellations* 21, no. 3 (2014): 327–37.

———. "Councils and Revolution: Participatory Democracy in Anarchist Thought and the New Social Movements." *Science & Society* 79, no. 2 (2015): 243–63.

McConkey, Mike. "On Arendt's Vision of the European Council Phenomenon: Critique from a Historical Perspective." *Dialectical Anthropology* 16 (1991): 15–31.

Medearis, John. "Lost or Obscured? How V. I. Lenin, Joseph Schumpeter and Hannah Arendt Misunderstood the Council Movement." *Polity* 36, no. 3 (2004): 447–76.

Mohanty, Manoranjan, Richard Baum, Rong Ma and George Mathew (eds). *Grass-roots Democracy in India and China: The Right to Participate*. New Delhi: Sage, 2007.

Moruzzi, Norma C. *Speaking Through the Mask: Hannah Arendt and the Politics of Social Identity*. Ithaca, NY and London: Cornell University Press, 2000.

The Movement for Black Lives. *Platform*. Accessed at https://policy.m4bl.org/platform/.

Muldoon, James. "The Lost Treasure of Arendt's Council System." *Critical Horizons* 12, no. 3 (2011): 396–417.

———. "The Origins of Hannah Arendt's Council System." *History of Political Thought* 37, no. 4 (2016): 761–89.

Pearce, Jenny (ed.). *Participation and Democracy in the Twenty-First Century City*. New York: Palgrave Macmillan, 2010.

Pettit, Philip. *Republicanism: A Theory of Freedom and Government*. New York: Oxford University Press, 1999.

Pitkin, Hannah F. *The Attack of the Blob: Hannah Arendt's Concept of the Social*. Chicago and London: University of Chicago Press, 1998.

Pocock, J. G. A. *The Machiavellian Moment: Florentine Political Thought and the Atlantic Republican Tradition*. Princeton, NJ: Princeton University Press, 1975.

Reinhardt, Mark. *The Art of Being Free: Taking Liberties with Tocqueville, Marx, and Arendt*. Ithaca, NY and London: Cornell University Press, 1997.

Ricoeur, Paul. "Power and Violence." In *Hannah Arendt: Critical Assessments of Leading Political Philosophers*, vol. 3: *Arendt and Philosophy*. Edited by Garrath Williams. 20–42. London and New York: Routledge, 2006.

Santos, Boaventura de Sousa (ed.). *Democratizing Democracy: Beyond the Liberal Democratic Canon*. London and New York: Verso, 2005.

Shipway, Mark. "Council Communism." In *Non-Market Socialism in the Nineteenth and Twentieth Centuries*. Edited by Maximilien Rubel and John Crump. 104–26. London: Macmillan Press, 1987.

Sitton, John F. "Hannah Arendt's Argument for Council Democracy." In *Hannah Arendt: Critical Essays*. Edited by Lewis P. Hinchman and Sandra K. Hinchman. 307–29. New York: State University of New York Press, 1994.

Skinner, Quentin. "Freedom as the Absence of Arbitrary Power." In *Republicanism and Political Theory*. Edited by Cecile Laborde and John Maynor. 83–101. Malden, MA: Blackwell Publishing, 2008.

———. *Liberty before Liberalism*. Cambridge: Cambridge University Press, 1998.

Stahler-Sholk, Richard, Harry E. Vanden and Glen David Kuecker (eds). *Latin American Social Movements in the Twenty-First Century: Resistance, Power, and Democracy*. Lanham, MD: Rowman & Littlefield Publishers, 2008.

Wampler, Brian and Leonardo Avritzer. "Participatory Publics: Civil Society and New Institutions in Democratic Brazil." *Comparative Politics* 36, no. 3 (2004): 291–312.

Winham, Ilya. "Rereading Hannah Arendt's 'What is Freedom?' Freedom as a Phenomenon of Political Virtuosity." *Theoria: A Journal of Social and Political Theory* 59, no. 131 (2012): 84–106.

Young-Bruehl, Elizabeth. *Hannah Arendt: For Love of the World*. New Haven, CT and London: Yale University Press, 2004.

9 The Self-Limiting Revolution and the Mixed Constitution of Socialist Democracy

Claude Lefort's Vision of Council Democracy

Benjamin Ask Popp-Madsen

Introduction

Claude Lefort's political thinking is best known for his idea of democracy as an "empty place" of power.[1] In a nutshell, Lefort's idea is that modern democracy is characterised by the condition that no one can speak authoritatively with the *true* voice of the people, because the people are always plural, divided and in conflict. No group or individual can fully incarnate the people, and as such the place of power becomes empty.[2] When Lefort introduces this idea, he notes how "there is no need to dwell on the details of the institutional apparatus" producing democracy's emptiness.[3] Hence, although Lefort's theorisation of democracy is appealing due to the stress on the open-endedness and pluralism of democracy, it is difficult to imagine the specificities of such a democratic regime. What is this "empty place"? How is it instituted and maintained?

This confusion is reproduced when discussing Lefort's political position. Can his political thinking best be associated with liberal democracy or radical democracy? In one reading, Lefort is a critic of revolutionary politics, and by contrasting democracy and totalitarianism, Lefort could be said to foster a reorientation from radical transformation to liberal constitutionalism.[4] As such, Lefort can be read as demonstrating the progressive nature of liberal democracy. The vacated parliament on election day is the best symbol of democracy's empty place, and representation ensures the distance between the principle of democracy (the government of the people) and its institutional realisation (the government by the representatives of the people). Liberal democracy and its key components of representation and periodic elections, Lefort could be taken to argue, deserves to be understood as the progressive regime that cut off the monarch's head and replaced it with the multi-headed people.

In another reading, Lefort's idea of democracy as an empty place signifies how democracy is always at odds with its specific, present institutionalisation. This idea of an irreducible gap between the principle of democracy and its institutionalisation has inspired theories of democracy as a radical project.[5] As such, Lefort can be taken to infuse the revolutionary tradition with a dose of anarchism. Whereas the revolutionary tradition has insisted on versions of organism and homogeneity, such as in Jean-Jacques Rousseau's general will, Karl Marx's communist revolution or V. I. Lenin's proletarian state, Lefort heeded the call of deepening democracy, but without sacrificing pluralism, internal conflict and difference. On this reading, Lefort's thinking acquires an anarchical bent, where democratic action is never able to stabilise itself, as it is hostile to any form of institutionalisation.[6] Lefort's thinking, as James Ingram has argued, contains the resources for both such political positions.[7]

My contribution in this chapter is to evaluate these questions through the lens of Lefort's writings on the council system and what he calls "socialist democracy." When discussing the council tradition, Lefort notes how the councils form the basis of a *socialist* democracy "infinitely more extensive than bourgeois democracy has ever been,"[8] but simultaneously upholding a differential, pluralist and conflictual nature of the people. Lefort's idea of a socialist democracy is built on an interpretation of the council system that stresses their self-limiting qualities. In the programmes of the Hungarian councils, Lefort detects a self-limiting ambition of creating a society where councils, parties and unions co-exist in institutionalised conflict. Instead of imagining a sovereign republic of councils, along the lines of Cornelius Castoriadis and Hannah Arendt, Lefort stresses that only by combining uneven and conflicting sources of power could freedom be secured and totalitarian tendencies held in check. In light of this analysis, I claim Lefort can be understood neither entirely as a liberal nor a radical democrat. On the one hand, Lefort's socialist council democracy offers a more widespread democratisation of the economy and civil society than that available within liberal democracy. On the other hand, such democratisation is achieved through the institutionalisation of democratic politics within parties, councils and unions, rather than through episodic and insurgent forms of politics occurring at the margins of a political system, as with certain varieties of radical democracy.[9]

Lefort's novel conception of councils, parties and unions working together in a mixed regime is neglected in the literature in a double sense. On the one hand, general accounts of "council communism" in the interwar years frequently mention how Lefort and Castoriadis are notable heirs to this tradition, but they fail to mention that Lefort welcomes a division of power between councils, parties and unions, whereas Castoriadis argues for the sovereignty of councils.[10]

On the other hand, in the English-speaking reception of Lefort's thought, his analyses of the council system are almost completely absent. Despite a few remarks by Andrew Arato,[11] one will hardly find any engagement with this theme. The only monograph on Lefort's thought, Bernard Flynn's otherwise excellent introduction to Lefort,[12] has nothing to say on the councils. Moreover, the only anthology featuring analyses of a range of different aspects of Lefort's thinking by leading Lefort scholars, *Claude Lefort: Thinker of the Political* (2013), also neglects Lefort's interpretations of the council system.[13] Analyses of Lefort by political theorists and intellectual historians such as Warren Breckman,[14] Samuel Moyn,[15] Oliver Marchart,[16] Raf Geenens[17] and Carlos Accetti[18] all aim to discuss Lefort's theory of democracy, but none reflect on Lefort's notion of socialist democracy or the self-limiting democracy of the councils.

To remedy this lack of engagement with Lefort's writings on the council tradition, and to bring out his idea of a socialist democracy of self-limiting councils, the chapter is structured the following way: I begin by providing Lefort's first analysis of the councils of the Hungarian Revolution, published in 1956. Here, Lefort rehearses the same arguments as Castoriadis and Arendt, which do not stray from the established tradition of council analysis. In the next section, I briefly lay out Lefort's theory of democracy as an empty place. Next, I proceed with an analysis of Lefort's second interpretation of Hungarian councils in the article "The Age of Novelty," published in 1976. In this article, Lefort departs from his early analysis and provides a novel reinterpretation of the council system. As Lefort's thoughts on this matter are tentative and not fully developed, I use the concepts of the *mixed constitution* and *self-limitation* to help reconstruct Lefort's position. Finally, in the concluding section, I argue that following a consideration of Lefort's council theory, he is best understood neither as a liberal nor radical democrat, but as a socialist democrat, who seeks to enhance both the radical democrat's desire for popular self-government and the liberal democrat's demand for societal pluralisation and difference.

Lefort's Early Analysis of the Council System

Lefort published his first analysis of the Hungarian councils in the article "The Hungarian Insurrection" in *Socialism ou Barberie* in December 1956. Here, Lefort conforms to the main principles of the council tradition from Karl Marx's interpretation of the Paris Commune to Castoriadis' 1956 article on the Hungarian Revolution, "The Proletarian Revolution against Democracy." In a 1975 interview, Lefort stated that

> in the face of the major events (French politics, East Berlin, de-Stalinization, Poland, Hungary and Algeria), Castoriadis and I found ourselves so close that the texts published by either of us were also in large part the product of the other.[19]

Lefort later dismisses his early interpretation of the council system on the grounds of his theory of democracy as an empty place, society's constitutive division and its haunting spectre of totalitarianism.

Lefort's early interpretation of the councils is a meticulous examination of the events in Hungary with special attention to the formation of councils and their political demands. He examines the council movement in Hungary as a whole, and argues that the revolutionaries "demanded the constitution of councils in all factories. This proves that the workers saw in their autonomous bodies a power that had universal meaning … they were tending toward a sort of republic of councils."[20] From this description we can already recognise the contours of earlier interpretations of the council system, as well as those provided by Castoriadis and Arendt: First, the councils originate in the production sphere, but their primary significance lies outside this milieu due to their "universal meaning." Second, the councils arise autonomously; they are products of the organisational qualities of the workers themselves. Third, from the dispersed struggles emerge a *republic* of councils, meaning that some kind of integration takes place – traditionally understood as federalisation. Such integration of the dispersed councils into a republic implies the creation of a new, sovereign council regime, i.e. the subordination of all other political forms to the councils.

Throughout the analysis, Lefort refers to the councils as both instruments of revolutionary struggle and an image of post-revolutionary society – and as such places himself firmly in the council tradition. In describing the councils as instruments of revolutionary struggle, Lefort mentions the spontaneity of their emergence[21] and their immediate attempt to federate.[22] Moreover, he describes how the councils in a revolutionary situation rise against the existing structures of political power, against the state and the parties, and co-ordinate the insurrection:

> A proletarian movement had emerged that found its true expression straightaway in the creation of councils and that constituted the *sole real* power … It was the Workers' Council that ran everything: it armed fighters, organized resupply, and presented political and economic demands.[23]

Among these demands were the "replacement of local Stalinist authorities, implementation of *workers' self-management*, and departure of Russian troops."[24] Lefort's italicisation of "workers' self-management" as a central demand of the Hungarian council movement brings him face to face with the classic formulations of council theory. Some agents – the parasitic state for Marx, the unions and parties for the interwar "council communists," bureaucracy for Castoriadis and the party system for Arendt – seek to deprive society of its constituent capabilities and deny "the proletariat," "the many" or "the people" the self-management of their own affairs. Lefort, in this 1956 article, agrees. Like Castoriadis, Lefort positions the councils as opposed to the bureaucratic division of directors and executors that *Socialisme ou Barbarie* had developed during the 1950s.[25] The way to overcome this division – an argument we are also familiar with from Castoriadis – is the self-management of workers through councils, as the

Hungarian insurrectionaries "specified that the workers alone, through their Council, are qualified to decide."[26]

Moreover, Lefort also provides the classic choice on how post-revolutionary society should be organised. Reminiscent of Arendt's dichotomy between councils and parties, between action and representation, Lefort argues the Hungarians were faced with a fundamental choice of government, "as the insurrection bore within itself the seeds of two absolutely different regimes."[27] Either, the Hungarians would start "a process leading to the rebuilding of a separate state apparatus opposed to the Councils, of a parliamentary 'democracy'," or they would deliver "the victory of workers' democracy, the takeover of factories by the Councils."[28] According to Lefort – and this point is crucial in relation to his later reinterpretation of the councils – "it would have been necessary for one solution to win out brutally at the expense of the other and for a bourgeois-type parliament *or* the Councils ... to win out."[29] This description is similar to the general narrative of the revolutionary tradition that Arendt provides in *On Revolution* (1963), and is of special importance, as Lefort twenty years later will label the councils' call for the co-existence of councils, parties and unions as the true novelty of the Hungarian councils.

As such, in his initial encounter with the council tradition Lefort reproduces the central tenets of the council theory. He highlights the spontaneity of their emergence, their impulse to federate, their negation of existing power structures, their demands for political and economic self-government, their expression of true proletarian power and their fundamental opposition to parliamentary democracy. All these elements have been central to the various analyses of council formations from the Paris Commune onwards. For a reader familiar with Lefort's democratic theory of the empty place, the language of Lefort's analysis of the Hungarian councils seems peculiar. How can a thinker of the constitutive division of society speak of a "true expression" of proletarian power? How can a thinker, who is most famously known for understanding democracy as an "empty place" due to the "disincarnation of power," let a substantive category such as "the proletariat" and a positive institutional form such as the council system fully occupy the place of power?

What these questions imply is that Lefort decisively changes his political thinking after his break with *Socialisme ou Barberie* in 1958. I argue that Lefort's assessment of the council movement changes due to his fundamental re-evaluation of democracy.

The *Ancien Régime*, Democracy and Totalitarianism: The Empty Space Explained

This re-evaluation starts from the argument that democracy and totalitarianism should be understood together.[30] For Lefort, democracy emerges from the break with the *Ancien Régime*, and totalitarianism is a revolt against the democratic experience. One way to understand Lefort's democratic theory is thus to briefly survey the central characteristics of these three regime forms. But first, it is necessary to understand what Lefort means by a "place of power." Lefort contends that every society is organised around a place of power, which gives it its unity and ensures that society does not fall into civil war.[31] This unity is strictly symbolic, it is external to reality, but nonetheless structures and forms it.[32]

Premodern society, according to Lefort, is unified in the figure of the king. Lefort follows Ernst Kantorowicz, who argued that in premodern societies, unity was created by reference to the dual body of the king:

> we thus have to recognize [in the king] a *twin person*, one descending from nature, the other from grace ... concerning one personality, he was, by nature, an individual man: concerning his other personality, he was, by grace, a *Christus*, that is, a God-man.[33]

Ultimately, the eternal body of the king is an earthly representative of the body of Christ. This ultimately means that premodern society grounds its order and unity in *another* and *fully occupied place*.

The radical break created by modern democracy is not that this place of power disappears, but instead that power cannot be incorporated in a body – in a determinate figure. Power, the democrat says, resides in "the people," but "the people" can never be totally present or speak with one voice. The place of power, hence, cannot be fully occupied by a corporate figure; power becomes *disincorporated*: "The modern democratic revolution is best recognized in this mutation: there is no power linked to a body."[34] Modern democracy is the only regime which openly acknowledges that the place of power is empty, meaning that order, unity and legitimacy are only periodically achieved and only partly justified.[35] Because there is no determinate figure of power, there is no final determination of society's foundations. "If we bear in mind the monarchical model of the *Ancien Régime*," Lefort argues, "the meaning of the transformation can be summarized as follows: democratic society is instituted without a body, as a society which undermines the representation of an organic totality."[36] The conflicts and disagreements which dominate every society are not concealed by the operation of power; instead modern democracy welcomes disagreement and conflict. The democratic regime is thus held together by a very peculiar force: democracy is unified around *nothing*, a void, an empty space:

> Power appears as an empty place and those who exercise it as mere mortals who occupy it only temporarily ... there is no law that can be fixed, whose articles cannot be contested, whose foundations are susceptible of being called into question. Lastly, there is no representation of a centre and of the contours of society: unity cannot now

> efface social division. Democracy inaugurates the experience of an ungraspable, uncontrollable society in which the people will be said to be sovereign, of course, but whose identity will constantly be open to question, whose identity will remain latent.[37]

Democracy can never achieve certainty regarding its values and principles. Instead, the key elements of the democratic experience are contestation of truths and hierarchies, debate on political principles, a vibrant public sphere and contest over the temporary occupation of the place of power.

In contrast, totalitarian society regards the democratic experience as scandalous, and cannot accept ambiguity of its own foundations.[38] "The people," which in the democratic discourse is an object of contestation, is understood as a realisable object in the totalitarian discourse. Power, which as a result of the democratic experience and society's constitutive division becomes disincorporated, is in totalitarianism again represented as a determined figure:

> A logic of identification is set in motion, and is governed by the representation of power as embodiment. The proletariat and the people are one; the party and the proletariat are one; the politbureau and, ultimately, the *egocrat*, and the party are one. Whilst there develops a representation of a homogenous and self-transparent society, of a People-as-One, social division, in all its modes, is denied, and at the same time all signs of differences of opinion, belief and mores are condemned.[39]

Totalitarianism cannot assent to the constitutive character of conflict and emptiness; for totalitarian society, unity is always threatened by conflict, by the intrusion of the Other (the Jews, the kulaks, the bourgeoisie etc.), which must be overcome at whatever price (mass extermination, mass deportation). As such, totalitarianism seeks to resurrect the premodern, fully incorporated figure of power in the figure of *Führer* or the Party, which will substantially occupy the place of power opened by the democratic revolution. Totalitarian society seeks to be in complete harmony with itself, and the fiction of the People-as-One lives on, as the gap between the symbolic referent of "the people" and empirical people is denied.

From Sovereignty to Self-Limitation: Reinterpreting the Hungarian Revolution

In "The Age of Novelty" (1976) Lefort once again turns to the Hungarian councils, only this time with different results. Whereas in the 1956 analysis, Lefort situated the councils and the parties in stark opposition, he now interprets the councils' struggle as one towards a mixed polity in which conflict between council system, party system and unions will be productively institutionalised. In 1956, Lefort stressed, in accordance with the council tradition, the councils' aspirations of complete sovereignty and their fundamental opposition to the state, parties and unions. By 1976, Lefort argues that "in adopting this language one could still allow part of the novelty to escape."[40] This novelty, Lefort contends, is the Hungarian councils' recognition of the hazards of constituting of a new polity; the revolutionaries knew of "the danger that was posed by a power ... that concentrated all the decisions affecting the fate of society." The revolutionaries reflectively "showed new insight into the danger which issued from the development of their own power."[41] In essence, the consequence of this insight is that "the idea of a new revolutionary power totally in the workers' hands was condemned because it would have a totalitarian bent."[42] Instead of aspiring to a total takeover of power through the councils – a republic of councils, a sovereign council state etc. – Lefort argues that the workers' councils themselves knew that such an aspiration would be totalitarian, and thus they refrained from it. Instead, the programmes issued by the Hungarian councils advocated for the establishment of councils as a *limited* political power existing side by side with parties and unions. Consequently, the experiences with totalitarianism made the Hungarian councils support a *self-limited* democracy.

Lefort finds evidence for this position in a discussion in the most powerful council, the Budapest Council, where participants renounced the idea of setting up a national council with delegates from local and regional councils, i.e. the classic pyramidal model of council organisation. The Budapest Council, according to Lefort, rejected such a step, because they were "haunted by the problem of their own representativity" and clearly "opposed the criterion of efficacy to that of democracy."[43] Although it might be more effective to have a national council assembling delegates from the entire country, it could not be the mandate of the Budapest Council – in their own self-understanding – to create such a national council. As such, according to Lefort, the councils deliberately placed themselves between responsibility and limitation. Emerging from a totalitarian society with a power totally occupying the place of power, the Hungarian councils wished to place limitations on power in a new regime.

Crucially, Lefort highlights three central demands by the Budapest Council, which were also proclaimed by many regional councils. According to the Budapest Council, three different institutions ought to constitute the polity after the revolution: First, workers' councils should direct the economy, decide on national investment, salaries, production norms and general conditions of working life. As an important site of domination, the economy would be fully democratised. Second, a multi-party system with free, general and secret elections to parliament would complement the councils' direction of the economy. Third, new trade unions would ensure the right of the individual worker to strike.[44] This division of the polity into three distinct institutions recognises, according to Lefort, that society cannot eradicate conflict, because "the worker is caught in at least three different webs of socialisation," and hence that "the fiction of unity must be realized."[45] In terms of production, the worker is represented by the councils; the individual as a citizen is represented in parliament; in terms of local working conditions, the so-called "worker-unionist-potential striker" is represented by the unions.[46] That the Hungarian councils argued for councils, parties and unions demonstrates for Lefort "the difference at the heart of the same individual," and how "the councils themselves do not constitute the entire working class."[47]

Lefort's novel interpretation of the council system lies in this principle of co-existing but conflicting powers. He summarises his position as follows:

> A new and very remarkable fact is the search for a new political model combining several types of power, which would in effect forbid a state apparatus to solidify and detach itself from civil society. We want a parliament elected by universal suffrage (whose effectiveness would be guaranteed by the existence of multiple parties in competition), a government elected by it and remaining under its control; we want a federation of workers' councils that governs national economic affairs – which obviously gives the councils a political role – and we also want democratic trade unions that defend the specific interests of workers.[48]

Such a divided polity is, for Lefort, "the formula for a *socialist democracy*, infinitely more extensive than bourgeois democracy has ever been."[49] This Lefortian socialist democracy grounded upon the self-limiting proposals of the Hungarian councils is indeed a different conceptualisation of the council system than that found in Marx, Arendt or Castoriadis. As Arato, who is one of the sole interpreters of Lefort to stress this issue, argues:

> By postulating the self-limitation of the council movement itself, the Hungarian Revolution, though involving councils, went beyond, according to Lefort, the famous counciliar model developed by Marx and reintegrated as such by his younger self [Lefort], as well as by Arendt and Castoriadis. It would have been as wrong for the councils to claim all power as it would for the old party.[50]

The crucial difference is this: the situation of *dual power* that historically existed between the Petrograd Soviet and the Provisional Government after the February Revolution in Russia in 1917, i.e. between the council system and the party system, is for Lefort a situation to be upheld and further developed rather than transcended in favour of the full sovereignty of a republic of councils. In their self-understanding, according to Lefort, the Hungarian councils rejected the idea that they incarnated the will of the people, or, in a more general manner, that any single institution could ever do so. This is because the councils "were outlining a new model for a division of power" that is "unknown in bourgeois democratic system" and which "alone would make socialism possible."[51]

Lefort immediately acknowledges that this new model of political division did not exist long enough to evaluate its viability, but "it is impossible to misconstrue its impulse," which consists in the idea "to combine authorities whose sources are openly recognized as dissimilar."[52] The result of such a deliberate combination of dissimilar sources of power "presupposes that there cannot exist a society in accord with itself, delivered once and for all from internal antagonisms."[53] By drawing power from different springs, adherence to society's fundamental division is upheld. Because the Hungarian councils emerge from the background of totalitarian society, they recognise the dangers of *one* source of power, be it from the People-as-One (popular sovereignty), race (Nazism) or from history itself (communism).

For other thinkers in the council tradition, the appraisal of combining councils, parties and unions would be a desperate confusion. It would signify the confused mixture of bureaucratic and self-governing elements (Castoriadis), the muddled combination of institutions of action and representation (Arendt), or a chaotic blend of revolutionary and counter-revolutionary forces (the Marxist tradition in general). As Lefort devotes only a couple of pages to his proposal of a self-limiting democracy, it is necessary to supplement the analysis with a discussion of the concepts of the *mixed constitution* and *self-limitation* in order to understand Lefort's proposal in more detail.

The Mixed Constitution

One concept through which Lefort's notion of a self-limited socialist democracy can be heuristically understood is "the mixed constitution." The mixed constitution traditionally refers to the typology of pure constitutions developed in Greek antiquity, where political regimes can be distinguished by who governs (the one, the few or the many) and how they govern (in accordance with the common good or self-interest). The result is three good forms of government – monarchy, aristocracy and democracy – and three vicious forms – tyranny, oligarchy and mob-rule. The theory of the mixed constitution argues that the ideally best form of government is established by combining monarchy, aristocracy and democracy into a mixed polity.[54] Obviously, the ancient idea of a mixed constitution and Lefort's proposed division between councils, parties and unions are miles apart. But when the perceived benefits of the mixed constitution, as well as its historical successor – the theory of unitary sovereignty – is taken into consideration, it is possible to interpret Lefort's later council theory through this concept.

In the classical argument, the reason for mixing the pure forms of government was to ensure that no individual or group would impose their will on the whole of society. The pure regime forms will always be corrupted, because power is undivided, but by mixing them, institutions will not alienate themselves from the people and dominate them.[55] No class of society will be able to govern society sovereignly, as forms of struggle and negotiation will be necessary for political decision-making. These reasons for mixing institutional forms fit well with Lefort's descriptions of the self-limiting ambitions of the Hungarian councils. For Lefort, the Hungarian councils favoured a mixed regime without the establishment of a firm locus of sovereignty because of their experiences with a regime form which favoured unity and homogeneity over division and conflict. The councils were afraid of every power, even their own, in its pure form. They were afraid that a sovereign council system, even with the mechanisms of instant recall and imperative mandate, would become an alien and dominating power. As Arato has aptly phrased it,

> this project had to and did involve the renunciation of the utopia of revolution in the sense of the dream of a single, imposed model of the good society that breaks completely with the present, that is beyond conflict and division."[56]

Another detour through the history of the mixed constitution might help detect the meaning of Lefort's interpretation. While the concept of the mixed constitution was repeated by many major political thinkers up until the Enlightenment, it gradually fell out of fashion as theories of sovereignty were formulated by absolutist thinkers such as Jean Bodin and Thomas Hobbes in the sixteenth and seventeenth centuries. As absolutist sovereignty gave way to popular sovereignty, another device for the division of powers was developed, as every true republic needed to divide its power into three distinct branches of government – legislative, executive and judicial power.[57] As such, theories of sovereignty, both absolutist and popular, were directly developed against the mixed constitution.[58] For both Bodin and Hobbes, something like a mixed constitution was a logical abomination as well as a political problem, as logically there had to be one place in the polity that was sovereign, otherwise anarchy would emerge. Viewed against the theory of unitary sovereignty, the mixed constitution essentially entails another understanding of sovereignty, namely *pluralistic* sovereignty. In the model of unitary sovereignty, the foundation of new political regimes is the result of the constituent power by the unitary people in a legal state of nature. In the *interregnum* between two systems of legality, the People-as-One emerge with a revolutionary programme and a determinate constituent will. This is the classical notion of the constituent power from Emmanuel Sieyès to Carl Schmitt, which is firmly located within the revolutionary tradition of the French Revolution.

In the proposals of the Hungarian councils, Lefort detects a different model of sovereignty, which shifts the emphasis from monism and unity to pluralism and difference. Whereas the unitary model of sovereignty is intimately linked with the state, Lefort's pluralist model prioritises civil society.[59] As such, the proposals of the Hungarian councils do not evolve around how to constitute themselves as new organs of state power, but are instead occupied with creating a self-democratising civil society with a host of institutions, associations and groups. By radicalising already existing institutions, Lefort envisioned a pluralistic constituent power, which never found itself in a legal state of nature. The novelty of the proposals of the Hungarian councils were the recognition of a plurality of constituting actors and of their fundamental different interests. Hence, in a way, the crux of Lefort's analysis is that the councils argued for a reconstitution of the polity through already constituted powers, not through the mythical fiction of constituting people outside legality. As such, the Hungarian Revolution in Lefort's rendition is

> not then conceptualized so much in terms of the sovereign power of the people, but rather in terms of freedoms and autonomy of those who make up the people. The sovereign people disappeared, and was replaced by a strategy demanding pluralization and automatization of different forms of life."[60]

Lefort's analysis of the councils through the concepts of the mixed constitution and its pluralistic sovereignty has affinities with Arendt's analysis of the revolutionary tradition. Arendt's ambition is also to develop a different kind of constituent power than the unitary, homogeneous and external version of the French Revolution, and the reason why she draws from the American, federal tradition is also that civil society and already constituted institutions were prioritised over statism and constituent power in a legal void. But in a sense, Lefort's proposal of mixing councils, parties and unions is both less and more radical than Arendt's advocacy for the council system. Less radical, because Lefort's proposal – precisely due to its status as a mixed regime – involves less self-government than Arendt's council system. But more radical, insofar as the principle of self-government is coupled with the principle of difference and conflict. According to Lefort, the proposals of the Hungarian councils show how self-government can be combined with pluralism. In the Hungarian councils, Lefort sees

> a democratic will affirmed very deliberately according to two poles which could not, in effect, be disassociated without being annihilated: the pole of collective organization [i.e. self-management in the councils] … and the pole of social differentiation which presupposes the recognition of the specificity of the domain of politics, economic, law, pedagogy, science, aesthetics etc.[61]

The politics proposed by the councils was "not only owing to the mobilization and the near-fusion of collective energies, but also owing to a new experience and an authentic desire for difference."[62] This dynamic can be captured by Lefort's idea of a *plural revolution*, which is meant to differentiate the proposals of the Hungarian councils from the notion of the singular revolution in French tradition. A plural revolution takes place in many different parts of society at once, and changes parts of society according to different logics. The result of a plural revolution is societal differentiation through the rejection of one logic governing all spheres of society. The Hungarian Revolution

> is a *plural* revolution that passes through multiple locations; it grows in factories, in the university, in the cultural and informational sectors, it sees the proliferation of committees in local factories and of soviets, of various associations, political parties, and popular assemblies. This wild process resembles the experiences in the first quarter of the century [i.e. the formation workers' councils across Europe]. The forms of organization and the methods of struggle particular to the workers' movement are spontaneously "rediscovered".[63]

As such, different modalities of power are created, and opposing political institutions are established. The multi-party system, the democratically managed economy through the workers' councils and the trade unions co-exist due to the pluralistic nature of the Hungarian Revolution. In this way no *one* institution can claim to speak with the voice of the people, no organ can claim to embody the will of the popular sovereign.

Self-Limitation

Together with the mixed constitution, the notion of *self-limitation* provides an opportunity to understand how Lefort differentiates himself from the council tradition, and how the idea of democracy as an empty place influences his evaluation of the councils. The notion of self-limitation is a refusal to impose fundamentalist projects on the rest of society. Hence, the self-limiting revolution is a revolution against "the metaphysics of the Jacobin-Bolshevik type of revolutions,"[64] which seeks to appropriate state power through a violent break with the former regime and a totalising vision of the future. Paul Blokker mentions how the self-limiting revolution can be seen as a "third way" between "liberal constitutionalism" and "permanent, totalizing revolution."[65] In a similar vein, Arato argues that the differences between a self-limited and an unlimited revolution is "the survival of its spirit beyond institutionalization," that is, "how to save something of the spirit of revolutionary public freedom in settled constitutions."[66] In the classic discourse on the councils, the council system was precisely understood as a third way beyond parliamentarianism and communist one-party rule. Both Castoriadis and Arendt understood it as one of the primary ambitions of the councils to preserve the constituent power in some de-revolutionised form in constituted politics. By placing the council system between liberal constitutionalism and permanent revolution, between society as instituting and as instituted, they thought the councils could do just that. With the idea of self-limitation, Lefort shares the ambition of Castoriadis and Arendt of going beyond the opposition of liberal democracy and the Jacobin imaginary of revolution, but his insistence on self-limitation makes it a harder task than Castoriadis and Arendt perceive it. While Castoriadis and Arendt seek to make one logic govern society – autonomy for Castoriadis, action for Arendt, self-government for the council tradition in general – Lefort is determined to induce society with conflicting logics. Although Castoriadis and Arendt distance themselves from the unitary subject due to the federalism of their council systems, they want to eradicate the multiplicity of differential logics of power that any mixed regime incorporates. Even though their projects are anti-statist, Castoriadis and Arendt nonetheless want the council system to become a new, sovereign system of government.[67]

Hence, according to Arato, Lefort had learned "the Tocquevillian lesson" not "to impose the logic of democratic coordination on all spheres," because "it is this outcome that leads to the collapse of the forms of self-organization that in many cases were the major carriers of the revolutionary process: revolutionary societies, associations, clubs, councils, movements."[68] In this way, Lefort's self-limiting council system serves as a corrective to Arendt's essentially tragic understanding of political modernity. For Arendt, the tragedy of modernity is that public freedom seldom survives for longer periods of time, as even the council system hasn't been able to stabilise itself in the face of representative government and permanent revolution. The way to pause the tragic oscillation between constituent and constituted politics that characterises modernity for Arendt is, according to Lefort, to carry the conflicting and different demands, which exist in any moment of revolution, into constituted politics.[69] This is what self-limitation means. In other words, "preservation of heterogeneity has priority over the construction of a unified discourse framework" of a pure council democracy.[70] This is essentially where Lefort differs from the council tradition, and from Castoriadis and Arendt. For Lefort, it is crucial to uphold the historical situation of dual power, and hence to combine the strengths and limit the weaknesses of different forms of the democracy (parliamentary democracy and council democracy).[71] According to Arato, "paradoxically then the self-limitation of the actors of a self-organizing society allows the continuation of their social role and influence beyond the foundation of a new form of power."[72] As such, it is the self-limited nature of the revolutionary actors which makes the revolutionary energy survive in constituted politics. Only by limiting themselves can the temporary forces of revolution become permanent forces of democracy.

With this idea, Lefort reorients the discourse of the council system from political society to civil society, that is, from an ambition of combining civil society and the functions of the state into one unified political society to an ambition of upholding the divide between civil society and the state, albeit further democratising both. One of the basic analytical tropes in the council tradition – starting with Marx's description of the state as a parasite that draws out the energy of society, and hence needs to be replaced with the commune, over Castoriadis' equation of the state with bureaucratic domination and forces of heteronomy, to Arendt's understanding of state sovereignty as pre-political relations of domination and obedience – is the ambition to eradicate the division between state and society. In the liberal tradition, much criticised by the council tradition, politics was located in the state, while in civil society individuals could pursue economic interests, partake in voluntary associations and enjoy family life. For previous council thinkers, this divide masked the state's domination of society, whereas for liberals society was an uncoerced space of individual liberty and the state was inhabited solely by citizens with equal rights. By destroying the state and politicising society, council thinkers imagined the council system as an expression of a fully democratised society, and hence a society without domination. The main ambition was to overcome a separation of society into a distinctly *political* and *non-political* sphere, including a separation between rulers and ruled and representatives and represented, since these forms of separation enabled domination. Hence, previous council thinkers conceptualised the council system as unifying the dispersed functions, tasks and activities of liberal society into *one* unified and self-managing system.

Lefort's conceptualisation of self-limitation upholds the division between the state and civil society. Civil society, instead, is democratised through the workers' councils and the trade unions, but it is not reduced to a political society governed exclusively by the logic of self-management. In this way, we are back to Lefort's idea of democracy as an empty place. I argue that the reason why Lefort appraises the proposals of the Hungarian councils – and why he decisively changes his analysis from the one he provided in 1956 – is that they represent Lefort's formulation of democracy as an empty place. By upholding the difference between the state and civil society, by refusing to supersede conflict with one governing logic, by denying the unitary voice of the popular sovereign and the fundamentalist impulse of the Jacobin tradition, the councils, according to Lefort, seek to institute a society of competing logics, conflicting institutions and a heterogeneity of demands and interests. These characteristics are those of a regime which is founded upon what Lefort understands as emptiness. Consequently, I argue that discussions on how Lefort's empty place of power is to be understood, how it is produced and sustained, could fruitfully consult his council writings.

Lefort argues that the self-limiting proposals of the Hungarian councils form the basis of what he calls a "socialist democracy." According to Lefort, the mixing of different institutional forms testifies to the fact that society cannot be relieved of antagonism and conflict, and that every individual has a number of different interests. In order to understand the general import of Lefort's analysis beyond the context of the Hungarian rebellion against totalitarianism, the concepts of the mixed constitution and self-limitation show how Lefort wants to break conclusively with any tradition of democratic politics in the register of sovereignty, unity and homogeneity. A society which mixes councilist forms of democracy with parliamentarian forms of democracy is indeed a society in conflict with itself.

Conclusion

Lefort has been associated with both a liberal democratic project that cautions against the dangers of popular sovereignty, but also with a radical democratic project, which stresses the inherent hostility of democracy to institutionalisation. This confusion, I argue, is due to the level of abstraction with which Lefort discusses his master concept of democracy as an empty place. Because Lefort does not spell out how democracy's emptiness is produced, his thinking is open to multiple interpretations.

In Lefort's analysis of the councils, he argues that a mixed regime of councils, parties and unions constitutes the basis for a *socialist democracy*, which cannot be entirely subsumed under either a liberal or a radical conception of democracy. This mixed regime of socialist democracy is, on the one hand, according to Lefort, more democratic than liberal democracy, because of its democratisation of the economy through the councils as well as its flourishing civil society in which individuals can participate through unions and other voluntary associations. On the other hand, it is less politicised and more institutionalised than most versions of radical democracy. Consequently, I argue that Lefort's vision of the mixed regime of socialist democracy is a pertinent way to understand the possible institutional form of a society founded upon an empty place. For a society to be democratic in the Lefortian register, it is not enough that representation and elections divide the principle of democracy from its actualisation (the liberal interpretation) or that the democracy is hostile to every form of institutionalisation (the radical interpretation). Instead, different and conflicting logics should be established in institutionalised conflict. Socialist democracy as institutionalised conflict between councils, parties and unions runs counter to both the liberal and radical interpretations of Lefort. Contrary to the liberal interpretation of Lefort, which highlights democracy's emptiness as primarily a result of the mechanism of representation, Lefort's socialist democracy includes a much wider democratisation of society along with collective ownership and self-management of economic production through the councils. In opposition to the radical democratic reading of Lefort, which interprets democracy's emptiness as emerging through an inherent hostility towards institutionalisation, Lefort's socialist democracy reveals that it is the conflict *between* institutions, not the *absence* of them, which continually produces and secures democracy's empty place of power. Socialist democracy in Lefort's conceptualisation is hence an *institutionalised* ideal of democracy rather than an anti-institutional model. Reading Lefort through his writings on the council system thus sheds new light upon his democratic theory as it demonstrates the limitations of both of the dominant interpretations of his work. The liberal and radical readings of Lefort's theory of democracy fail to capture the important institutional and socialist dimensions of his preferred interpretation of a socialist democracy as a self-limiting and power-dispersing mixed regime of parties, unions and councils in institutionalised conflict.

Lefort's reinterpretation of the Hungarian Revolution also contributes new theoretical elements to the council tradition. Although he shares many of the ambitions of the other council thinkers, such as the desire for political institutions not to dominate the people and to democratise spheres of domination – and although he shares Castoriadis' and Arendt's ambitions of developing an alternative to revolution in the Jacobin tradition, as well as finding ways to de-revolutionise the constituent power and incorporate its revolutionary energy in settled constitutions – Lefort's proposals for doing this are remarkably different from other thinkers of the councils.

The difference resides in the idea of mixing conflicting modes of power into a divided whole. Whereas for most other thinkers of the councils, the historical situation of *dual power*, which has existed in every revolution involving council-like formations, is one to be transcended, hopefully with the councils' victory over the *Ancien Régime* and the party system. By advocating for a republic of councils, thinkers of the councils such as Marx, Castoriadis and Arendt argue for the sovereignty of the council system, and hence for the logic of self-government to pervade all spheres of society. Lefort's novel vision for the council system is the insight that its sovereign aspirations represent a potentially undemocratic force, as every sovereign political form, according to Lefort, envisions society as a totality, which can be governed according to one logic. The novelty of Lefort's interpretation is thus to appraise the situation of dual power, to stabilise and institutionalise it through the mixed regime of councils, parties and unions. The essence of Lefort's self-limited council system is the awareness that to stipulate the sovereignty of the council system is to partake in a political tradition which believes that conflict and division are temporary obstacles on the road to perfect autonomy and freedom. Hence, the Lefortian council system is one where self-government, societal conflict and pluralism are combined into a conglomerated polity through the plural revolution of society and its institutions.

Notes

1 Claude Lefort, "The Question of Democracy," in *Democracy and Political Theory*, 9–20.
2 Ibid., 17–18.
3 Ibid., 17.
4 Michael Scott Christofferson, *French Intellectuals Against the Left*.
5 Ernesto Laclau and Chantal Mouffe, *Hegemony and Socialist Strategy*; Jean-Luc Nancy and Philippe Lacoue-Labarthe, *Retreating the Political*; Miguel Abensour, *Democracy Against the State*.
6 Abensour, *Democracy Against the State*.
7 James Ingram, "The Politics of Claude Lefort's Political."
8 Claude Lefort, "La question de la revolution," 211.
9 See, for example, Sheldon Wolin, "Fugitive Democracy," in Seyla Benhabib (ed.), *Democracy and Difference*; Jacques Rancière, *Disagreement*.
10 Darrow Schecter, *Radical Theories*, 100–1; Richard Gombin, *The Origins of Modern Leftism*, 102–3.
11 Andrew Arato, "Lefort, the Philosopher of 1989," in Martin Plot (ed.), *Claude Lefort*, 116–17.
12 Bernard Flynn, *The Philosophy of Claude Lefort*.
13 Andrew Arato's brief remarks in ch. 8 of the volume are an exception; see "Lefort, the Philosopher of 1989."
14 Warren Breckman, *Adventures of the Symbolic*.
15 Samuel Moyn, "Marxism and Alterity," in *The Modernist Imagination*, 99–116.
16 Oliver Marchart, *Post-Foundational Political Thought*.
17 Raf Geenens, "Contingency *and* Universality?," 443–55.
18 Carlos Ancetti, "Claude Lefort," in Breaugh *et al.* (eds), *Thinking Radical Democracy*, 121–40.
19 Claude Lefort, "Interview with Lefort," 177.
20 Claude Lefort, "The Hungarian Insurrection," in *A Socialisme ou Barbarie Anthology*, 212.
21 Ibid., 209.
22 Ibid., 210.
23 Ibid., 209, italics added.
24 Ibid., italics in original.
25 Ibid., 213.
26 Ibid., 214.
27 Ibid., 223.
28 Ibid., 223, 222.
29 Ibid., 223, italics in original.
30 Claude Lefort, "The Image of the Body and Totalitarianism," in *The Political Forms of Modern Society*, 301; Lefort, "The Question of Democracy," 12.
31 Lefort, "The Question of Democracy," 11–12.
32 Claude Lefort, "The Permanence of the Theologico-Political?" in *Democracy and Political Theory*, 225; Flynn, *The Philosophy of Claude Lefort*, 131.
33 Ernst Kantorowicz, *The King's Two Bodies*, 46, italics in original.
34 Lefort, "The Image of the Body and Totalitarianism," 303.
35 Ibid., 303.

36 Lefort, "The Question of Democracy," 18.
37 Lefort, "The Image of the Body and Totalitarianism," 303–4.
38 Lefort, "The Question of Democracy," 12–13.
39 Ibid., 13.
40 Claude Lefort, "The Age of Novelty," 34.
41 Ibid., 34.
42 Ibid., 35.
43 Ibid., 34.
44 Ibid., 35.
45 Ibid.
46 Ibid.
47 Ibid.
48 Lefort, "La question de la revolution," 211. My translation.
49 Ibid., 211. My translation, italics added.
50 Arato, "Lefort, the Philosopher of 1989," 116.
51 Lefort, "The Age of Novelty," 35.
52 Ibid.
53 Ibid.
54 Mogens Herman Hansen, "The Mixed Constitution Versus the Separation of Powers," 522–3.
55 Philip Pettit, *On the People's Terms*, 220–5.
56 Andrew Arato, "Thinking the Present," 26.
57 Hansen, "The Mixed Constitution Versus the Separation of Powers," 510.
58 Pettit, *On the People's Terms*, 220–5.
59 See Paul Blokker, "Democracy through the Lens of 1989," 282–5, for similar arguments concerning the "velvet" revolutions of 1989.
60 Jiri Priban, *Dissidents of Law*, 44.
61 Lefort, "The Age of Novelty," 37.
62 Ibid., 38.
63 Lefort, "La question de la revolution," 211. My translation.
64 Blokker, "Democracy through the Lens of 1989," 10.
65 Ibid., 9.
66 Arato, "Thinking the Present," 30.
67 To some readers, the slightest connection between Castoriadis and Arendt and the concept of sovereignty would be highly objectionable. Arendt, for her part, argued that the concept of sovereignty was alien to the council system, and neither Castoriadis nor Arendt can be counted as monist thinkers due to their celebration of plurality and the federal nature of the council system. Nonetheless, both Castoriadis and Arendt argued that the council system could not exist alongside the party system and other similar political forms because they disclosed radically different political principles. Hence, they wanted to place the council system in a superior position in relation to other political forms (bureaucracy for Castoriadis; representation for Arendt), whereas Lefort wanted to institutionalise conflict between different institutional and political logics.
68 Arato, "Thinking the Present," 26.
69 Arendt could be interpreted as having the same ambition, but whereas Lefort seeks to uphold the situation of dual power in post-revolutionary times, Arendt sought to disperse constituent power between the councils, a Constitution

and a Supreme Court. See James Muldoon, "Arendt's Revolutionary Constitutionalism," 596–607.

70 Priban, *Dissidents of Law*, 50.

71 Arato, "The Democratic Theory of the Polish Opposition," 3–6.

72 Ibid., 26.

References

Abensour, Miguel. *Democracy against the State: Marx and the Machiavellian Moment*. Cambridge: Polity, 2011.

Ancetti, Carlos. "Claude Lefort: Democracy as the Empty Place of Power." In *Thinking Radical Democracy: The Return to Politics in Post-War France*. Edited by Martin Breaugh, Christopher Holman, Rachel Magnusson, Paul Mazzocchi and Devin Penner. 121–40. Toronto: Toronto University Press, 2015.

Arato, Andrew. "The Democratic Theory of the Polish Opposition: Normative Intentions and Strategic Ambiguities." *Kellogg Institute of International Studies*, Working Paper 15 (1984): 1–32.

———. "Lefort, the Philosopher of 1989." In Martin Plot (ed.), *Claude Lefort: Thinker of the Political*. 114–23. New York: Palgrave Macmillan, 2013.

———. "Thinking the Present: Revolution in Eastern Europe. Revolution, Civil Society and Democracy." *Praxis International* 10, no. 1/2 (1990): 25–38.

Blokker, Paul. "Democracy Through the Lens of 1989: Liberal Triumph or Radical Turn?" *International Journal of Politics, Culture, and Society* 22 (2009): 273–90.

Breckman, Warren. *Adventures of the Symbolic: Post-Marxism and Radical Democracy*. New York: Columbia University Press, 2013.

Christofferson, Michael Scott. *French Intellectuals against the Left: The Antitotalitarian Moment of the 1970s*. Oxford: Berghahn Books, 2004.

Flynn, Bernard. *The Philosophy of Claude Lefort*. Chicago, IL: Northwestern University Press, 2005.

Geenens, Raf. "Contingency *and* Universality? Lefort's Ambiguous Justification of Democracy." *Research in Phenomenology* 37 (2007): 443–55.

Gombin, Richard. *The Origins of Modern Leftism*. Harmondsworth: Pelican Books, 1975.

Hansen, Mogens Herman. "The Mixed Constitution Versus the Separation of Powers." *History of Political Thought* 31, no. 3 (2010): 509–31.

Ingram, James. "The Politics of Claude Lefort's Political: Between Liberalism and Radical Democracy." *Thesis Eleven* 87 (2006): 33–50.

Kantorowicz, Ernst. *The King's Two Bodies: A Study in Medieval Political Thought*. Princeton, NJ: Princeton University Press, 1957.

Laclau, Ernesto and Chantal Mouffe. *Hegemony and Socialist Strategy*. London: Verso, 1985.

Lefort, Claude. "The Age of Novelty." *Telos* 29 (1976a): 23–38.

———. "The Hungarian Insurrection." In *A Socialisme ou Barbarie Anthology: Autonomy, Critique, and Revolution in the Age of Bureaucratic Capitalism*. 201–23. Accessed at http://notbored.org/SouBA.pdf.

———. "The Image of the Body and Totalitarianism." In *The Political Forms of Modern Society*. 292–306. Cambridge, MA: The MIT Press, 1986.

———. "Interview with Lefort." *Anti-Mythes* 14 (1975): 173–92.

———. "The Permanence of the Theologico-Political?" In *Democracy and Political Theory*. 213–55. Cambridge: Polity Press, 1988b.

———. "La question de la revolution." *Esprit* 460, no. 9 (1976b): 206–12.

———. "The Question of Democracy" In *Democracy and Political Theory*. 9–20. Cambridge: Polity Press, 1988a.

Marchart, Oliver. *Post-Foundational Political Thought: Political Difference in Nancy, Lefort, Badiou and Laclau*. Edinburgh: Edinburgh University Press, 2007.

Moyn, Samuel. "Marxism and Alterity: Claude Lefort and the Critique of Totality." In *The Modernist Imagination*. 99–116. Oxford: Berghahn Books, 2009.

Muldoon, James. "Arendt's Revolutionary Constitutionalism: Between Constituent Power and Constitutional Form." *Constellations* 23, no. 4 (2016): 596–607.

Nancy, Jean-Luc and Philippe Lacoue-Labarthe. *Retreating the Political*. London: Routledge, 1997.

Pettit, Philip. *On the People's Terms: A Republican Theory and Model of Democracy*. Cambridge: Cambridge University Press, 2012.

Priban, Jiri. *Dissidents of Law*. Farnham: Ashgate, 2002.

Rancière, Jacques. *Disagreement: Politics and Philosophy*. Minneapolis: University of Minnesota Press, 2004.

Schecter, Darrow. *Radical Theories: Paths Beyond Marxism and Social Democracy*. Manchester: Manchester University Press, 1994.

Wolin, Sheldon. "Fugitive Democracy." In *Democracy and Difference: Contesting the Boundaries of the Political*. Edited by Seyla Benhabib. 31–45. Princeton, NJ: Princeton University Press, 1996.

Part IV

Beyond the Councils

10 After the Councils

Opposing Domination and Developing Democratic Agency

John Medearis

Introduction

For much of the history of what we now call – by means of a retrospective artifice – "democratic theory," it seemed clear that democracy should be conceptualised in integral connection with historically evolving structures of inequality and power in the economy. It was widely recognised that the rise of democracy as a movement, an ideology and a political arrangement was rooted in these changing institutions and forces, and that the political economy was a significant part of democracy's indigenous habitat. Figures from Aristotle to Joseph Schumpeter viewed markets, firms and workplaces as integral topics under the broad subject matter of democracy. Yet much democratic theory in the last 30 years has emphasised "modes" of democratic activity, rather than exploring the "sectors" of social life, such as the economy, that might fruitfully be democratised.[1] Deliberative democratic theory, for example, has had little to say about the idea that the political economy and its characteristic institutions might or should be democratised. Instead, the emphasis has been on elucidating deliberation as a mode of democratic activity – or more recently, on how deliberative politics might be achieved even through many un-deliberative practices. And agonistic democratic theory has similarly focused more on a distinct view of what it means to act or think democratically and less on what sectors of social life are ripe for democratisation.

From the standpoint of these more recent approaches to democratic theory, generally subordinating consideration of the "sectors" of democratic activity to consideration of "modes" of democratic practice, it would be quite difficult to grasp the significance of the council era in Central Europe at the end of the First World War. One can hardly begin to say what the councils were and what they intended without naming the particular social locations in which the spontaneously elected committees sprang up: especially military barracks and factories. And, in any case, it would not be possible to identify the council movement with just one "mode" of action. For what the soldiers' councils, factory councils and local workers' and soldiers' councils did, the practices in which they engaged, varied as much as the places in which they did it. They debated the political issues of the time, issued demands and petitioned existing governments and politicians, but they also took over the management of idled factories and of practical local efforts, such as dealing with food shortages and other dislocating effects of the war's end.

In this chapter, I take up the tradition that, in general, views the "sectors" of potential democratic activity as crucial and that, particularly, is concerned with economic democracy. And, drawing on the council era, I reflect especially on the legacy of *factory* or *works* councils and the expectations some of their participants – and some of their observers – had for them and for their possible effects on the structure of the broader political economy. I aim to place those expectations in historical context – not by delving deeply and exclusively into the post-war setting, or staying within its horizons, but rather by calling attention to the significant ways that our contemporary political economy seems to differ from that of the early twentieth century. I am interested, finally, in the significant question: what might the future of economic democracy be, and more broadly, what are the issues we should be focused upon if we are to arrive at an integral and compelling answer to this question?

My assessment of developments in the modern political economy long after the council era points to the conclusion that one of the core institutional innovations of the time, factory councils – and more broadly, the goal of democratising the political economy by democratising factories or workplaces – may not be a sufficient response to the challenges today's economic structures and forces pose to democratic life.

The best way to understand the reasons for this is to return to the programme of council democracy, which included, among other strategies and goals: the establishment of factory councils, intended to democratise the political economy by democratising individual workplaces or firms; opposing domination by taking the democratic battle to those sites at which the power resided to change politics, society and the economy; and developing the democratic agency of ordinary people. As long as the factory, individual workplace or firm remained a crucial nexus of power in the political economy, these three elements of the council programme harmonised well. Democratising individual workplaces could clearly help workers exercise and develop their agency, while it also took the democratic struggle to agents with considerable power – to institutional sites whose restructuring would have repercussions across the entire political economy. But developments in the last few decades have challenged the centrality of the individual workplace for many sectors of the political economy, making many workplaces or enterprises far less viable targets for democratisation. Democratising individual workplaces, while a tested way of building democratic institutions that can foster the agency of ordinary workers, is no longer a sure way to challenge today's domination.

And this is not just an inference on my part from political economic developments – though I shall try to delineate the basis for such an inference. It is also a conclusion supported by a reading of a contemporary debate about democracy and the future of the labour movement. On one side of this debate are advocates of strategies for countering or opposing contemporary forms of domination in the economy, strategies that quite clearly neglect promoting the democratic agency of workers themselves. On the other side are advocates of a renewed push to organise workers at the enterprise level. These approaches emphasise nurturing the democratic agency of workers, but fail to account for structural changes in the political economy of employment. The way these two sides talk past each other is a symptom, I contend, of the decline of the individual workplace or enterprise as a nexus of power.

Recognition of the failings of this contemporary debate – and the root cause of these failings – point to the need to find new strategies, practices and programmes for democratising the political economy that can at once develop the agency of workers, and counter today's forms of domination.

In the next section of this chapter, I quickly review the essentials of the council era in Central Europe, then draw from the councils' doings and their historical context some basic characteristics and aims which I sum up as the council democratic programme. Beyond the institutional innovation of councils themselves, some of the most important of these aims or principles include: opposing domination, and building the democratic agency of ordinary people. After reviewing these aims and practices of the councils, I raise an important question: What historical and structural conditions made it possible for this programme to cohere with or take shape in the specific institutional mechanism of the factory or works council – both in the minds of some council participants and of some later interpreters? The answer, I contend, is that the factory, the large individual productive work site, occupied a crucial position in the political economy that it had not before the Industrial Revolution was well under way.

An exploration of the political economy of the machine age points to a sequel subject for the next section: an analytical review of developments in late capitalism, and the effects they have had on the structures of work and employment since the 1980s, making the individual workplace less central, putting distance between those with power and resources in the political economy and the sites where much work takes place, attenuating the employment relation, and making employment less certain and secure.

These developments set the stage for critically analysing, in the following section, a recent debate about democracy and the labour movement, one roughly between advocates of "new labour" or "alt-labour" strategies that are less centred on fighting for democratic representation in individual workplaces, and those who call for a redoubling of such traditional stratagems. The debate is not focused specifically on councils, of course, but its stakes include democratic aims familiar to the councils, especially challenging institutions and forces that dominate ordinary people and allowing such people to exercise, experience and develop their democratic agency. In many precincts of the present political economy, I argue, these aims are today in some practical tension with each other, with the some of the most effective strategies that have been proposed for responding to contemporary forms of domination seeming to require the sacrifice of the most familiar strategies for allowing workers to become more effective democratic agents – and vice versa. I bring the chapter to a close with a critical review of strategies and approaches for democratising the political economy, exploring the degree to which they meet two of the most important criteria established by the council era: both opposing domination and enhancing the democratic agency of ordinary people.

The Councils, Economic Democracy and the Political Economy of the Machine Age

One of the most striking features of the council era was diversity – diversity, especially, in where the councils arose and, relatedly, what they did. Councils were elected or deployed in factories, barracks and city halls. They took part in the creation of political institutions that replaced the old regime; guided the direction of factories and of local governments; and formulated democratic political programmes, such as the Hamburg Points.

Yet this diversity should not hide the fact that during the entire council era there was a recurrent focus on the factory itself as a source or nexus of power and an institution requiring democratisation. This was perhaps clearest in Russia, where factory committees in 1905 and 1917 tried to achieve workers' control, calling for the dismissal of certain managers and making demands of management, but rarely attempting to seize enterprises outright.[2] But the emphasis on the factory as source and object of power was not limited to Russia. In Central Europe, workers' councils were most often elected from factories. And months after the Armistice, many German workers, once they believed the course had been set for a thorough post-war democratisation of the state, turned their attention back "to struggles in the workplace," which they pursued locally, in part through strikes and other work stoppages.[3] In 1919 in the Ruhr region, workers in the mines organising strikes and other actions pushed local workers' and soldiers' councils, especially the one in Essen, towards plans for a rapid socialisation, whose institutional form would have been based on mine councils.[4] And railway workers in Frankfurt formed a council that claimed and won a right to participate in the management of the regional railway.[5]

I set out to draw lessons from the council era, but not by describing the movement and its aims straight away in the most abstract terms possible, such as freedom or equality, with the thought that such concepts, if sufficiently stripped of concrete detail, are universally applicable. My approach instead is to consider how the characteristic practices of the movement were both reflections of its motivating ideals and responses to the political and economic structures and forces of its time. Drawing out, in this way, all the basic democratic characteristics and aims of the council movement, as comprehensively as possible, helps us distinguish the more important and less important expressions of the council movement, the deeper and more enduring commitments from ones that responded to what we can now see were changeable features of the political economy. This is an indispensable preliminary step towards considering how similar aims might be shaped today, when the structures and forces we face are different.

It is simplest to begin by reflecting on: (a) the council form, and the formation of councils. Participants in the movement began to act primarily by electing representatives to committees, bodies that were to meet regularly for a period of time to debate, advise and decide about a range of matters. What sort of matters they were to take up had much to do with where they were elected or were to meet. In factories, councils sought sometimes to oust managers and sometimes to redirect management decisions. Workers' and soldiers' councils, though elected *from* factories and barracks, were generally elected *to* the local city hall, where they sometimes sought to replace and sometimes only to supervise the local civil servants of the old regime.

In either case, there was clearly a sense that these particular locations required a reconfiguring that the councils could accomplish. And the means by which the councils were created – democratic election – clearly signified the sort of reshaping the movement had in mind: democratic reshaping. The councils were generally quite conscious of this second, fundamental aim of the movement: (b) democratisation. Elizabeth Tobin argues that the "minimal program common to nearly every council was 'democratization' of the government, economy, society, and military."[6] And Eberhard Kolb similarly interprets the Hamburg Points, adopted by the Congress of Workers' and Soldiers' Councils, as articulating a programme of " 'democratisation' of the army (especially), the civil service and the economy."[7]

The type of democratisation that is most significant for this chapter is economic democratisation, and more particularly: (c) the factory council as a specific, local strategy for achieving economic democratisation. As we have seen, the Ruhr miners favoured the establishment of mine councils, which they saw as an institutional prerequisite for democratising and socialising the mining industry. And in fact many interpreters of the council movement, both sympathetic and hostile, also assumed that democratising every plant or workplace through the establishment of councils was both central to the meaning and purpose of the council movement and a crucial mechanism for socialising the mining industry. This was certainly the view of Otto Bauer, the Austrian Social Democrat.[8] Indeed, Bauer believed worker self-organisation at the factory level to be so central to the council movement's aims and practices that he felt it necessary to sketch out how democratisation in the factory should be integrated into a system that also guaranteed democratic participation and representation by peasants and consumers. And Joseph Schumpeter, though he thought conditions were not yet ripe for socialism, followed Bauer in emphasising councils as already engaged precisely in transforming the political economy by transforming the factory. Just as the historical process of political democratisation had focused on the state, he thought, the process of economic democratisation would focus on the factory.[9] It is crucial to emphasise that the aim of democratising the economy by democratising firms and workplaces also connects the council movement and its interpreters to a long, rich tradition of workplace and economic democracy, a point to which I shall return.

A theme that underlies council efforts in the factory and elsewhere, recognition of which can deepen our sense of what democratisation meant to the council movement, is (d): the attention the movement devoted not simply to institutions that were undemocratic, but to social structures and forces characterised by domination – ones that, especially in the war years, clearly had come deeply to overshadow the agency of ordinary people and to impose necessities on them.[10] The military, the state apparatus and the industrial economy of Central Europe all shared this characteristic, and in overlapping ways. (As hierarchical and undemocratic as the factory had always been, it became more so under the conditions of wartime production.) Domination in these interconnected social spheres helps explain why the council movement focused its attention on barracks, local governments and factories.

And this leads us to another theme – already mentioned but not yet separately and distinctly highlighted: (e) the council movement sought to *transform* these structures, democratically. Or, to put this differently, it saw democracy as transformative. This is especially important in the case of transforming the political economy, because it highlights the fact that participants in the council movement favoured *democratic* socialism, and that this meant for them a form of socialism with specific democratic mechanisms and features, including the democratised factory or workplace. The emphasis on democratic transformation differentiates the council movement from later mainstream approaches to democratic theory that overlook the radical implications of introducing democratic practices where they do not already exist. And it distinguishes the movement's participants, as well, from socialists who favoured or entertained undemocratic means to revolutionise the political economy.

The rather direct way in which participants in the movement, by electing councils, took on for themselves new, challenging and essential tasks points to another characteristic aim of the movement: (f) the attempt to develop and sustain the democratic agency of ordinary people. This may only have been an implicit theme of the many formal statements of councils across Central Europe. But those statements themselves are a clear demonstration that people who had been political bystanders or subordinates had taken the stage as actors. And at least some interpreters and interlocutors of the movement remarked on this explicitly. Bauer, for example, insisted on seeing councils as "a potent agency for the self-education of the masses" that could widen their horizons.[11]

A final democratic characteristic of the council era – one already implicit and implied in the last few sentences, but still in need of articulation – is (g) the oppositional stance of the councils. Clearly enough, the democratic practices and institutions the councils introduced were intended to counteract the domination ordinary Central Europeans experienced in the economy, as political subjects and as soldiers and other participants in war. The oppositional stance of the councils is also indicated by the fact that the councils generally did not attempt fully to supplant parliamentary democratic institutions. Instead, they sought to work alongside these other institutions and forge a popular democratic practice of continual opposition to undemocratic power.

I think it is fair to understand these democratic characteristics and aims of the council movement as representing, together, a set of democratic principles: the programme of council democracy.[12] Viewed together, the principles were obviously somewhat heterogeneous, with some referring primarily to what the movement hoped to accomplish, some to how they hoped to accomplish it, and some to how they understood their activities in relation to the economic and political context of the time. And so it is useful to ask: how did they fit together – and more specifically, what made it possible for at least some council participants and interpreters to view the creation of factory councils, in particular, as a way to democratise the political economy, to challenge effectively the domination workers experienced, to become effective political agents? And what made the factory – the individual workplace or employer – appear to them to be a particularly significant site of potential democratisation?

In brief, the answer is that in the political economy of the time, individual factories were in fact crucial, nodal sites both for production and for the relationship between labour and capital. The development of the factory system took place over many decades, beginning in the earliest phase of the Industrial Revolution. At the outset of the process, the putting-out system still dominated; production was dispersed among many small workshops and households, and merchants, rather than artisans, were the key agents who owned the materials and co-ordinated the movement of finished and unfinished goods.[13] But by the late nineteenth century, the scene in many parts of Europe and America was dominated by the factory system, in which the manufacturer owned the materials and tools and controlled labour processes. The factory system embraced both large, integrated manufacturing corporations, on the one hand, and smaller, single plants, on the other.[14] And it is worth noting that whatever advantages the factory system may have had for capital, factory production also enabled effective organisation of workers with similar interests, and placed near at hand to them a nexus of power, the management of which was worth contesting.

The decades-long position of the individual workplace or firm as a crucial nexus, a centre of power in the political economy, surely helps explain why it is that workplace democracy has been such a prominent theme in the history of democratic theory. Theorists from John Stuart Mill to Carole Pateman and Robert Dahl have offered two types of justifications for workplace democracy: ones holding that by right, the firm, like any authority structure, should be democratised, and ones arguing that democratising the institutions in which people live their daily lives will make them more effective democratic agents more broadly.[15] It is not too much to say that for many such thinkers, democratising the political economy has been almost synonymous with democratising workplaces or firms. And while firm-level collective bargaining is often seen as only a pale approximation of full workplace democracy, proponents of collective bargaining have shared this view connecting democratic practices in the workplace to the democratisation of the whole political economy. If changes in the structure of the political economy now mean that democratising workplaces, however valuable an achievement, might still leave the goal of a truly democratic political economy unaddressed, this is a significant fact.

Employment and the Changing Political Economy of the Late Twentieth and Early Twenty-First Centuries

It is not difficult to list the most important developments of the last three to four decades for labour, democracy and the political economy. Many observers could agree on the following: an intensification of globalisation, measured in greater international flows of goods, capital and people; a second facet of globalisation, the development of truly worldwide production and supply chains, with much manufacturing moving to regions with lower labour costs; the growing size and reach of the internet and digital economies; weakening government regulation of labour and the environment; increased hostility to organised labour, both from employers and from the political right; the related rise of neoliberal ideology; the weakening of the labour movement; and increasing economic inequality. The question at hand, though, is how these different trends relate to each other – and how some of them are linked to significant changes in workplaces and in relations of employment. In what follows, I shall focus, first, on two types of technological changes that have led, next, to three types of transformations in the political economy of work.

The first type of technological change includes developments that have made it much cheaper to move goods and capital around the world, and so at the same time to divide up production processes and disperse them regionally or globally. This set of changes includes the transformation in shipping brought about by "intermodal containers," the ubiquitous, large, standard-size metal shipping boxes that can be transferred readily from truck to ship to train – and parallel developments in computing and telecommunications that simultaneously made it less expensive to move both goods and capital.[16] These are the developments, jointly, that have made today's long global supply chains possible, although this is not their only significance.

A second crucial set of technological changes, especially in computerised design and manufacture, have changed the face of production in a different way, making it less stable, more competitive, and taking away many of the advantages once enjoyed by large, oligopolistic manufacturers.[17] Such developments have not, of course, done away with factories. But they have contributed to a restructuring of the economic and technological ecosystem factories inhabit, a process that in some ways reverses the much earlier changes that tended to concentrate complex production processes in single factories and in integrated firms.

These technological changes have put greater pressure on businesses everywhere to cut labour costs drastically and to maximise benefits to shareholders – while enabling businesses to respond to these cost and profit pressures by moving production processes and making use of cheaper and more remote labour. Another broad effect of these technological changes has been simply the shifting of much manufacturing away from developed countries such as the United States – leaving behind fewer employers that might have fit the old model of factory production.

The cost and profit pressures, in turn, have also triggered a whole series of momentous changes in the structure of employment. A first set of resulting developments in the political economy of work has been a distancing or disassociation of the firms and agents that allocate capital and make decisions affecting the structure of industries from the workplace level, where labour is directed and individuals are hired and fired. The most obvious example of this is subcontracting, in which a firm allocates work or processes once performed internally to another firm entirely.[18] Businesses have begun ever more frequently to subcontract even core tasks and processes – in order to reduce costs, or to insulate themselves from some of the responsibilities, liabilities and risks of direct employment. The result is that an increasing proportion of workers are employed directly by firms that have limited resources and less ability to make strategic decisions, firms that face severe cost pressures – along with incentives to offer low pay, minimal benefits and little job security.[19]

"Temporary" work is at least in part a particular extension of the subcontracting model.[20] From a limited mechanism for filling short-term vacancies, "temporary" work has grown into something far more pervasive and quite different. ("Temps" now constitute as much as 5 per cent of the US workforce.) Regardless of who employs a temporary worker, the practice shifts many of the risks of commerce and manufacturing from firms to workers. And the large subset of temps who actually work for temporary agencies face, as well, a situation similar to that of workers who are employed by a subcontractor – a division between themselves and the firm or agents that really control relevant business decisions.

The growth of employment by franchisees, especially in the service economy, presents a picture similar to subcontracting and temporary work. The franchisers, often large corporations such as McDonalds, determine many aspects of the business of small franchisees, such as recipes, operating procedures and marketing – but are institutionally separate from them, and they avoid most of the risks of employment that franchisees must take on. At the same time, franchisers' fees and their control over many aspects of business force franchisees to focus on cutting labour costs.[21] As a result, workers again face direct employers – many thousands of them across the economy – with limited ability to improve pay, benefits and working conditions.

The rise of "platform" firms such as Uber and Task Rabbit presents a second broad type of structural challenge. Such businesses argue that they are just technology firms, not transportation or service companies at all. Their web "platforms," they say, simply allow drivers and personal assistants, working as independent contractors, to connect with customers. New software, communications and data-analysis technologies have allowed the very firms that make the decisions that structure the platform economy, that have access to financial markets and that amass vast revenues from platform workers, simultaneously to insulate themselves from the risks and responsibilities of employment. This is the crux of the problem for platform workers. Uber drivers, for example, are legally self-employed, even though they are arguably an "underclass of sorts" that is quite "subject to the company's whims."[22] Reclassification of drivers as employees would bring them under the protection of labour law, including collective bargaining law – but could cost Uber $4 billion per year, according to one estimate.[23] So well before any unionisation effort could begin, a legal transformation would be required that the company is highly motivated to resist with all its means.

A third set of developments in the contemporary political economy has undermined and attenuated the relationship between buyer and seller of labour, making employment less secure and workers more isolated. These developments include freelancing and technology-aided work-scheduling practices that make workers' hours volatile and uncertain.[24] Even where they have not been walled off institutionally from resources and strategic decision-making – as those who work for franchisees, temp agencies and subcontractors have been – workers subject to these practices find that their relationship to an employer is no longer a reliable, predictable, long-term one.

Alongside and intertwined with all the changes discussed so far, the political economy of work has also been affected by ideological and political developments. The relevant movement is most often summed up under the heading of the rise of neoliberal ideology, or just neoliberalism.[25] On the one hand, neoliberal ideology has promoted a variety of policies, most especially different forms of deregulation, that could facilitate and hasten the technological changes just described. On the other hand, precisely those economic interests that would benefit from globalisation – "those in competitive and technologically advanced industries" – were the ones that "fought for liberalization and economic integration" – that is, for neoliberal policies.[26] And neoliberal ideology is the language in which the increasingly hostile attitude of business towards labour is most often expressed.

In common, all these changes in the contemporary political economy have made the individual employer, the individual workplace, a much less viable target for democratic transformation. Democratising a subcontractor has far less value for workers if that firm itself occupies a relatively weak and dependent position in the new political economy – if it is not in a position to change its practices and strategies in response to the demands of workers. And democratising a thousand hard-pressed franchisees spread across a region or nation is often far more challenging than targeting a single larger business once was. Moreover, in the era of neoliberal ideology, any such moves towards democratisation are aggressively resisted by business. And to the degree that democratising individual firms becomes a less viable strategy, tensions between the principles of council democracy – of which democratising individual workplaces was just one – become more apparent.

The Alt-Labour Debate and Contemporary Tensions between the Principles of Council Democracy

The profound changes to the political economy of work that I have just described provide a key to help make sense of a contemporary debate between engaged intellectuals about the future of democracy and the labour movement. And assessing the debate alongside the democratic programme of the councils clarifies what is at issue between the disputants. The debate pits proponents of fundamental change in the strategies, practices and goals of the labour movement – advocates of a range of ideas variously grouped under the headings of "alt" or "new" labour – against proponents of a renewed commitment to a model of organising associated with twentieth-century industrial unionism. Clearly the debate is not explicitly about councils or the council movement, but one evident stake is the goal that motivated factory councils: democratising the political economy by democratising workplaces. Also at issue are strategies for countering contemporary forms of domination in the economy, and for developing the democratic agency of workers and other ordinary people. The debate makes clear that these three practices and aims of council democracy no longer harmonise easily. Since the workplace is not as pivotal in many crucial sectors of the political economy as it once was, it is no longer clear that democratising the workplace will serve both effectively to counteract contemporary forms of economic domination and to develop the agency of workers.

And so the contemporary debate offers a distressing contrast. One side is deeply concerned with understanding the new political economy and the forms of domination characteristic of it – and devising new strategies to respond to such domination – but seemingly indifferent, even hostile, to developing the agency of workers, and disdainful of organising focused on individual workplaces. The other side is acutely focused on developing the agency of workers – especially by organising the workplaces that are ripe for such attention – but it sidesteps sober analysis of changes in the political economy of work and of the new forms of domination associated with those changes.

Proponents of the newer strategies – whose most visible current spokesperson is David Rolf – emphasise structural changes in the political economy of work, along with growing anti-labour intransigence of business and its political allies. They attempt to respond to economic domination as many workers, such as those in the fast food industry and the platform economy, now experience it, a condition epitomised, Rolf notes, by "an often tenuous connection to a subcontractor, a temp agency, an erratically scheduled part-time job, a contract, or a gig."[27] They are closely attuned, that is, to contemporary social structures and forces that overwhelm workers' capacities to act and that impose dire necessities on them. But they argue that in a political economy characterised by subcontracting, franchising, global supply chains and platform technologies, dominating forces are not all centred in workers' direct employers. So instead of building on the effort and power of workers themselves in their daily work habitats, the new strategies depend heavily on professional staffs of highly skilled researchers to analyse how industries are structured and how they work, so it is possible to identify firms and other actors – usually not direct employers – with the capacity to improve the lot of workers, as well as to locate political pressure points to encourage them to do so. The real focus of such efforts may be on passing legislation, or on a "corporate" publicity campaign to embarrass a business. Such strategies themselves may often involve workers only for hearings and press conferences. Frequently cited and undeniably inventive efforts on behalf of airport workers in Seattle and fast food workers in the United States and Europe fit this description.[28] Some proponents of these strategies explicitly advocate redirecting efforts away from "enterprise-based collective bargaining" – a practice that, for all its faults, engages workers democratically, at least some to extent, right where they are – with no clear plan to build or cultivate new democratic, participatory structures of labour to replace it. Such workplace- or firm-level bargaining, in Rolf's view, is now "inherently weak" and strategies to revive it are "unlikely to prevail in the 21st century."[29] Indeed, at least some proponents of these newer labour strategies think promoting bottom-up union democracy can only come at the cost of forsaking the anti-domination strategies they favour. In part, this is based on research that shows that the unions that have tried to organise new groups of workers in recent decades often have done so when locals were run in a top-down fashion.[30] In the view of Rolf and some other proponents of these newer strategies, union democracy hampers "unions' ability to re-allocate resources, from serving their existing members, to organizing new ones."[31] Such writers seem to believe that democratising the political economy of work can refer only to establishing democratic procedures within unions – and these they associate with lethargy and self-centredness, and so an inability to meet current challenges of domination.

Contemporary proponents of traditional labour organising centre their arguments precisely on a critique of these "new" or "alt" labour arguments. Jane McAlevey, perhaps the best-known advocate of the traditionalist approach, effectively recovers two elements of the council democratic programme: an emphasis on introducing democratic practices – in this case, collective bargaining – into individual workplaces, and doing so through campaigns that emphasise developing the democratic agency of workers. She favours relying on "large numbers of people whose power is derived from their ability to withdraw labour or other cooperation from those who rely on them" as well as developing the skills of "organic leaders" found among ordinary people.[32] The approach focuses on the "agency" of workers themselves, she argues – especially their ability to exercise this agency within a specific "structure," the workplace.[33] She contends that her favoured approach, which she readily agrees derives from the industrial unionism of the early and middle twentieth century, can work in industries still characterised, for varying reasons, by relatively immobile capital, production, activity or jobs.

But McAlevey's argument is formulated in two ways to sidestep analysis of the changing character of domination in the contemporary economy, and the strategies needed to respond to that change. First, she limits the scope of her argument to sectors of the economy that have not undergone the kinds of profound change Rolf emphasises. Labour organising of the kind she favours should focus, she says, on workers in health and education, because in these sectors "there can be no exit threat" by employers, no danger that they will move in search of cheaper or more pliable labour. In this way, she at once acknowledges one aspect of structural change in the political economy – capital mobility made possible by technological changes – while at the same time she declines to address what might make it possible to organise workers actually affected by this and related developments. McAlevey also circumvents direct consideration of important changes in the political economy of labour and the character of economic domination by attributing the weakness of the contemporary labour movement chiefly to insidious ideological developments and unprincipled strategic decisions by the labour movement.

This debate is not simply about whether to organise at the workplace or some higher, broader level. Were that the only issue, the simple and obvious answer would be: both. Instead, the debate reflects a practical tension between strategies that target individual workplaces and employers – attempting to transform the political economy through transforming these individual sites – and strategies that attempt to counteract domination by targeting new and different nexuses of power, businesses or entities that are not necessarily direct employers at all. It is between organising workers largely to engage in or threaten job actions in their workplaces and bringing political, commercial or publicity pressures to bear on actors in quite different locales. It is between relying upon and helping to develop the agency of workers, on the one hand, and heavy use of experts, researchers, professional campaign staff and lobbyists, on the other.

The debate over the future of the labour movement and economic democracy in America is characterised by a contemporary fracturing of the old council democratic programme. And while there are weaknesses in the arguments on each side, arguments embracing just part of council democracy, it is not, in the end, these errors that are most revealing for us. For what makes these particular oversights meaningful – what produces tension between elements of the old council democratic programme and sets the stage for these errors – is profound changes in the political economy of labour in recent decades.

New Approaches to Workplace Democracy

Missing from the contemporary debate is a commitment to realising the programme and principles of council democracy as comprehensively as possible, even in an era when the individual workplace is losing the crucial position it once held in the political economy. Yet the council movement had good reason to value both the nurturing of democratic agency on the part of ordinary participants in the economy, and effective strategies for countering domination as it exists at any time. It is not, I think, for scholars of democratic theory to invent new programmes and courses of action for others to enact. But it is feasible and appropriate critically to evaluate some of the strategies, practices and institutional mechanisms that are most widely discussed in terms of their ability both to resist contemporary economic domination and to nurture democratic agency.

One of the most ambitious goals Rolf has proposed is sectoral collective bargaining – bargaining covering an entire industry, nationwide. If achieved, a legal system enacting sectoral bargaining could address new forms of domination not centred in individual workplaces, because it could leverage the power of the state to force changes in the practices of those agents who have the capacity and resources to improve conditions of employment. But even though sectoral bargaining, where it exists in Europe, usually exists alongside mechanisms for participation of workers in unions or works councils, it does not always in itself foster wide worker participation and the resulting development of worker agency. After all, the bargaining of terms for one industry in one country necessarily plays out at a considerable distance from ordinary workers. The experience of France is highly suggestive. There, collective bargaining agreements cover 98 per cent of workers, but only 8 per cent of workers are members of unions.[34] For those not in unions, collective bargaining terms are merely imposed from above. So even in countries that have already achieved sectoral bargaining, something more is apparently needed to encourage democratic agency. Perhaps an even more poignant problem is that it is precisely in the many countries that do not have sectoral bargaining – including the United States, the United Kingdom, Japan, Mexico, Poland, Malaysia and many others – that labour movements are weakest, hardly in a position to bring about such a consequential reform.[35] That is not to say the goal should be written off. But it is well to keep in mind that the programme of council democracy, in total, embraced not just a set of distant ideals but an integrated set of goals and closely related means for achieving them. The question, from this perspective, is not whether sectoral bargaining would be an improvement, but rather: What is the democratic programme or strategy that involves workers actively in a campaign to achieve sectoral or national bargaining?

Much easier to bring about would be a widespread system of voluntary worker associations that could enforce labour standards. Such associations are or would be chiefly for workers in industries like fast food whose structures make them almost impervious to unionisation.[36] And in many places, they would likely support many immigrant workers, and many who are not yet fluent in the dominant language where they live. Dozens of such associations already exist. They educate workers about their rights, help them take legal action to recover unpaid wages and connect them to services. They have demonstrated "great skill at creative means of recruitment, leadership development, and democratic participation," according to one interpreter, but they are still small relative to the population they could serve, they have mostly succeeded where they could spur policy changes by sympathetic elected officials and they "have not obviated the need for massive unionization of low-wage immigrant workers."[37] Again, for our purposes the same criteria – the same principles of council democracy – should apply to these efforts. Such associations do seem oriented towards developing the democratic agency of those they reach. But on their own they do not yet seem to represent a formula for mounting potent challenges to current forms of economic domination.

It would be possible to evaluate other extant proposals and stratagems, such as establishing a system for labelling and certification of ethical labour practices. But the essential point would remain the same: the goal should be to analyse proposed new practices, strategies and institutions from the standpoint of both the principles of council democracy embraced (if separately) by Rolf and McAlevey: both fighting domination and building the democratic agency of ordinary people. Approaches that target new forms of domination without recruiting and involving most ordinary workers in the effort risk becoming bureaucratic remote, elitist and democratically moribund. Approaches that build the agency of workers in their workplaces without effectively countering dominating power where it now exists risk becoming feeble and ultimately disillusioning for their participants. Only efforts that combine these goals of the council movement are likely to become, in John Dewey's phrase, "buoyant, crusading, and militant" ones.[38]

It may seem that in formulating the analysis of this chapter, I myself have given short shrift to an element of the council democratic programme, as I have described it – namely transformation. After all, many participants in the council movement, and especially in workers' and factory councils, thought their actions could lay the groundwork for a transformation to socialism. The contemporary debate I analyse in the last section of this chapter seems by contrast much less ambitious, focused only on the creation of a robust labour movement. But transformations may range from relatively modest to radical and complete. Certainly, as compared to our present circumstances, the winning of a more democratic political economy in which workers and other ordinary participants have a powerful, durable position would constitute a significant transformation. What is more, we can never be sure what the outcome of our principled interventions may be, especially in a social world that is constantly undergoing significant structural change. In the era of the council movement, the contrast between capitalism and socialism – each fairly clearly defined – substantially defined the alternatives agents could envision, and the durability of capitalism seemed, at best, highly questionable, even to its defenders. A hundred years later, it is clearer to us that significant transformation of the political economy is always under way, so that the relevant choice is not between transformation and stasis, but between forms and directions of change. With respect to that choice, it is clear that both the council movement's participants and most contributors to the contemporary debate about labour's future favour some version of democratic transformation. Exactly where such transformation will take us, if we are able to secure it, is a question beyond the scope of this chapter.

A dominant theme of this chapter is that, on its own, the idea animating the factory council – transforming the economy through a focus on democratically transforming individual workplaces – seems less sufficient as a means of achieving a democratic economy in light of late-twentieth and early-twenty-first-century developments. But in truth, as the first section of the chapter showed, factory councils were far from the only element of the council democratic programme. And relatedly, even the council movement embraced other strategies for democratising the political economy. The council era was also punctuated by general strikes, which organised workers across an entire region. And even the Ruhr coal workers, who saw factory councils as crucial to their vision of a future democratic economy, planned to get to that future not only through the creation of such councils, but also through the activities of workers' and soldiers' councils. Something similar could be said of the era of labour organising in the United States in the 1930s. Even the movement phase that culminated in obtaining collective bargaining rights, to be recognised and enacted in each workplace, involved general strikes and even broader strike waves that created a national sense of crisis to which elected governments – not just individual employers – responded. The idea that economic democracy might require more than just enterprise-level democratic institutions and activities was always there alongside factory councils.

Yet it must be said again that exactly what future mechanisms, practices and strategies can respect and enact both the aims of opposing domination and building democratic agency is yet to be determined. Regrounding ourselves in the experience of the councils provides us with vivid democratic criteria rather than fixed democratic formulas or solutions.

Notes

1 Jeffrey Hilmer, "The State of Participatory Democratic Theory," 46.
2 Gennady Shkliarevsky, *Labour in the Russian Revolution*, 5–9, 16–17.
3 Elizabeth H. Tobin, "Revolution and Alienation," in M. Dobkowski and I. Wallimann (eds), *Toward the Holocaust*, 159.
4 F. L. Carsten, *Revolution in Central Europe, 1918–1919*, 153–4.
5 Ibid., 161.
6 Tobin, "Revolution and Alienation," 158.
7 Eberhard Kolb, *The Weimar Republic*, 15.
8 Otto Bauer, "Der Weg zum Sozialismus," in Hugo Pepper (ed.), *Otto Bauer*, 104–5, 107.
9 Joseph Schumpeter, "Sozialistische Möglichkeiten von heute," 336–8. For a fuller discussion of both Bauer's and Schumpeter's view of the council movement and economic democratisation, see John Medearis, *Joseph Schumpeter's Two Theories of Democracy*, 46–64.
10 This understanding of domination is further elaborated in John Medearis, *Why Democracy Is Oppositional*, 102–6.
11 Otto Bauer, *The Austrian Revolution*, 170.
12 Elsewhere, I have argued that the most of important of these principles – especially those emphasising democracy as rising in opposition to domination or dominating social structures and forces, democracy as oppositional, and democracy as focused on a particular understanding of collective agency, and the enrichment of such agency – actually offer deep insight into democracy, *tout court*. See Medearis, *Why Democracy Is Oppositional*.
13 S. R. H. Jones, "The Rise of the Factory System in Britain" in Paul L. Robertson (ed.), *Authority and Control in Modern Industry*, 17–44.

14 Sachio Kaku, "Management and Labour in German Chemical Companies before World War One," in Robertson (ed.), *Authority and Control in Modern Industry*, 203–20.
15 John Stuart Mill, *Principles of Political Economy, with Some of Their Application to Social Philosophy*, 759–94; Carole Pateman, *Participation and Democratic Theory*; Robert A. Dahl, *A Preface to Economic Democracy*.
16 Robert B. Reich, *Supercapitalism*, 60–3.
17 Ibid., 64–5.
18 David Rolf, *The Fight for Fifteen*, 24–5.
19 Ibid., 24.
20 My discussion of temporary work draws on ibid., 29–32.
21 Ibid., 29.
22 Brishen Rogers, "Employment Rights in the Platform Economy."
23 Ibid., 481.
24 Rolf, *The Fight for Fifteen*, 32–6.
25 Jeffry A. Frieden, *Global Capitalism*, 397–400, 401; David Harvey, *A Brief History of Neoliberalism*, 2.
26 Frieden, *Global Capitalism*, 401.
27 Rolf, *Fight for Fifteen*, 23.
28 Harold Meyerson, "The Seeds of a New Labour Movement"; Rolf, *Fight for Fifteen*, chs. 4, 6.
29 David Rolf, "Toward a 21st-Century Labor Movement."
30 Kim Voss and Rachel Sherman, "Breaking the Iron Law of Oligarchy."
31 Meyerson, "The Seeds of a New Labour Movement."
32 Jane F. McAlevey, *No Shortcuts*, 11–12.
33 Ibid., 28, 12.
34 Udo Rehfeldt, "The French System of Collective Bargaining."
35 See Jelle Visser, ICTWS Database.
36 The key work on these associations is Janice Fine's *Worker Centers*.
37 Ibid., 5, 266.
38 John Dewey, "Democracy Is Radical," 299.

References

Bauer, Otto. *The Austrian Revolution*. New York: Burt Franklin, 1970.

———. "Der Weg zum Sozialismus." In *Otto Bauer: Werkausgabe*, vol. 2. 89–131. Edited by Hugo Pepper. Vienna: Europaverlag, 1976.

Carsten, F. L. *Revolution in Central Europe, 1918–1919*. Berkeley and Los Angeles: University of California Press, 1972.

Dahl, Robert A. *A Preface to Economic Democracy*. Berkeley and Los Angeles: University of California Press, 1985.

Dewey, John. "Democracy Is Radical." In *The Later Works, 1925–1953*, vol. 11: *1935–1937*. Edited by J. Boydston. 296–9. Carbondale, IL: Southern Illinois University Press, 1987.

Fine, Janice. *Worker Centers: Organizing Communities at the Edge of the Dream*. Ithaca, NY: Cornell University Press, 2005.

Frieden, Jeffry A. *Global Capitalism: Its Fall and Rise in the Twentieth Century*. New York: Norton, 2006.

Harvey, David. *A Brief History of Neoliberalism.* Oxford: Oxford University Press, 2005.

Hilmer, Jeffrey D. "The State of Participatory Democratic Theory." *New Political Science* 32, no. 1 (2010): 43–63.

Jones, S. R. H. "The Rise of the Factory System in Britain: Efficiency or Exploitation?" In *Authority and Control in Modern Industry: Theoretical and Empirical Perspectives*. Edited by Paul L. Robertson. 17–44. Abingdon: Routledge, 2015.

Kaku, Sachio. "Management and Labour in German Chemical Companies before World War One." In *Authority and Control in Modern Industry: Theoretical and Empirical Perspectives*. Edited by Paul L. Robertson. 203–20. Abingdon: Routledge, 2015.

Kolb, Eberhard. *The Weimar Republic*. London: Allen & Unwin, 1988.

McAlevey, Jane F. *No Shortcuts.* Oxford: Oxford University Press, 2016.

Medearis, John. *Joseph Schumpeter's Two Theories of Democracy.* Cambridge, MA: Harvard University Press, 2001.

———. *Why Democracy Is Oppositional.* Cambridge, MA: Harvard University Press, 2015.

Meyerson, Harold. "The Seeds of a New Labour Movement." Accessed at http://prospect.org/article/labour-crossroads-seeds-new-movement.

Mill, John Stuart. *Principles of Political Economy, With Some of Their Applications to Social Philosophy*. Edited by J. M. Robson. *Collected Works of John Stuart Mill*. Vols. 2 and 3. Toronto: University of Toronto Press, 1965.

Pateman, Carole. *Participation and Democratic Theory*. Cambridge: Cambridge University Press, 1970.

Rehfeldt, Udo. "The French System of Collective Bargaining." Accessed at www.socialeurope.eu/the-french-system-of-collective-bargaining.

Reich, Robert B. *Supercapitalism: The Transformation of Business, Democracy, and Everyday Life.* New York: Vintage. 2007.

Rogers, Brishen. "Employment Rights in the Platform Economy: Getting Back to Basics." *Harvard Law and Policy Review* 10 (2016): 479–520.

Rolf, David. *The Fight for Fifteen: The Right Wage for Working America.* New York: The New Press, 2016.

———. "Toward a 21st-Century Labor Movement." Accessed at http://prospect.org/article/toward-21st-century-labor-movement.

Schumpeter, Joseph. "Sozialistische Möglichkeiten von heute." *Archiv für Sozialwissenschaft und Sozialpolitik* 48 (1920–1): 305–60.

Shkliarevsky, Gennady. *Labour in the Russian Revolution: Factory Committees and Trade Unions, 1917–1918.* New York: St. Martin's Press, 1993.

Tobin, Elizabeth H. "Revolution and Alienation: The Foundations of Weimar." In *Toward the Holocaust: The Social and Economic Collapse of the Weimar Republic.* Edited by M. Dobkowski and I. Wallimann. Westport, CT: Greenwood Press, 1983.

Visser, Jelle. ICTWSS Database, version 5.1. Amsterdam: Amsterdam Institute for Advanced Labour Studies (AIAS), University of Amsterdam. September 2016.

Voss, Kim and Rachel Sherman. "Breaking the Iron Law of Oligarchy: Union Revitalization in the American Labour Movement." *American Journal of Sociology* 106, no. 3 (2000): 303–49.

11 The Case for Workplace Democracy

David Ellerman

Introduction

In this chapter I seek to provide a theoretical defence of workplace democracy that is independent from and outside the lineage of Marxist and communist theory. Common to the council movements, anarcho-syndicalism and many other forms of libertarian socialism was the idea "that workers' self-management was central."[1] Yet the idea of workers' control has not been subject to the same theoretical development as Marx's theory, not to mention capitalist economic theory. This chapter aims to contribute at a theoretical level by providing a justification and defence of self-managed workplaces that is independent of the particular historical tradition of the council movements.

There is a clear and definitive case for workplace democracy based on first principles that descends to modern times through the Reformation and Enlightenment in the abolitionist, democratic and feminist movements. By the twentieth century, the arguments had been scattered and lost – like the bones of some ancient beast scattered in a desert – partly due to misconceptions, mental blocks and misinterpretations embodied in Marxism, liberalism and economic theory. When one has worked through some of these intellectual roadblocks, then one may be better able to reassemble the case for workplace democracy from well-known first principles developed in the abolitionist, democratic and feminist movements.

The Basic Misconception of Liberalism

The modern liberal consciousness was formed in the nineteenth century with the abolition of slavery and the triumph of political democracy as the normative ideal in the West. Both changes were interpreted as moving from a coercive system to a system based on consent. Thus "consent" became the root principle of liberalism (always in the European sense of classical liberalism), a principle further exemplified with the post-socialist resurgence of market societies.

But this "liberal principle of consent" is both a conceptual oversimplification of the issues as well as a historical falsification of the debates. There were always sophisticated arguments for slavery and for non-democratic forms of government *based on consent*. The advances in anti-slavery arguments and democratic arguments based on the inalienable rights arguments of the Reformation and Enlightenment were made against those liberal defences of slavery and autocracy based on consent. These inalienable rights arguments have been largely lost to modern liberalism (not to mention, neoclassical economics) with its dumbed-down dichotomy of "coercion versus consent." Of course, there were always illiberal defences of slavery and autocracy (e.g. racist arguments or divine-right theories), and those are precisely the ones propped up as strawmen and then batted down by liberal philosophers and intellectual historians as they portray the triumphal march "from Status to Contract."[2]

Slavery

Take slavery. The contractual arguments for slavery go back even to antiquity. In Justinian's codification of Roman law, each of the three legal means of becoming a slave had an incidence of contract. One means was an explicit contract to sell one's labour services all at once, the self-sale contract. Another means was the practice of allowing prisoners of war to plea bargain a lifetime of labour instead of being executed. Finally, those who were born slaves received food, clothing and shelter from their masters and they could (by manumission) pay off this liability inherited from their mothers' contractual condition, or they could continue the arrangement for another generation.

Frank Knight pointed out that the foundations of classical liberalism were laid well before Adam Smith: "Interestingly enough, the political and legal theory had been stated in a series of classics, well in advance of the formulation of the economic theory by Smith. The leading names are, of course, Locke, Montesquieu, and Blackstone."[3] All three of these classical liberal writers accepted a voluntary slavery contract as long as there was some semblance of rights on both sides, for example, so that a master may not arbitrarily kill his slave. Here are the three pertinent quotations:

> For, if once *Compact* enter between them, and make an agreement for a limited Power on the one side, and Obedience on the other, the State of War and *Slavery* ceases, as long as the Compact endures … I confess, we find among the *Jews*, as well as other Nations, that Men did sell themselves; but, 'tis plain, this was only to *Drudgery, not to Slavery*. For, it is evident, the Person sold was not under an Absolute, Arbitrary, Despotical Power.[4]
>
> This is the true and rational origin of that mild law of slavery which obtains in some countries; and mild it ought to be, as founded on the

> free choice a man makes of a master, for his own benefit; which forms a mutual convention between two parties.[5]
>
> Yet, with regard to any right which the master may have lawfully acquired to the perpetual service of John or Thomas, this will remain exactly in the same state as before: for this is no more than the same state of subjection for life, which every apprentice submits to for the space of seven years, or sometimes for a longer term.[6]

In the American debates over slavery, people like Reverend Samuel Seabury gave perfectly liberal contractarian defences of slavery – while George Fitzhugh and a host of others gave illiberal and racist arguments.[7] The reader is invited to see which strawmen are propped up and batted down in the standard histories of the slavery debates. For instance, modern liberal scholars of pro-slavery thought can't seem to find Seabury or any of the earlier contractarian defences. Eric McKitrick collects essays of 15 pro-slavery writers;[8] Harvard University's current president, Drew Gilpin Faust,[9] collects essays from seven pro-slavery writers; and Paul Finkelman collects 17 excerpts from pro-slavery writings.[10] But *none* of them include a single writer who argues to allow slavery on a contractual basis such as Seabury – not to mention Grotius, Pufendorf, Locke, Blackstone, Montesquieu and a host of Scholastics such as Jean Gerson, Luis de Molina and Francisco Suarez.[11]

As was pointed out by some pro-slavery writers, the essential economic difference between the slave and the hireling is the amount of labour purchased at once:

> With us this property does not consist in human "flesh" … Our property in man is a right and a title to human labor. And where is it that this right and title does not exist on the part of those who have the money to buy it? *The only difference in any two cases is the tenure … Our slave-property lies only incidentally in the person of the slave but essentially in his labor*. Who buys a slave except he has work for him? His person is held as the only sure means of obtaining his labor. The proprietorship of his person extends only so far as the derivation of a fair amount of labor. The value of the slave is determined by the sort and amount of labor he is capable of and it is according to these that he is bought and sold; and it is undeniable that these are the same conditions which determined the hireling's wages.[12]

Or as James Mill, the utilitarian liberal and father of John Stuart Mill, pointed out:

> The labourer, who receives wages sells his labour for a day, a week, a month, or a year, as the case may be. The manufacturer, who pays these wages, buys the labour, for the day, the year, or whatever period

> it may be. He is equally therefore the owner of the labour, with the manufacturer who operates with slaves. The only difference is, in the mode of purchasing. The owner of the slave purchases, at once, the whole of the labour, which the man can ever perform: he, who pays wages, purchases only so much of a man's labour as he can perform in a day, or any other stipulated time.[13]

If a contractual relationship to buy "the whole of the labour, which the man can ever perform" was morally wrong in spite of being voluntary, then the current economic system based on the voluntary contract for the shorter-term purchase of labour "for the day, the year, or whatever period it may be" might be put in moral jeopardy. Hence responsible intellectual historians and liberal scholars just cannot go there.

Today, the reigning social model finds its "scientific" expression in the neoclassical model of competitive capitalism which not only allows, but requires for efficiency, complete future markets in all goods and services including labour. Although self-sale contracts were outlawed when slavery was abolished, the shining exemplar of liberal thought (the neoclassical economic model) requires that such lifetime labour contracts be re-allowed in order to get the basic efficiency results.

> Now it is time to state the conditions under which private property and free contract will lead to an optimal allocation of resources … The institution of private property and free contract as we know it is modified to permit individuals to sell or mortgage their persons in return for present and/or future benefits.[14]

To place emphasis on the libertarian logic of freedom, the late Harvard philosopher, Robert Nozick, has argued that a free system would allow an individual "to sell himself into slavery." As if to emphasise the modern learned ignorance of Enlightenment inalienable rights doctrine, Nozick even reinterprets an "inalienable" right as a right that one may not give up without consent – which just identifies "inalienable rights" with "rights" as opposed to privileges. Nozick thus has no notion whatever of "inalienable rights" in the original sense of a right that one may not give up even with consent (e.g. due to the inherent invalidity of the contract to alienate any rights one has *qua* person).

Non-democratic Government

The contractual arguments for allowing non-democratic government also go back to antiquity and continue down to Nozick. Any rulership that existed as a settled condition was interpreted as based on an implicit contract or covenant with the people – settled by the prescription of time. In the *Institutes* of Justinian, we find that the Roman people have by the *lex regia* enacted the *imperium* of the ruler. The German legal scholar, Otto Gierke, finds that by the late Middle Ages, it was propounded as a philosophical axiom that rulership was based on a voluntary contractual alienation of rights from the ruled to the ruler, the contract of subjection or *pactum subjectionis*.[15] Or as medieval scholar Brian Tierney pointed out: "The idea that licit rulership was conferred by consent of the community to be ruled was fairly commonplace at the beginning of the fourteenth century."[16] Surely the best-known version of this doctrine was Thomas Hobbes' theory of contractual autocracy. To avoid the war of all against all that would make life "nasty, brutish, and short," each along with the other would alienate the right of self-determination to the sovereign. This liberal tradition of non-democratic government based on the "consent of the governed" continues down to Harvard's poster-child for free-market principles whose libertarian vision of a free system would allow the *pactum subjectionis* where individuals contract away their governance rights to a "dominant protective association."[17]

This completes the summary of the basic misconception of liberalism, that the abolition of slavery and the triumph of political democracy represented a decision for consent over coercion. The older non-trivial debate, lost to modern liberalism, was *not* between consent and coercion but between two opposite forms of consensual arrangements. It was between a Hobbesian contract to *alienate* the rights of self-determination and a democratic constitution to secure those rights which are only *delegated* to the governors/managers.

> During the Middle Ages the question was much debated whether the *lex regia* effected an absolute alienation (*translatio*) of the legislative power to the Emperor, or was a revocable delegation (*cessio*). The champions of popular sovereignty at the end of this period, like Marsiglio of Padua in his *Defensor Pacis*, took the latter view.[18]

The non-trivial argument for democracy was not the usual liberal stance in favour of consent instead of coercion, but the inalienable rights argument against the voluntary alienation contract and in favour of the voluntary delegation contract.

> There is, at least, *one* right that cannot be ceded or abandoned: the right to personality. Arguing upon this principle the most influential writers on politics in the seventeenth century rejected the conclusions drawn by Hobbes. They charged the great logician with a contradiction in terms … There is no *pactum subjectionis,* no act of submission by which man can give up the state of free agent and enslave himself. For by such an act of renunciation he would give up that very character which constitutes his nature and essence: he would lose his humanity.[19]

It means, as the examples of modern economics and philosophical libertarianism illustrate, that the non-trivial inalienable rights arguments against such alienation contracts have been "forgotten." And for good reason. As Philmore put it, perhaps ironically:

> Contractual slavery and constitutional non-democratic government are, respectively, the individual and social extensions of the employer–employee contract. Any thorough and decisive critique of voluntary slavery or constitutional non-democratic government would carry over to the employment contract – which is the voluntary contractual basis for the free market free enterprise system.[20]

Thus the "problem" is that when the old inalienable rights arguments are understood in clear and modern terms, then it is quickly seen that the arguments cut far deeper than just ruling out *buying* other people and *political* autocracy – they also rule out the renting of persons and the workplace *pactum subjectionis* of the employment contract.

A Linguistic Glass Wall in Capitalist Talk

Let us pause to consider an amusing invisible barrier in "capitalist talk." Suppose a person lived in the middle of a slave society (e.g. the antebellum American South). Surely when asked if they knew of a society based on owning other human beings, they would recognise their own society as an example. Now consider present-day society and consider the following experiment the author has conducted with economics students.

First the students are told about the system of chattel slavery where workers are bought and sold as moveable property. But just as a house or a car can be bought and sold, so one can also rent a house or car. Now instead of buying workers as in a slavery system, suppose we consider a system of renting workers. The students are asked if anyone knows an economic system based on the renting of workers. There is usually a puzzled silence. A Black student might point out that during slack times in the period of slavery, plantation slaves were rented out to work as stevedores, as hands in factories (e.g. turpentine or sugar mills) or as common labourers. The professor agrees, but asks again for an example of a whole economic system based on renting people. After another pause, some students offer, "well, what about feudalism?" The professor responds that feudalism might be seen as based on the voluntary homage contract that permanently attached the serf to the manor and was not a temporary rental contract. Thus we still need an example of a system of renting people. After more embarrassed silence and shuffling feet, finally a student, by the process of elimination if by no other logic, offers: "Well, isn't that sort of like what we have now?"[21]

Yes, except that we use the word "hiring" or some other euphemism ("employing" or "giving a job") instead of "renting" when people are rented in an employment contract. Economists can sometimes be quite frank about the matter. As the late dean of neoclassical economics, Paul Samuelson, put it: "Since slavery was abolished, human earning power is forbidden by law to be capitalised. A man is not even free to sell himself: he must *rent* himself at a wage."[22] Or as other neoclassicals put it:

> To clarify our discussion of capital we … emphasize two crucial distinctions: between *stocks* and *flows*, and between *rental payments* and *asset prices*. We begin with the example of labour input … The labour market trades a commodity called "hours of labour services." The corresponding price is the hourly wage rate. Rather loosely, we sometimes call this the "price of labour." Strictly speaking, the hourly wage is the *rental payment* that firms pay to hire an hour of labour. There is no asset price for the durable physical asset called a "worker" because modern societies do not allow slavery, the institution by which firms actually own workers.[23]

Hiring and renting are used interchangeably when referring to cars (e.g. "hire-car" in the UK instead of "rental-car" in the US), but not for people. Learning this unwritten rule is part of being socialised into a society based on renting human beings. Try it on your friends.

The "R"-Word That Cannot Be Spoken in Economics

The "science" of economics has even stronger unwritten rules as to what words and concepts can be used. Certain facts, known to all, are quite unmentionable in this "science." For instance, we all know that only people can be blamed or held responsible for anything. We all might occasionally indulge animistic metaphors about "things" being blamed for some outcome, but we are well aware of the metaphor. We know, for example, that when a crime is committed, the responsibility for the crime must be imputed back through the tools or instruments to the human users. When we do not blame the knife or gun for a crime, we do not think for a moment that the instrument was therefore of no "help" to the perpetrator in the commission of the crime (and thus some crimes and many accidents might be prevented if such tools were scarcer). Of course, such instruments have some efficacy in crimes; otherwise they would not be used. But we have no trouble differentiating that efficacy from responsibility for the crime. No trouble, that is, unless one is a professional economist who must, in the interests of science, "overlook" what everyone knows.

This simple and definitive differentiation of human actions from the services of things on the basis of the "R"-word, "responsibility," has been lost to economics for the whole twentieth century. In economics, human actions and the services of things are seen alike as having a causal efficacy called "productivity" and they are represented symmetrically as input services in "production functions." Economists flip-flop between two symmetrical pictures of the production process. When feeling scientific, economists adopt an engineering mentality and a passive voice; the inputs are technologically transformed into the outputs. When economists wax poetical, then all the inputs (such as land, labour and capital) co-operate together to produce the product. "Together, the man and shovel can dig my cellar" and "land and labor together produce the corn harvest."[24] At all costs, the asymmetrical picture is avoided where persons use up materials and the services of the instrument to produce the outputs – thereby producing the "whole product" (see below) with its negative and positive components.

Long years of rigorous economic training are necessary in order to "forget" such an obvious difference between persons and things. The payoff from this rigorous indoctrination can be seen by investigating any economics textbook. Before the twentieth century, there was a darkness over the land and muddle-headed political economists like Thomas Hodgskin and other classical labourists had some sort of "labour theory" that tried to treat labour as having some "mysterious" attribute fundamentally different from the services of things.[25] What could it be? Then around the turn of the twentieth century, a light burst over the land as the theory of marginal productivity emerged to solve the "problem of imputation." Every principles text, from Marshall's and Samuelson's to their vast contemporary progeny, discusses (and dismisses) the "labour theory" and presents marginal productivity theory.

The reader is invited to try to find a single economics text in the entire twentieth century which even mentions the simple fact that only human actions (labour services) are imputable – that responsibility must be imputed back through whichever instruments and tools to the human users. For a couple of decades, I have offered any fellow economist a free lunch if they find such a text, but to no avail. Failing that, one begins to appreciate the power of capitalist indoctrination in the "science" of economics.

One has to go back to the legally trained nineteenth-century Austrian economist, Friedrich von Wieser, to find any non-metaphorical mention of the R-word in the economics literature:

> The judge … who, in his narrowly-defined task, is only concerned with the *legal imputation*, confines himself to the discovery of the legally responsible factor, – that person, in fact, who is threatened with the legal punishment. On him will rightly be laid the whole burden of the consequences, although he could never by himself alone – without instruments and all the other conditions – have committed the crime. The imputation takes for granted physical causality … If it is the moral imputation that is in question, then certainly no one but the labourer could be named. Land and capital have no merit that they bring forth fruit; they are dead tools in the hand of man; and the man is responsible for the use he makes of them.[26]

There is a common pose that orthodox economists are scientifically judging the existing human rental system according to some normative principles such as Pareto optimality – analogous to the political economists, jurisprudents and philosophers in the antebellum American South who pretended to be judging their peculiar institution according to some moral principles and who unsurprisingly never supported any knock-down inalienable rights arguments against the institution. The social role of "economics" in our society based on human rentals suggests the opposite direction of causality. Normative principles are judged according to whether or not they align with the social role of orthodox economics in giving a "scientific account" of the existing or perhaps an idealised human rental system.

For instance, Wieser actually summarises the essentials of the labour theory of property (juridical imputation principle) critique of the employment system: "Land and capital have no merit that they bring forth fruit; they are dead tools in the hand of man; and the man is responsible for the use he makes of them."[27] But that gives Wieser no second thoughts about the system of renting human beings; it only proves that the usual moral (factual) or legal notions of imputation *obviously* do not apply! Apparently, the usual moral/legal notions of imputation and responsibility apply to some other world than the world with which economists deal. It would be an economic *reductio ad absurdum* to apply the usual moral/legal notion of imputation to production since it conflicts with the liberty of renting human beings in the free market free enterprise system! The social role of economics in the human rental system demands a new notion of "economic imputation" in accordance with another new notion of economic responsibility: "In the division of the return from production, we have to deal similarly … with an imputation, – save that it is from the economic, not the judicial point of view."[28] By defining "economic responsibility" in terms of the animistic version of marginal productivity, Wieser and later orthodox economists can finally draw the conclusion demanded by their professional vocation: to show that the competitive human rental system "economically" imputes the product in accordance with "economic" responsibility.

Thus we arrive at one of the high points of neoclassical microeconomics: trying to justify a metaphorical imputation of "distributive shares" in the product rights with a metaphorical notion of "responsibility." In contrast, the modern treatment of the labour theory of property (i.e. based on the juridical imputation principle) deals with the imputation of the "return from production" precisely from the moral, legal or "juridical point of view."

The Fundamental Myth of Capitalist Property Rights

The last ideological misconception that we can consider is about the structure of property rights in production. The labour theory of property is about the appropriation of newly produced property. The standard view pretends that no appropriation takes place in capitalist production since the right to the product is supposedly already part of the "private ownership of the means of production." Any appropriation, where the labour theory might be applied, could only be situated in some original state of nature when the first means of production were being appropriated, and in any case all that is lost in the mists of the past.

But the "story" is false from the beginning. The rights to the product are not part of the "ownership of the means of production" (private or otherwise); that is the *fundamental myth* sponsored by Marxist as well as orthodox economists. Appropriation does take place in normal production, not just in some original state of nature. Indeed, there is a market mechanism of appropriation quite unnoticed by conventional economics which buys the myth that the product is already part of the "ownership of the means of production."

Consider a technically defined production opportunity wherein people use some materials and a widget-maker machine to produce widgets. The "fundamental myth" is that the right to the product is part and parcel of the ownership of the capital good, the widget-maker machine. In this simple form, the myth is easy to defeat. Have labour hire capital or have some third party hire both. Then the hiring party would own the product, not the owner of the machine.

But that insight is much more "difficult" to grasp if we put the capital assets inside a corporate shell. Incorporate a company and have the owner of the widget-maker machine contribute it to the company in return for the only shares. Then he is the owner of the company and would "supposedly" be the owner of whatever is produced using the capital assets of the company (that is, the widget-maker machine). Isn't that what corporate ownership means? But that is again false for the same reasons. The machine can be rented out by the company. When the machine is rented out, then the company would not be the owner of the product produced using the company's capital assets (the machine). The company would only be an input-supplier to the "firm" or "enterprise" using the machine. Yet the original owner of the machine is still the owner of the company. This is a point about the structure of property rights, not marketplace power relations. The ownership of the product produced with a company's capital assets is not part and parcel of the ownership of the company. That is the fundamental myth about capitalist property rights.

It is the direction of the hiring contracts (who hires what or whom) that determines who bears the input-liabilities and who thus appropriates the output-assets – not the "ownership of the means of production." One party buys or already owns all the inputs to be used up in production and then, having absorbed those input-liabilities, can lay sole legal claim on the new produced assets.

The idea that the product was part of the "ownership of the means of production" was crystallised by Marx and thus he named the system "capitalism." It is a misnomer. The product rights are not part of capital. Both Marxists (and by virtue most council theorists) and the defenders of "capitalism" agreed on the myth that the owner of capital was the "owner of the firm"; they agreed to disagree on whether that "owner" should be public or private – so that the Cold War was much like a modern version of the Peloponnesian War between the Athenians who had privately owned slaves and the Spartans who had publicly owned slaves.

The Case for Workplace Democracy

The Labour Theory of Property

We are now in a position to briefly state the case for the democratic firm based on ordinary jurisprudence. I will state the case based on the "labour theory of property" – which is just the ordinary juridical principle of assigning legal responsibility in accordance with de facto or factual responsibility.

Regardless of the productivity of the instruments and materials of production, only the human beings involved in the firm can be de facto responsible for producing the product. But hordes of textbook-trained economists immediately throw up their hands and point out that you can't impute the entire output to labour ("labour" = "managers and workers"); the product must be divided to account for the income to the other inputs! But they are wrong; they just think too positively. They must learn to think negatively. There is also a negative product. Labour does not produce the product *ex nihilo*; labour produces the product by using up the input materials and the services of the capital instruments. And thus labour is also de facto responsible for that negative product (and the satisfaction of those input-liabilities accounts for the other factor incomes). The positive and negative product, the (undivided) produced assets and input-liabilities, make what we might call the *whole product*.[29] It is not described by a number but by an ordered list of positive and negative numbers, a "vector."

The imputation principle (assign the legal responsibility to the de facto responsible party) implies that labour should have the legal responsibility for the positive and negative fruits of their labour. In the nineteenth century, Hodgskin and others asserted "Labour's Right to the Whole Product."[30] Labour should be legally liable for the used-up inputs and should legally own the produced outputs; labour should be the firm. The net value of whole product is the "residual," so the responsibility argument concludes that labour ought to be the residual claimant.

The Analogous Case for Abolishing the Coverture Marriage Contract

Historical examples of voluntary contracts that have been abolished due to the abolitionist, democratic and feminist movements are, respectively, the voluntary slavery contract, the non-democratic political constitution (*pactum subjectionis*) and the coverture marriage contract. Since the coverture contract is the most recent example, it may be useful to review the inalienable rights argument against that free and voluntary contract. Note that we are *not* playing the usual left-wing parlour game of escalating one's notion of "voluntariness" until the contract we want to rule out is seen as being "involuntary." The inalienable rights critique applies even if it is perfectly voluntary.

Normally, to establish a legal guardian relationship of one adult as guardian over another adult as dependant, there must be some *factual* condition on the part of the dependant such as some mental disability, insanity or senility that needs to be certified. Yet the coverture marriage contract established the husband as the "Lord and Baron" or, in less flowery language, guardian over the *feme covert* who had no independent legal personality and thus could not make contracts or own property except in the name of the husband:

> By marriage, the husband and wife are one person in law: that is, the very being or legal existence of the woman is suspended during the marriage, or at least is incorporated and consolidated into that of the husband; under whose wing, protection, and cover, she performs everything; and is therefore called in our law-French, a *feme covert*, and is said to be under the protection and influence of her husband, her baron, or lord; and her condition during her marriage is called her coverture.[31]

In an adult woman of normal capacity, that factual capacity is factually inalienable in the sense that the woman cannot by voluntary agreement actually alienate that capacity and factually become a person of diminished capacity, a dependant, factually suitable for a guardianship relation. Yet the coverture contract gave her precisely that *legal* position (note that the point is the contrast between the factual and the legal situation). Since the woman is just as much a de facto capacitated adult as before voluntarily agreeing to the contract, the coverture contract was essentially an institutional fraud sponsored by the legal system in a patriarchal society that allowed the reduction of married women to the status of legal dependants to parade in the form of a voluntary contract. The critique of the human rental or employment contract is entirely analogous using the usual notions of factual and legal responsibility as applied to the appropriation of the liabilities and assets created in production.

The Case for Abolishing the Human Rental Contract

The inalienable rights argument against not only buying but renting people can be illustrated with a simple story. Suppose that an entrepreneur hired an employee for general services (no intimations of criminal intent). The entrepreneur similarly hired a van, and the owner of the van was not otherwise involved in the entrepreneur's activities. Eventually the entrepreneur decided to use the factor services he had purchased (man-hours and van-hours) to rob a bank. After being caught, the entrepreneur and the employee were charged with the crime. In court, the worker argued that he was just as innocent as the van owner. Both had sold the services of factors they owned to the entrepreneur. "Labor Service is a Commodity."[32] The use the entrepreneur makes of these commodities is his own business.

The judge would, no doubt, be unmoved by these arguments. The judge would point out it was plausible that the van owner was not responsible. He had given up and transferred the use of his van to the entrepreneur, so unless the van owner was otherwise *personally* involved, his absentee ownership of the factor would not give him any responsibility for the results of the enterprise. But man-hours are a peculiar commodity in comparison with van-hours. The worker cannot "give up and transfer" the use of his own person, as the van owner can the van. Employment contract or not, the worker remained a fully responsible agent knowingly co-operating with the entrepreneur. The employee and the employer share the de facto responsibility for the results of their joint activity, and the law will impute legal responsibility accordingly:

> All who participate in a crime with a guilty intent are liable to punishment. A master and servant who so participate in a crime are liable criminally, not because they are master and servant, but because they jointly carried out a criminal venture and are both criminous.[33]

Unless one wants to argue that employees suddenly become robots or some sort of non-responsible instruments to be "employed" by the "employer" when the venture "they jointly carried out" was non-criminal, then the employees (and working employer) in an enterprise are jointly factually responsible for using up the inputs (i.e. creating the input-liabilities) and producing the products (i.e. the output-assets) that make up the negative and positive components in the "whole product" representing the whole results in a productive opportunity.

Thus, by the usual juridical norm of imputation, they should *jointly* have the legal liabilities for using up the inputs and the legal ownership of the produced outputs. Yet, the employees, *qua* employees, have 0 per cent of the input-liabilities charged against them and 0 per cent of the produced outputs owned by them, which is exactly the legal role of a rented non-responsible instrument. Anyone who can tell the difference between 0 per cent and 100 per cent can see that the whole "distributive shares" in the product are only metaphorical property rights. The employer holds 100 per cent of the input-liabilities and owns 100 per cent of the produced outputs. Yet the employees are as inextricably and inalienably co-responsible (in factual terms) as in the case of the criminal venture. That is (one form of) the inalienable rights argument that descends from the Reformation (where it took the form of the "inalienability of conscience") and the Enlightenment.

The employees cannot by any voluntary act turn themselves into de facto non-responsible instruments, just as the married woman cannot voluntarily alienate her adult capacity to become a de facto dependant. The whole contract to rent human beings is another institutional fraud legally sponsored by a society based on renting (instead of owning) other humans so that the positive and negative fruits of the rented people can be appropriated by the employer. Thus the neo-abolitionist claim that the employer–employee contract for the renting of human beings is inherently invalid.[34]

Generalising from these two cases, one can see the general form of the inalienability argument against personal alienation contracts. Any contract that puts a normally capacitated person in the legal position of a person of diminished capacity or non-capacity cannot actually be voluntarily fulfilled to factually justify that legal role. The person remains a person. Hence the legal authorities always must have an alternative factual performance that will legally count as "fulfilling" the contract, and that factual performance always has the same form: obey your master, obey your ruler, obey your husband or obey your employer. The resulting legal contract is only an institutionalised fraud parading on the stage as a voluntary contract (i.e. with voluntary *obedience*) to allow the "legalised" treatment of normal persons as having only diminished or no capacity.

Unlike the coverture marriage contract, the human rental contract is still legally valid. Perhaps 100 or even 50 years from now, today's good-hearted orthodox economists, lawyers, political scientists and liberal intellectuals will be looked back upon and asked *in absentia*: "Just which part of renting human beings didn't you understand?"

Notice that this argument is entirely independent of the size of the wage or quality of working conditions, and has no connection to any theory of price or value including any so-called "labour theory of value."[35] The parallel argument from democratic theory arrives at the same conclusion about the employment contract except that it is then viewed as the *private* Hobbesian *pactum subjectionis* of the workplace. The fact that a whole economic civilisation is founded on a bogus "contract" (the contract to rent human beings) to transfer what is untransferable is "unbelievable" to most people – which is why so much false consciousness needs to be socially constructed to sustain the system. While the earlier systems of legalised violations of human rights had their platoons of intellectual mercenaries, no previous system had anything approaching the sophistication of orthodox economics, political science, legal theory and the other social sciences.

Justice and Injustice

Whenever two things ought to match, like being a legal and factual dependant or being legally and factually responsible for something, then there are two ways to have a mismatch – like the type I and type II errors in statistics. It is an injustice when there is a mismatch. For instance, when a factually guilty person is judged legally not guilty, that is a miscarriage of justice – analogous to a type I error of rejecting a true hypothesis. Or when a factually innocent person is found to be legally guilty, that is also a miscarriage of justice – like the type II error of accepting a false hypothesis.

In the case at hand, both errors occur. The factually responsible party or association, the people working within a firm, do not get the legal responsibility for the whole product, and the party or association that does get the legal responsibility, such as the corporate shareholders in the employing corporation, do not have the factual responsibility. In a remarkable case of courage and clarity, the British Conservative minister and writer, Lord Eustace Percy, precisely pointed this out in 1944:

> Here is the most urgent challenge to political invention ever offered to the jurist and the statesman. The human association which in fact produces and distributes wealth, the association of workmen, managers, technicians and directors, is not an association recognised by the law. The association which the law does recognise – the association of shareholders, creditors and directors – is incapable of production and is not expected by the law to perform these functions. We have to give law to the real association, and to withdraw meaningless privilege from the imaginary one.[36]

Conclusion

The workers' councils of the European council movements can be seen as the self-conscious eruption in history of what Percy called the "human association which in fact produces and distributes wealth, the association of workmen, managers, technicians and directors."[37]

"For many, the workers councils became a viable alternative to the capitalist economic system and the established political order, the cells of a future self-managed society."[38] Yet no matter how attractive the direct action and general strike strategies have been to express left-wing enthusiasms and being-against-the-system posturing, they have hardly proved successful as a shortcut through history. Particularly now in the twenty-first century, after the collapse of much of the Left in the late twentieth century, there seems to be no real alternative to Rudi Dutschke's "long march through the institutions of power." This includes refounding the intellectual case of workplace democracy – our task here – in a way quite distinct from and for the most part antithetical to Marxist theory, not to mention "real-existing Marxist socialism."[39]

Notes

1 Ralf Hoffrogge, *Working Class Politics in the German Revolution*, 111.
2 Henry Maine, *Ancient Law*, 100.
3 Frank Knight, *Freedom and Reform*, 27, fn. 4.
4 John Locke, *Two Treatises on Government, Second Treatise*, §24.
5 Baron de Montesquieu, *The Spirit of the Laws*, Vol. I, Bk. XV, Ch. V.
6 William Blackstone, *Ehrlich's Blackstone*, section on "Master and Servant."
7 Samuel Seabury, *American Slavery Justified by the Law of Nature.*
8 Eric McKitrick, *Slavery Defended.*
9 Drew Faust, *The Ideology of Slavery.*
10 Paul Finkelman (ed.), *Defending Slavery.*
11 On the Scholastics, see Richard Tuck, *Natural Rights Theories.*
12 Edward Bryan, *Letters to the Southern People*, 10 (italics in original); partly quoted in J. Philmore, "The Libertarian Case for Slavery," 43.
13 James Mill, *Elements of Political Economy*, ch. I, section II.
14 Carl Christ, "The Competitive Market and Optimal Allocative Efficiency," 334; quoted in Philmore, "The Libertarian Case for Slavery," 52.
15 Otto von Gierke, *Political Theories of the Middle Age.*
16 Brian Tierney, *The Idea of Natural Rights*, 182.
17 Robert Nozick, *Anarchy, State, and Utopia*, 15, 113.
18 Edward S. Corwin, *The "Higher Law" Background of American Constitutional Law*, 4.
19 Ernst Cassirer, *The Myth of the State*, 175.
20 Philmore, "The Libertarian Case for Slavery," 55.
21 Stanley Engerman, "Some Considerations Relating to Property Rights in Man," 43–65.
22 Paul A. Samuelson, *Economics*, 52, italics in original.
23 David Begg *et al.*, *Economics*, 201.
24 Samuelson, *Economics*, 536–7.
25 Hodgskin, *The Natural and Artificial Right of Property Contrasted.*
26 Friedrich von Wieser, *Natural Value*, 76–9.
27 Ibid.
28 Ibid., 76.
29 In the neoclassical literature, this standard vector is called the "input–output vector" as in James Quirk and Rubin Saposnik, *Introduction to General Equilibrium Theory and Welfare Economics*, 27; or "production vector" or just "production."
30 Anton Menger, *The Right to the Whole Produce of Labour*. See also David Ellerman, *Property & Contract in Economics*; David Ellerman, "The Labour Theory of Property and Marginal Productivity Theory"; David Ellerman, "On the Labor Theory of Property"
31 Blackstone, *Ehrlich's Blackstone.*
32 Armen Alchian and William R. Allen, *Exchange and Production*, 469.
33 Francis Batt, *The Law of Master and Servant*, 612.

34 David Ellerman, "On the Renting of Persons."
35 David Ellerman, "Marxism as a Capitalist Tool."
36 Eustace Percy, *The Unknown State*, 38.
37 Ibid.
38 Comack, *Wild Socialism*, 75.
39 There is also the task of rethinking the legal structure of the self-managed democratic firm to avoid the problems of the hybrid "socialist" firms in the only previous historical example of a country attempting to be politically and economically self-managed, the Socialist Federal Republic of Yugoslavia. See David Ellerman, *The Democratic Worker-Owned Firm*.

References

Alchian, Armen and William R. Allen. *Exchange and Production: Theory in Use*. Belmont, CA: Wadsworth, 1969.

Batt, Francis. *The Law of Master and Servant*. 5th edn. London: Pitman, 1967.

Begg, David, Stanley Fischer and Rudiger Dornbusch. *Economics*. 5th edn. London: McGraw-Hill Co., 1997.

Blackstone, William. *Ehrlich's Blackstone*. Edited by J. W. Ehrlich. New York: Capricorn Books, 1959.

Bryan, Edward B. *Letters to the Southern People*. Charleston, SC: Walker, Evans & Co., 1858.

Cassirer, Ernst. *The Myth of the State*. New Haven, CT: Yale University Press, 1963.

Christ, Carl F. "The Competitive Market and Optimal Allocative Efficiency." In *Competing Philosophies in American Political Economics*. Edited by John Elliott and John Cownie. 332–8. Pacific Palisades, CA: Goodyear, 1975.

Comack, Martin. *Wild Socialism: Workers Councils in Revolutionary Berlin 1918–21*. Lanham, MD: University Press of America, 2012.

Corwin, Edward S. *The "Higher Law" Background of American Constitutional Law*. Ithaca, NY: Cornell University Press, 1955.

Ellerman, David. *The Democratic Worker-Owned Firm*. London: Unwin-Hyman Academic, 1990. Accessed at www.ellerman.org.

———. "On the Labor Theory of Property: Is the Problem Distribution or Predistribution?" *Challenge: The Magazine of Economic Affairs* 60, no. 2 (2017): 171–88.

———. "The Labour Theory of Property and Marginal Productivity Theory." *Economic Thought* 5, no. 1 (2016): 19–36.

———. "Marxism as a Capitalist Tool." *Journal of Socio-Economics* 39, no. 6 (December 2010): 696–700.

———. *Property & Contract in Economics: The Case for Economic Democracy*. Cambridge, MA: Blackwell, 1993.

———. "On the Renting of Persons: The Neo-Abolitionist Case Against Today's Peculiar Institution." *Economic Thought* 4, no. 1 (2015): 1–20.

Engerman, Stanley. "Some Considerations Relating to Property Rights in Man." *Journal of Economic History* 33, no. 1 (1973): 43–65.

Faust, Drew Gilpin (ed.). *The Ideology of Slavery: Proslavery Thought in the Antebellum South, 1830–1860*. Baton Rouge, LA: Louisiana State University Press, 1981.

Finkelman, Paul (ed.). *Defending Slavery: Proslavery Thought in the Old South – A Brief History with Documents*. Boston, MA: Bedford/St. Martin's, 2003.

Gierke, Otto von. *Political Theories of the Middle Age*. Translated by F. W. Maitland. Boston, MA: Beacon Press, 1958.

Hodgskin, Thomas. *The Natural and Artificial Right of Property Contrasted*. Clifton, NJ: Augustus M. Kelley, 1973 [1832].

Hoffrogge, Ralf. *Working Class Politics in the German Revolution: Richard Müller, the Revolutionary Shop Stewards and the Origins of the Council Movement*. Translated by Joseph B. Keady. Leiden: Brill, 2015.

Knight, Frank. *Freedom and Reform*. New York: Harper & Row, 1947.

Locke, John. *Two Treatises on Government*. New York: New American Library, 1960 [1690].

McKitrick, Eric. *Slavery Defended: The Views of the Old South*. Englewood Cliffs, NJ: Prentice-Hall, 1963.

Maine, Henry. *Ancient Law*. London: Dent, 1972.

Menger, Anton. *The Right to the Whole Produce of Labour: The Origin and Development of the Theory of Labour's Claim to the Whole Product of Industry*. Translated by M. E. Tanner. New York: Augustus M. Kelley, 1970 [1899].

Mill, James. *Elements of Political Economy*. 3rd edn. London: Baldwin, Cradock, and Joy, 1826.

Montesquieu, Baron de. *The Spirit of the Laws*. Translated by Thomas Nugent. New York: Appleton, 1912 [1748].

Nozick, Robert. *Anarchy, State, and Utopia*. New York: Basic Books, 1974.

Pannekoek, Anton. *Workers' Councils*. Edited by Robert F. Barsky. Oakland, CA: AK Press, 2003.

Percy, Eustace. *The Unknown State: 16th Riddell Memorial Lectures*. London: Oxford University Press, 1944.

Philmore, J. "The Libertarian Case for Slavery: A Note on Nozick." *Philosophical Forum* 14 (1982): 43–58.

Quirk, James and Rubin Saposnik. *Introduction to General Equilibrium Theory and Welfare Economics*. New York: McGraw-Hill, 1968.

Samuelson, Paul A. *Economics*. 10th edn. New York: McGraw-Hill, 1976.

Seabury, Samuel. *American Slavery Justified by the Law of Nature*. Miami, FL: Mnemosyne Publishing Company, 1969.

Tierney, Brian. *The Idea of Natural Rights: Studies on Natural Rights, Natural Law, and Church Law 1150–1625*. Grand Rapids, MI: William B. Eerdmans Publishing, 1997.

Tuck, Richard. *Natural Rights Theories*. Cambridge: Cambridge University Press, 1979.

Wieser, Friedrich von. *Natural Value*. Translated by C. A. Malloch. New York: G. E. Stechert and Company, 1930 [1889].

12 The Legacy of Workers' Councils in Contemporary Social Movements

Dario Azzellini

Introduction

Over the "short twentieth century," the common and majoritarian frameworks for economic and social struggles – as well as for social and political organisation – were the union, the political party and the nation-state. These forms were invariably based on the principle of representation. Socialist and communist movements were no exception to that, even if, in its origins, socialism was grounded in a "communitarian impetus."[1] The workers' councils of the early twentieth century (and of the aftermath of the Spanish Civil War) seemed to represent the last massive upsurge of "commune socialism."[2] Until the revolutions of the early twentieth century in Europe, the only archetype of socialist transformation had been the Paris Commune, which was grounded in self-organisation, imperative mandate and the direct exercise of power by the Communards. The present chapter explores how and to what extent worker-recuperated companies (WRCs) and forms of local self-administration (referred to here as communes) draw – intentionally or otherwise – on the historical legacy of council democracy, from the Paris Commune to the workers' councils of the early twentieth century.

WRCs[3] are companies that were closed down, leading to a struggle on the part of the workers to restart operations under collective and democratic self-management. Workplace occupations with the aim of placing the company under workers' self-management have occurred repeatedly in history. This practice became widespread with the 2000/2001 crisis in Argentina, when workers occupied their closing workplaces. The occupations also spread to Uruguay, Brazil and Venezuela. After 2010, in the wake of the 2008 global economic crisis, this practice spread to Europe and North Africa. Countries where one or more WRCs are currently in operation include Italy, France, Greece, Bosnia, Croatia, Tunisia, Egypt, the United States and Turkey. Since 2008, there have been around 120 new takeovers in Argentina and about 25 in Venezuela; among them there are food, chemical and metal industries, shoe and textile factories, print shops, media outlets and even fast food restaurants. Altogether, in 2017 there existed 400

WRCs in Argentina, employing more than 15,000 workers; at least 78 in Brazil, with more than 12,000 workers; 22 in Uruguay and approximately 80 in Venezuela. Aside from the new WRCs mentioned, more exist in other Latin American countries, India and Southeast Asia.[4] Considering that systematic research and data are available only for Argentina, Brazil and Uruguay, it is probable that more WRCs exist.

For the first time after the fall of real socialism, local self-administration through direct democracy with a socialist outlook emerged in an indigenous context, with the struggle of the Zapatistas in Chiapas, Mexico. The 1994 Zapatista uprising led to the creation of 32 "Autonomous Zapatista Municipalities in Rebellion," each consisting of a number of Autonomous Communities. The example of the Zapatistas led to the proclamation of self-administered communities in Oaxaca and Guerrero. Since then, similar approaches promoting the political organisation of socialist societies into federations of municipalities have emerged in various parts of the world.[5] Here I will concentrate on Venezuela and on Rojava, Kurdistan.

In Venezuela, from the year 2000 onwards, popular organisations, communities and even some institutions started to develop various local self-government initiatives. From those experiences communal councils arose in 2005 as a form of self-administration at the neighbourhood level, followed by the communes in 2007, as a higher tier of self-government. The idea of local self-administration is rooted in the historical experiences of indigenous people and Afro-Venezuelans, in the thought of certain Latin American Marxists, such as Peruvian José Carlos Mariátegui, in the concept of *popular power* (*poder popular*) and in different socialist and councilist currents. Another key theoretical reference is Istvan Mészáros' "communal system."[6] The structures of self-administration have a complex relationship of co-operation and conflict with the institutions of representative democracy. The latter co-exist with the former, but maintain a dominant position in an asymmetric power relationship; even though they officially support the development of self-administration, they often interfere with it and obstruct it.

In Kurdistan, as well, self-administration builds both on local communitarian traditions and on socialist concepts. In the late 1990s, formerly Marxist-Leninist national liberation movement PKK (Kurdistan Workers' Party) reoriented itself towards the democratic confederalism of Murray Bookchin, as theorised in the Kurdish context by PKK leader Abdullah Öcalan. In 2005, PKK and the numerous organisations around it were reorganised as KCK, Association of Kurdistan Communities.[7] This was followed by the establishment of clandestine council structures in Turkish Kurdistan, which are still in operation today. In 2007, mainly under the guidance of the Democratic Union Party (PYD), clandestine council structures expanded to West Kurdistan, in northern Syria, and became public after the collapse of Syrian government control in 2011.[8] In 2013, the PYD and other organisations established the Movement for a Democratic Society (TEV-DEM), which is based on popular assemblies. In March 2016, Syrian Turkmen, Arab, Aramaic/Assyrian and Kurdish organisations and officials founded the Democratic Federation of Northern Syria (DFNS), also known as Rojava, as a council system based on popular assemblies.

Evidently, the present context and circumstances differ from those a century ago; it is, therefore, not possible to base the comparison on trying to identify the same expressions of political and social organisation that were present during the earlier council movements. Council theorists such as Karl Korsch warned against fetishising the council form, since its character depends very much on the political and historical context.[9] As council theorist Ernst Däumig pointed out:

> [t]he councils concept is in its pure and consequential application practical socialism ... Since the *council organization* is the child of revolutionary epochs, it will never enter fixed and complete ... into beautifully paragraphed phrases, but will take its external form and tactical tasks according to the process of revolutionary development and the demands of the current revolutionary situation to which it *must conform*.[10]

The question, then, is how the aforementioned practices and movements can be understood as an updated and adapted concept of council democracy, and where the differences lie.

First, I will attempt to highlight the important differences between council democracy and the early twentieth century's workers' councils, and outline some of the contradictions the latter faced. Then, I will proceed to analyse the main characteristics of council democracy and of workers' councils, and examine how these characteristics resurface in WRCs and communes. I will end the chapter with some preliminary conclusions.

Workers' Councils and Council Democracy: Limitations, Contradictions and Renewal

Before summarising the main characteristics of council democracy, the limited character of early-twentieth-century workers' councils should be pointed out. In contrast to Marx's descriptions of the Paris Commune, where the councils were territorial decision-making and executive bodies, membership to later councils was limited to workers (and in some cases, for a limited period, to soldiers). Workers' councils did not necessarily self-manage their workplaces. In Germany, for instance, they were only electing the directors who would manage the factory.

There are many important contradictions that could not be solved either by workers' councils over the course of their brief existence or by council theorists in the debates following their defeat. Councilists deemed it necessary to concentrate all the power in the hands of productive workers: "Only the proletariat can carry the council idea, that is, all manual and intellectual workers forced to sell their labor to capital in order to survive."[11] Broadening the category of "workers" entailed the contradiction of diluting class divisions and obscuring the fact that the various sectors that participate in the production process have specific interests, which may affect decisions. On the other hand, the expansion of the council system beyond the shop floor to other sectors of society bore the danger of perpetuating class division and sectoral interests. Most council theorists were well aware of these contradictions and therefore regarded workers' councils merely as a transitional form of struggle towards socialism.[12] Similarly, Marx did not consider the Commune a final form but "the organised means of action. The Commune does not [do] away with the class struggles, through which the working classes strive to the abolition of all classes and, therefore, of all class rule." The "superseding of the economical conditions of the slavery of labour by the conditions of free and associated labour" was "the progressive work of time."[13]

Between then and today, several different movements, uprisings and revolts have renewed the idea of council democracy. This is most obvious in the praxis of workers' control. Takeover of production facilities and collective self-management has generally taken place during economic crises (i.e. in France and Japan after the Second World War; in Argentina, Brazil and Uruguay on account of the 2000/2001 crisis), political crises (i.e. around the May 1968 revolt in France) and social crises (i.e. in the United Kingdom and Canada during neoliberal restructuring in the 1970s and early 1980s); in the context of anti-colonial struggles (Indonesia, Algeria and other countries); under state socialism (i.e. in Hungary in 1956, in Czechoslovakia in 1968 and in Poland in the early 1980s); and during democratic revolutions (i.e. in Chile in the early 1970s, in Portugal in 1974).[14] Practices based on council democracy were also found in movements such as the global uprisings of 1968 and in Latin American social movements in the 1980s, as well as in indigenous movements in Latin America and Asia since the 1990s. It is obviously impossible to follow all these different lines of enquiry, and therefore, for the purposes of this chapter, I will examine the main characteristics of council democracy as exemplified in the practices of the Paris Commune and the workers' councils of the early twentieth century.

Main Characteristics of Council Democracy

General Participation Not Along Pre-established Groups or Parties

In the Paris Commune, participation was open to everyone and – to the best of our knowledge – there was no fracturing along pre-established political orientations (although it influenced choices and positions). In the workers' councils, the situation was more contradictory. Council theorists argued that

> [since] the idea of the councils is the liberation of the whole proletariat from capitalist exploitation, the organisation of the councils cannot be the domain of a single party or a single professional group, it has to encompass the proletariat as a whole.[15]

In addition, "[the] totality of the collaborative workers" would participate in decision-making.[16] At the same time, theorists saw a problem in having to deal with non- or counter-revolutionary forces in the councils, therefore Adler also proposed that only socialists should be participating in the councils. Council theorists argued that once workers begin to discuss their needs, aspirations and strategies in assemblies on the shop floor, party affiliation no longer matters: workers develop autonomy.[17] In the councils, differences between parties and professions would fade away.[18] Nevertheless, they observed that, over time, the parties strengthened their ideological grip on the workers and workers started following party lines, which, in the case of Germany, lead to the de facto self-elimination of councils by way of a majority vote of social democratic workers.

Non-representational Democracy and Immediate Accountability

In council democracy, deputies or delegates do not represent; rather, they execute the will and decisions of the electors or the assembly. They perform their duties publicly, they are absolutely and immediately accountable, and they can be recalled at any time by the very people who entrusted them with the responsibility of performing their duties. "Democracy is therefore a matter of creating the socio-political conditions that impede the development of political power."[19] At the workplace, the highest authority is the general assembly of all workers, the workers' council. At workplaces with a huge number of workers, departmental assemblies are constituted, which send delegates to a central delegate assembly or committee. Delegates have no power to make their own decisions but transmit departmental decisions to the delegate assembly and send back matters to be discussed at the department.[20]

Challenging the Division into Spheres

Council democracy challenges and overcomes the construction of the economic, the political and the social as supposedly distinct and autonomous spheres. This separation is foundational to capitalism and the bourgeois state, which exclude the economic and the social sphere from democracy. When the social division of labour is overcome, the social and the political are not separate spheres any more. The political potential of constituent power is no longer split off from political power or absorbed by the representative system, which neutralises constituent power as the most important motor of change. To overcome the split between the social and the political means to overcome the difference between governed and governors and the difference between civil society and political society. In council democracy, there is no political body that makes decisions detached from society. Democracy is no longer limited to a political regime: it becomes a principle that determines every sphere of life.

No Separation of Powers

The Paris Commune and the later councilists rejected the bourgeois separation of powers. As Marx stated, the Commune "was to be a working, not a parliamentary, body."[21] The elected committees of the Commune had both legislative and executive functions; only the judiciary was separated, nevertheless it was equally elected, accountable and recallable at any time. Council theorist Adler considered that the separation of powers, "as a principle harmful to democracy, had to be overcome."[22] Strongly influenced by Rousseau, he argued that the separation of powers was not compatible with the sovereignty of the people. In fact, from the viewpoint of democratic theory, it is antagonistic to it: If constituent power is almighty, is the source of legitimacy of constituted power and resides in the sovereign, how can the separation of legislative power from executive power be justified?[23]

Socialisation: Neither Private Nor State-Owned

The society envisioned by council theorists was based on a form of socialisation that today would be described as "commons," since it does not entail nationalisation under state control:

> When "socialization" is demanded today, the word no longer merely invokes the universal and abstract demand for the transfer of the means of production into the possession of the whole public. Rather the demand for the socialization today has solidified into the more concrete demand that the transfer of the means of production into public property takes place in such a way that everywhere the masses of workers themselves will receive the administration of their places to work, or at least will receive the decisive part of the control of his administration.[24]

Different workplaces co-ordinate to plan production to satisfy social needs, but they do not own the means of production, not even collectively:

> In the case of *direct* socialization, land and equipment are also merely lent to the working production participants at an individual workplace

> (branch of production). As the socio-economic basis of the entire process of production and consumption, they do not belong to any individual group of workers but to the combined community of all single groups.[25]

The objective is what Marx defined as the construction of "a community of free individuals, carrying on their work with the means of production in common, in which the labour power of all the different individuals is consciously applied as the combined labour power of the community."[26] Korsch also pointed out that workers' control of the production process could not be achieved by decree or at once, but it could only be the result of tenacious class struggle against capital in every single workplace.

Council Democracy: Neither Government Nor State

Were the Commune and the workers' councils anti-state movements or were they in favour of a "proletarian state"? Is a council administration tantamount to a government? These are some of the most controversial matters in the council debate. Much of the confusion is due to the inaccurate use of the terms "state" and "government" by many council theorists and to the fact that Marx did not elaborate a theory of the state. Judging by the assertions spread throughout his work, he was increasingly critical of the state form. In his description of the Paris Commune, Marx stated:

> It was a Revolution against the *State* itself, this supernaturalist abortion of society, a resumption by the people for the people, of its own social life. It was not a revolution to transfer it from one fraction of the ruling classes to the other, but a Revolution to break down this horrid machinery of Class domination itself … The Commune – the reabsorption of the State power by society, as its own living forces instead of as forces controlling and subduing it, by the popular masses themselves, forming their own force instead of the organized force of their suppression – the political force of their social emancipation.[27]

This included replacing the standing army with a popular militia and police functions with civil engagement. Marx never used the term "proletarian state" when describing the Commune. If, as Marx wrote, "not only municipal administration, but the whole initiative hitherto exercised by the State was laid into the hands of the Commune," it seems clear that the former state was not replaced by a "proletarian state."[28]

Up until the emergence of the doctrine of "socialism in one country" (triggered by the defeat of revolutionary movements in Western Europe), communist movements were not oriented towards the nation-state. The Paris Commune followed the idea of a Federation of Communes and the co-ordination on a national level through a Communal Constitution.

Workers' councils referred to the "bourgeois state," which had to be destroyed. But they were theorising a transition phase in the midst of turmoil, while losing ground to moderate and reactionary forces. Däumig stated: "A councils organization can only be related to proletarian socialist struggle that is determined to eliminate capitalist production and the state erected on it – even when it has a republican façade – and to put in its place a socialist production and a self-administered public community."[29] In 1922, Korsch used the term "proletarian state" to differentiate it from the bourgeois state.[30] However, affected by the authoritarian turn in Russia and later by the revolutionary movement in Spain, he moved to more radical positions and identified the autonomy of the workers' councils and their defence against the state as a central imperative. On Spain he wrote: "The energy of the anti-state attitude of the revolutionary Spanish proletariat, unhampered by self-created organizational or ideological obstacles, explains all their surprising successes in the face of overwhelming difficulties."[31]

Since the state is based on the division into different spheres, by challenging these divisions, council democracy also challenges, by extension, the state.[32] The Commune eliminated what Marx considered the central features of the state. According to contemporary definitions of the state – from an affirmative bourgeois analysis to a (much more evolved) critical Marxist definition – the form of administration emerging out of council democracy is not a state. This is not altered by the fact that, in absence of a better term for naming the structures of co-ordination, the term "state" was – and still is – used. This is not merely a question of semantics: the term "state" is connected to a whole set of preconceptions, and is therefore not adequate for capturing what a wider co-ordination in a council democracy could be like.

Marx's use of the term "government" was more imprecise than that of council theorists. He wrote that the Communards were "displacing the State machinery, the governmental machinery of the ruling classes by a governmental machinery of their own."[33] Council theorists often used the term self-government, but at the same time they did not consider the councils tantamount to a government. "The councils are no politicians, no government. They are messengers."[34] Government was linked to "mock democracy," the political democracy:

> Under council organization political democracy has disappeared, because politics itself disappeared and gave way to social economy … The councils are no government; not even the most central councils bear a governmental character … Governments … assumed administrative functions in increasing measure; but their chief character as power structures was determined by the necessity of upholding class domination. Now that the necessity has vanished, the instrument, too, has disappeared. What remains is administration.[35]

There was, therefore, no need for "government." All necessary functions were assumed by elected officials of the communes, who were paid the same as any other worker and mandated by the communes.

The Legacy of Council Democracy in Contemporary Movements

Evidently, there are profound differences between the circumstances prevalent 100 years ago and the ones experienced by contemporary movements. Today, workplace recuperations are the result of self-organisation of workers largely abandoned by unions, parties and institutions. Furthermore, the construction of alternatives today mainly has the character of resistance, most of the time in defensive situations. Only Rojava can be construed as a revolutionary context. Venezuela can be described as a more favourable context for self-administration, but both processes are under constant attack from the outside. In Venezuela there is also considerable opposition to the communes and – especially – to workers' control from inside the supposedly favourable government.[36]

Before examining in more detail how contemporary movements further the legacy of the workers' councils, it is important to establish whether these movements actually pursue a systemic change, the same way the Paris Commune and the workers' councils did. Especially in reference to WRCs, this is not a mandatory conclusion and it is often questioned. In the case of the communes this is more obvious, especially where self-administration structures replace representative structures (e.g. in Rojava and Chiapas).

The economic programme of the Democratic Federation of Northern Syria (DFNS) declares as a goal the construction of a social economy based on ethical values, in which use-value dominates over exchange-value. In Venezuela, councilist structures, built parallel to the still existing structures of representative democracy, are understood as the basis of Venezuelan socialism-in-progress; it is proposed that through their mutual co-operation and co-ordination at a higher level, the bourgeois state can be replaced by what has been called a "communal state." Councils in Venezuela and Rojava consider themselves explicitly anti-capitalist. They both engage in setting up collective and self-administered forms of work and production guided by needs and not by the market, maintaining their end goal of transforming the relations of production and overcoming the capitalist economic model.[37]

Regarding WRCs, most see themselves as part of a broader movement and pursue the idea of building a whole new society, starting with the relations of production. As Makis Anagnostou, from Greek WRC Vio. Me. explains:

> if the gears of the working class start turning, this might help the other smaller gears within society to turn. This way we could set the clockwork into motion, restart production, put society itself into motion,

> so society starts establishing assemblies in the neighbourhoods, in collectives. So we can take decisions collectively and manage our own affairs, exactly what the social movement was seeking in 2010–2012: how we can manage our affairs ourselves, and not delegate them to other people.[38]

Generally, WRCs collaborate with other social movements, offer their space to them and to community projects, support other labour struggles, have political and business relations with each other, build international networks, support each other beyond economic interests and increasingly engage in organic production, recycling and tackling environmental problems. They meet regularly at regional and global *Workers' Economy Gatherings*.[39]

Worker-Recuperated Companies

WRCs bring together all workers on the shop floor beyond their prior political orientation or union affiliation. Given the declining membership of workers in strong leftist parties or other ideological political organisations, and the fact that parties and unions are largely absent from these struggles, there is more heterogeneity in WRCs than in the councils of the early twentieth century. WRCs are administered collectively through mechanisms of direct democracy. Some name their structures councils, others name them committees or assemblies. In addition to the general assemblies, many WRCs have brief daily department meetings and workgroups for specific areas. Same as the historical workers' councils, bigger companies have departmental assemblies that co-ordinate in different ways. Nevertheless, the general assembly of all workers remains the highest authority. All WRCs operate with spokespeople that can be recalled at any time. Contrary to most traditional co-operatives, general assemblies have a central role and do not only meet once a year to elect a board of directors. In Argentina, 88 per cent of WRCs conduct regular assemblies; 44 per cent of them meet weekly.[40] In Brazilian WRCs, assemblies are held less frequently; nevertheless, just as in other countries, regular co-ordination sessions take place. Moreover, 75 per cent of Brazil's WRCs have wall newspapers, 43 per cent have regular departmental meetings and 11 per cent have internal publications.[41] Smaller WRCs in Argentina and in Europe make decisions according to the principle of consensus;[42] this is also the case with smaller WRCs I visited in Venezuela and Uruguay. In larger companies, consensus is usually a goal, but more often than not decisions are made by large majorities.[43]

Through their praxis, WRCs challenge the division into spheres and the separation of powers. They reject the notion that the economy is an autonomous sphere, separate from politics and society. The workers of WRCs do not wait for the political sphere (or the judicial system) to act on their behalf; rather, they resort to direct action through self-organisation. The tactics of their struggle – which involve the occupation of the company and an attempt to turn the legal question into a political one – expressly challenge the private ownership of the means of production. They subordinate questions of production to the interests of society. Since they are operating in a capitalist system, economic viability is important, but it is intrinsically connected with the aims of democratisation, solidarity, justice, dignity, alternative value production and overcoming workers' alienation. Most WRCs offer their spaces for neighbourhood and social movements' activities, and almost all engage in active support of other labour struggles during "worktime."[44]

WRCs are products of a struggle and thus have their origins in the contradiction between capital and labour. Individual private ownership of the means of production is transformed into collective property with a social purpose. Apart from very few companies with a complicated legal situation, WRCs do not adopt models of individual ownership, unequal distribution of shares or external investors. WRCs socialise what was formerly private capitalist property.[45]

Communes

Starting in 2005, people in Venezuela organised themselves in communal councils, a non-representative form of local self-government based on assemblies and direct democracy. In urban areas, each communal council (CC) comprises between 150 and 400 households, while in rural areas they comprise around 30 and in indigenous areas 10 to 20. The council is the community assembly of all inhabitants. The community appoints committees and elects spokespeople for each workgroup, and designates a technical organising committee for the council. Committees and spokespeople have no decision-making power; all decisions are made by the CC. Committees elaborate proposals in their respective fields, which are submitted to the CC for approval. In 2007, the communes emerged from below. A commune is made up of various communal councils (around 10 in rural areas and 20 to 40 in urban areas) and other organisations within the same territory; it can develop longer-term projects and extend over a wider area, while the decisions continue to be taken in the communal council assemblies. Communes co-ordinate the communal councils, social missions and grass-roots organisation so that projects are planned, implemented and assessed jointly.[46] Both CCs and communes strive for consensus. Individual decisions are also voted on, but rarely decided by a simple majority. Spokespeople, co-ordinators and people in charge of defined tasks are elected. They usually have no (or limited) decision-making power and can be recalled at any time by the assembly which elected them. The operation of self-administration structures has so far been satisfactory.[47]

Affinity-based councils have been created by fishermen, peasants, students, the disabled and others. Most of them did not evolve into structures of broad participation. In 2007, Venezuelan president Hugo Chávez launched the idea of communal cities as a level of self-administration above the communes. Communal cities consist in the co-ordination of communes within a self-defined territory. Although in some rural regions communes started to co-ordinate and declared themselves communal cities, no broader public debate or law followed. To this day, the discussion – as well as the practice – revolves mainly around the communes. By the end of 2017, the official number of CCs had reached 47,203, while the number of communes was 1,862.[48] The councils structure exists parallel to the structures of representative democracy. Communal councils are recognised by law and their projects are funded extensively by different state institutions (mainly from the central state level, in order to avoid dependence on local and regional governments). Nevertheless, their boundaries of responsibilities are unclear, while their relations with old institutions are flexible and constantly redefined.

In Venezuela (as well as in Chiapas and Guerrero), as a first step in overcoming the separation of spheres and of powers by local self-administration endeavours, the inhabitants of the communities, from the lowest level to the highest, determine the reference territory and their affiliation themselves.[49] The new boundaries refer to the (relational) socio-cultural-economic space that derives from everyday life and not to the existing political-administrative space.[50] Moreover, both the communal councils and the communes developed from below; although their massive expansion was due to formal support by the state, the laws regulating them were devised after they had become a widespread practice. In council structures, the division into separate political, social and economic spheres has been abolished. Nevertheless, their existence alongside a representative democracy and a private and state-owned economy means that the councils are engaged in a constant struggle to challenge the separation of spheres.

In 2008, CCs and communes started to establish *communal enterprises of social production* (*Empresas de Producción Social Comunal*, EPSC). These are co-operatives founded and administered collectively by the CC or the commune. The necessity of forming community-controlled companies as an alternative to traditional worker-controlled co-operatives emerged in 2006. By then, as result of institutional programmes and incentives, more than 70,000 traditional co-operatives were in operation; however, these did not permit advance planning of a communal production cycle (production, transformation and distribution). Their work did not necessarily correspond to the interests of the communities. Often, they did not contribute to the development of a communal economy.

Over the years, thousands of EPSC have been founded. They principally operate in sectors that respond to pressing social needs, such as food and construction materials production or transport services; textile manufacturers, agricultural companies, bakeries and shoemakers are also common. Larger EPSC also exist, such as one dedicated to the production of prefabricated houses.[51]

Although the declared goals of the government are to shift the ownership and administration of the means of production towards a worker- and community-controlled model and to cultivate the formation of workers' councils in all state-administered enterprises, the great majority of all non-private companies are under the supervision of state institutions. As a consequence, workers' struggles have emerged in most nationalised companies, in other state companies and also within state institutions. Conflicts revolve around the issue of participation of the labour force in the organisation of work and the administration of companies. Some struggles originate from a perspective of workers' control, while others develop that perspective during the conflict.

In the "Organic Law of Communes," the envisioned communal state is defined as:

> [a] form of socio-political organisation, founded in the Social State of Law and Justice established in the Constitution of the Bolivarian Republic of Venezuela, in which power is exercised directly by the people, by means of communal self-governments with an economic model of social property and endogenous and sustainable development that permits the achievement of supreme social happiness of Venezuelans in the socialist society. The basic structural cell of the communal state is the Commune.[52]

This implies a profound transformation of constituted power and a re-signification of the state. By this definition, the communal state would be more a non-state than a state.

The administration of the DFNS is based on a council system that is very similar to the Venezuelan model, although in the DFNS no other parallel structure exists. The smallest unit is the commune based on the neighbourhood assembly which – depending on the size of the community – may encompass between 30 and 150 households. The councils are open for participation to everyone in the neighbourhood, including teenagers. Every participant has equal voice and vote. More often than not, decisions are not made by majority vote, as most councils strive for consensus decisions. Councils are free to establish the frequency of their meetings themselves, although most meet once a week. In addition, affinity-based councils exist (e.g. women, youth). Councils send delegates to larger bodies; the next level of organisational authority is the district in urban areas or the village community (comprising seven to ten villages) in rural areas; higher up are the three cantons, and the highest instance is the Supreme Council of the Cantons.[53] Although the larger bodies have mainly co-ordinating functions, delegates can make decisions. However, "all decisions from these 'upper councils' must be formally adopted by the local councils to be binding for their constituents."[54] This administrative structure aims to overcome the separation between a political and a social sphere. Self-administration through the council network resembles neither a state nor a government. Former US diplomat Carney Ross observed: "I found it confusing: I kept looking for a hierarchy, the singular leader, or signs of a government line, when, in fact, there was none; there were just groups."[55]

The economic programme of the DFNS strongly challenges the assumption that the economic sphere is separate and autonomous, and embarks on a broad programme of socialisation. This economic orientation has been defined as a social economy, explicitly anti-liberal while not centrally planned. Since 2012, the construction of co-operatives has been promoted in all sectors, and after 2014 there has been an exponential growth in their numbers.[56] In about a third of enterprises, workers' councils have been created, which – just as with the co-operatives – are accountable to local councils. In late 2012, the principle of "ownership by use" was implemented for land, buildings and infrastructure, thus abolishing "absolute" private property. "Ownership by use" means that as long as the building, land or infrastructure is in use by the owner(s), ownership is not questioned and cannot be overturned by the councils, but neither is the owner allowed to sell the "property" on the market. All land, buildings and infrastructure that are not in use are under the control of the councils, which can assign them to new users; in effect, they become commons. According to economic co-minister of the DFNS, Ahmad Yousef, "three quarters of traditional private property is being used as commons and one quarter is still being owned by use of individuals."[57]

The justice system under construction in the DFNS is an example of an effort to partially overcome the separation of powers. The need to quickly rebuild a legal system has allowed little space for broad discussion, therefore much is yet to be defined and the whole system is subject to constant change. Given that the three cantons comprising the DFNS consider themselves an autonomous and democratic part of the Syrian state, they have generally adopted the Syrian law, changing, abolishing and rewriting parts of it and adding new elements, as deemed necessary for the construction of a democratic society. The death penalty has been abolished, while life imprisonment – for a maximum term of 20 years – can be imposed only in cases of murder, torture or terrorism.

At the level of the commune (the lowest organisational structure), district and village Peace and Consensus Committees are created, which make group decisions through consensus procedures on minor criminal cases and disputes; in addition, separate women's committees resolve issues of specific concern to women's rights, such as patriarchal violence and marriage. The Peace and Consensus Committees are chosen when the people's court meets with the delegates of the commune. At the next level, in the big central city of the area, there are the people's courts, which are appointed by justice councils created by the people and their members do not have to be jurists. Higher up, the justice system of the DFNS is very similar to conventional ones, with separate appeal courts, regional courts and constitutional courts that deal with higher-level legal proceedings and whose members have to be jurists. However, what differentiates the legal system of the DNFS from others is the institution of the Justice Parliament, which lies at the summit of the legal system in each canton. The Justice Parliaments consist of 23 representatives from different administration branches; the government of the day has very little influence over them.[58]

Conclusions

This analysis of the WRCs and the two examples of local self-administration with the main characteristics of council democracy has sought to demonstrate that these further the legacy of the Commune and workers' councils. They build forms of non-representative democracy with immediate accountability and are open to general participation. They challenge the division into spheres and the separation of powers, and build commons – or, as council theorists advocated, engage in socialisation and create direct social ownership (as opposed to private or state ownership). The administration model they propose is akin to neither a government nor a state; rather, it envisions the abolition of politics.

These endeavours take place under adverse conditions. Self-administration is usually dealt with by force when it questions private property and the sovereignty of the state. WRCs have to resist bourgeois legality, eviction attempts by the police and, in some cases, also the violence of the ex-owners. Local self-administration usually faces state repression: in the DFNS it takes the form of military attacks by all surrounding states and different armed factions, as well as of restrictions and legal persecution by other states; in the case of Venezuela, it takes the form of opposition by right-wing paramilitary groups, capitalist entrepreneurs and international governments. In implementing their ideas and decisions, self-administration structures in Venezuela often come into conflict with state institutions, which are not doing what they are supposed to do, impose their own priorities or attempt to co-opt the self-governing structures. Self-administered communities regard access to the socially produced wealth as a right, but insist on their autonomy vis-à-vis state institutions and parties. This seems to be the reason why most CCs and communes regard their socio-productive development as necessary to cease being dependent on the state.[59]

Despite the adversities, WRCs and contemporary communes help advance the principles of council democracy and deepen its praxis. While WRCs may not be as comprehensive a phenomenon as the workers' councils, since they are not formed during revolutionary upsurges and don't have the perspective of imminent system change, they are, nevertheless, much longer-lasting. To be sure, having to survive in a capitalist economy without sharing its logic and values presents them with difficulties and contradictions; however, it also gives them the possibility to gain experience in many fields, from democratic decision-making to labour processes. Worker recuperations entail the transformation of hierarchically structured capitalist businesses, which primarily pursue the increase of surplus value, into democratically self-managed companies with the workers' well-being at their centre. Almost everything changes: the workers' subjectivities; social relations among the workers; labour processes; internal dynamics and the relationship with providers, customers and communities. WRCs engage with problematics the workers' councils did not engage with: from reconciling the differing interests of producers and consumers or monitoring the conditions of production of their raw materials, to issues related to ecology and the socialisation of reproduction.[60]

The new communes are more comprehensive than WRCs. The political organisation adopted by twenty-first-century socialist societies, that of a horizontal confederation of communities or a network of social organisations, has appeared and been implemented – often independently – in different contexts around the world. As Esteva writes of Mexico, "The communities appear as an alternative because in them the union between politics and place is re-established, and the people [*pueblo*] acquire a form in which they can exercise their power, without needing to yield to the state."[61] Similarly, the council models of Venezuela and even more so of Kurdistan open the possibility of understanding the "state" as consisting of certain limited, democratically legitimated functions, which can co-exist with the autonomy of the communities.[62]

The reappearance of central ideas and practices of council democracy in contemporary movements means neither that these are guided directly by the workers' councils example nor that contemporary movements build a common front. However, setting aside any differences, these practices share certain basic common characteristics. They build spaces of production of social alternatives based on similar premises and with similar goals. These practices also reference each other; they are connected with each other and form new spatial configurations. I perceive worker-recuperated companies and the different systems of local self-government as parts of a global non-state-centred perspective of social transformation. In this context, we can also include the new global movements since 2008, and especially since 2010.[63] This may indicate a paradigm shift in the predominant forms and practices of organisation, which has the capacity to put council democracy back on the agenda.

Notes

1 Gustavo Esteva, "Otra mirada, otra democracia."
2 Workers' councils had a problematic and conflictive relationship with the parties they were stemming from. See Pietro Di Paola, "Factory Councils in

Turin, 1919–1920"; Peter Haumer, "The Austrian Revolution of 1918–1919 and Working Class Autonomy"; Ralf Hoffrogge, *Working-Class Politics in the German Revolution*; David Mandel, "The Factory Committee Movement in the Russian Revolution."

3 From the Spanish *Empresas Recuperadas por sus Trabajadores*, defined in Argentina and adopted in Uruguay and Brazil.

4 Dario Azzellini, *An Alternative Labour History*; Azzellini, "Besetzen, Widerstand leisten, produzieren"; CDER, *Nuevas Empresas Recuperadas 2010–2013*; Flávio Henriques Chedid *et al.*, *Empresas Recuperadas por Trabalhadores no Brasil*; Immanuel Ness and Dario Azzellini, *Ours to Master and to Own*, and additional own research.

5 Including Oaxaca, the capital of the eponymous Mexican state, which was self-administered for almost four-and-a-half months before it was stormed by special police forces. During a general uprising in 14 June 2006, the people had driven the police and city administration out of the 600,000-inhabitant city. See Carlos Beas Torres, "La batalla por Oaxaca." Local self-administrations in Mexico are strongly influenced by indigenous thinking and resistance experiences. They have much in common with the socialist communal tradition and also stem from dissident socialist currents such as council communism, libertarian socialism (in Oaxaca especially from *Magonism*, an anarcho-communist precursor of the Mexican Revolution of 1910, based on the ideas of Ricardo Flores Magón) and anarcho-syndicalism.

6 Istvan Mészáros, *Beyond Capital*, 739–70.

7 Joost Jongerden and Ahmet Hamdi Akkaya, "Democratic Confederalism as a Kurdish Spring."

8 Anja Flach *et al.*, *Revolution in Rojava*; Jongerden and Hamdi, "Democratic Confederalism."

9 Karl Korsch, "Revolutionary Commune."

10 Ernst Däumig, "Der Rätegedanke und seine Verwirklichung," in Schneider and Kuda, *Arbeiterräte*, 69–70. English translation given in Karl Korsch, *Revolutionary Theory*, 18–19.

11 Ibid., 52.

12 Max Adler, "Demokratie und Rätesystem"; Däumig, "Der Rätegedanke und seine Verwirklichung"; Karl Korsch, "Die Sozialisierungsfrage vor und nach der Revolution"; Anton Pannekoek, "Arbeiterräte." For a detailed analysis of council theorists' debates and the inherent contradictions and limitations of early-twentieth-century workers' councils, see Alex Demirovic, "Council Democracy, or the End of the Political."

13 Karl Marx, "First Draft of The Civil War in France," 490–1.

14 See Azzellini, *An Alternative Labour History*; Ness and Azzellini, *Ours to Master and to Own*.

15 Däumig, "Der Rätegedanke und seine Verwirklichung," 81.

16 Pannekoek, "Arbeiterräte," 40.

17 Which was undoubtedly a central reason for the parties' mistrust towards the councils.

18 Adler, "Demokratie und Rätesystem," 149, 159.

19 Demirovic, "Council Democracy, or the End of the Political," 45.

20 Pannekoek, "Arbeiterräte," 40.

21 Karl Marx, "Second Draft of The Civil War in France," 537.

22 Adler, "Demokratie und Rätesystem," 206.
23 For an overview of the main arguments against the separation of powers and of why liberals claim that the separation is the guarantee for democratic rights, see Demirovic, "Council Democracy, or the End of the Political," 43–5.
24 Korsch, "Die Sozialisierungsfrage," English translation given in Korsch, *Revolutionary Theory*, 22–3.
25 Korsch, "Sozialisierung und Arbeiterbewegung," 90.
26 Karl Marx, *Capital*, 82–3.
27 Marx "First Draft of The Civil War in France," 486–7.
28 Karl Marx, "The Civil War in France," 331.
29 Däumig, "Der Rätegedanke," 69. English translation given in Korsch, *Revolutionary Theory*, p. 19.
30 Karl Korsch, *Arbeitsrecht für Betriebsräte*.
31 Karl Korsch, "Collectivization in Spain."
32 Demirovic, "Council Democracy, or the End of the Political," 34.
33 Marx, "First Draft of The Civil War in France," 498.
34 Anton Pannekoek, *Workers' Councils*, 45.
35 Ibid., 48–9.
36 Regarding the internal contradictions of the Bolivarian process, see Dario Azzellini, "Class Struggle in the Bolivarian Process"; Dario Azzellini, "Venezuela's Social Transformation and Growing Class Struggle."
37 Dario Azzellini, *Communes and Workers' Control in Venezuela*, 243–62; Jongerden and Hamdi, "Democratic Confederalism," 172; Interview, Atenéa Jiménez.
38 Dario Azzellini and Oliver Ressler, *Occupy, Resist, Produce – Vio.Me.*
39 Dario Azzellini, *Vom Protest zum sozialen Prozess.*
40 PFA, *Las Empresas Recuperadas en la Argentina*, 47.
41 Chedid Henriques *et al.*, *Empresas Recuperadas por Trabalhadores no Brasil*, 124.
42 Azzellini, *An Alternative Labour History*; Interview, Andrés Ruggeri.
43 Chedid Henriques *et al.*, *Empresas Recuperadas por Trabalhadores no Brasil*, 114–32; Interview, Ruggeri.
44 Azzellini, *An Alternative Labour History*; CDER, *Nuevas Empresas Recuperadas 2010–2013*; Chedid Henriques *et al.*, *Empresas Recuperadas por Trabalhadores no Brasil*.
45 Dario Azzellini, "Labour as a Commons."
46 Azzellini, *Communes and Workers' Control in Venezuela*, 81–124, 243–51.
47 Ibid., 124–56; Dario Azzellini and Oliver Ressler, *Comuna under Construction*, Interview, Jiménez. A very similar structure and practice has also been working well in Chiapas and Guerrero. See Leandro Vergara-Camus, *Land and Freedom*; Giovanna Gasparello, "Policía comunitaria de guerrero."
48 See the list of communal councils and communes officially registered on the website of the Ministerio del Poder Popular para las Comunas, 25 December 2017, at: http://consulta.mpcomunas.gob.ve/.
49 Azzellini, *Communes and Workers' Control in Venezuela*, 124–56; Flach *et al.*, *Revolution in Rojava*.
50 David Harvey, *Spaces of Global Capitalism*, 119–48.
51 Azzellini, *Communes and Workers' Control in Venezuela*, 124–56; Interview, Jiménez.

52 LOC (Ley Orgánica de las Comunas).
53 Ercan Ayboğa, "Das neue Rechtssystem in Rojava"; Flach *et al.*, *Revolution in Rojava*; Strangers in a Tangled Wilderness, *A Mountain River Has Many Bends.*
54 Strangers in a Tangled Wilderness, *A Mountain River Has Many Bends*, 20.
55 Carne Ross, "The Kurds' Democratic Experiment."
56 Flach *et al.*, *Revolution in Rojava*, 251–3.
57 Strangers in a Tangled Wilderness, *A Mountain River Has Many Bends*, 26.
58 Ayboğa, "Das neue Rechtssystem in Rojava."
59 Azzellini, *Communes and Workers' Control in Venezuela*, 124–56; Azzellini and Ressler, *Comuna under Construction*, Interview, Jiménez.
60 Azzellini, *An Alternative Labour History*; CDER, *Nuevas Empresas Recuperadas 2010–2013*; Chedid Henriques *et al.*, *Empresas Recuperadas por Trabalhadores no Brasil*; Ness and Azzellini, *Ours to Master and to Own.*
61 Esteva, "Otra mirada, otra democracia."
62 Ibid.
63 Azzellini, *Vom Protest zum sozialen Prozess*; Marina Sitrin and Dario Azzellini, *They Can't Represent Us!*

References

Adler, Max. "Demokratie und Rätesystem." In *Max Adler: Ausgewählte Schriften.* Edited by Norbert Leser and Alfred Pfabigan. 133–62. Vienna: Österreichischer Bundesverlag, 1981 [1919].

La Asamblea Nacional de la República Bolivariana de Venezuela. *LOC (Ley Orgánica de las Comunas).* Caracas: Asamblea Nacional de la República Bolivariana de Venezuela, 2010.

Ayboğa, Ercan. "Das neue Rechtssystem in Rojava." *Kurdistan Report* 75 (2014): 34–7.

Azzellini, Dario. *An Alternative Labour History: Worker Control and Workplace Democracy.* London: Zed Books, 2015.

———. "Besetzen, Widerstand leisten, produzieren: Betriebsbesetzungen in Argentinien, Brasilien, Uruguay und Venezuela." *JEP, Journal für Entwicklungspolitik* 31, no. 2 (2015): 79–105.

———. "Class Struggle in the Bolivarian Process: Workers' Control and Workers' Councils." *Latin American Perspectives* 44, no. 1 (2017): 126–39.

———. *Communes and Workers' Control in Venezuela: Building 21st Century Socialism from Below.* Amsterdam: Brill, 2017.

———. "Labour as a Commons: The Example of Worker-Recuperated Companies." *Critical Sociology* (2016): 1–14.

———. "Venezuela's Social Transformation and Growing Class Struggle." In *Crisis and Contradiction: Marxist Perspectives on Latin America in the Global Economy.* Edited by Susan Spronk and Jeffery R. Webber. 138–62. Leiden: Brill Press, 2015.

———. *Vom Protest zum sozialen Prozess: Betriebsbesetzungen und Arbeiten in Selbstverwaltung.* Hamburg: VSA, 2018.

Azzellini, Dario and Oliver Ressler. *Comuna under Construction.* Berlin: good!movies, film, 94 min., 2010.

———. *Occupy, Resist, Produce – Vio.Me.* Berlin/Vienna: good!movies, film, 30 min., 2015.

Beas Torres, Carlos. "La batalla por Oaxaca." In *La batalla por Oaxaca*. 21–79. Oaxaca: Yope Power, 2007.

CDER (Centro de Documentación de Empresas Recuperadas). *Nuevas Empresas Recuperadas 2010–2013*. Buenos Aires: Continente, 2014.

Chedid Henriques, Flávio, Vanessa Moreira Sígolo, Sandra Rufino, Fernanda Santos Araújo, Vicente Nepomuceno, Mariana Baptista Girotto, Maria Alejandra Paulucci, Thiago Nogueira Rodrigues, Maíra Rocha Cavalcanti and Maurício Sardá de Faria. *Empresas Recuperadas por Trabalhadores no Brasil: Resultados de um Levantamento Nacional*. Rio de Janeiro: Editorial Multifoco, 2013.

Däumig, Ernst. "Der Rätegedanke und seine Verwirklichung." In *Theorie und Praxis der direkten Demokratie*. Edited by Udo Bermbach. 79–87. Opladen: Westdeutscher Verlag, 1973 [1920].

Demirovic, Alex. "Council Democracy, or the End of the Political." In *An Alternative Labour History: Worker Control and Workplace Democracy*. Edited by Dario Azzellini. 31–66. London: Zed Books, 2015.

Di Paola, Pietro. "Factory Councils in Turin, 1919–1920: 'The Sole and Authentic Social Representatives of the Proletarian Class'." In *Ours to Master and to Own: Workers' Control from the Commune to the Present*. Edited by Immanuel Ness and Dario Azzellini. 130–47. Chicago: Haymarket, 2011.

Esteva, Gustavo. "Otra mirada, otra democracia." *Rebelión.org*. (2009). Accessed at www.rebelion.org/noticia.php?id=80143.

Flach, Anja, Ercan Ayboğa and Michael Knapp. *Revolution in Rojava: Frauenbewegung und Kommunalismus zwischen Krieg und Embargo*. Hamburg: VSA, 2015.

Gasparello, Giovanna. "Policía comunitaria de guerrero, investigación y autonomía." *Política y Cultura* 32 (2009): 61–78.

Harvey, David. *Spaces of Global Capitalism: Towards a Theory of Uneven Geographical Development*. London and New York: Verso, 2006.

Haumer, Peter. "The Austrian Revolution of 1918–1919 and Working Class Autonomy." In *An Alternative Labour History: Worker Control and Workplace Democracy*. Edited by Dario Azzellini. 120–56. London: Zed Books, 2015.

Hoffrogge, Ralf. *Working Class Politics in the German Revolution: Richard Müller, the Revolutionary Shop Stewards and the Origins of the Council Movement*. Amsterdam: Brill, 2014.

Jongerden, Joost and Ahmet Hamdi Akkaya. "Democratic Confederalism as a Kurdish Spring: The PKK and the Quest for Radical Democracy." In *The Kurdish Spring: Geopolitical Changes and the Kurds*. Edited by Michael M. Gunter and Mohammed M. A. Ahmed. 163–85. Costa Mesa, CA: Mazda Publishers, 2013.

Korsch, Karl. *Arbeitsrecht für Betriebsräte*. Frankfurt: EVA, 1968 [1922].

———. "Collectivization in Spain." *Living Marxism* 4, no. 6 (April 1939): 178–82.

———. "Revolutionary Commune." Translated by Andrew Giles-Peters and Karl-Heinz Otto. *Die Aktion*, no. 19. Accessed at www.marxists.org/archive/korsch/1929/commune.htm.

———. *Revolutionary Theory*. Edited by Douglas Kellner. Austin, TX and London: University of Texas Press, 1977.

———. "Sozialisierung und Arbeiterbewegung." In *Gesamtausgabe, Bd. 2: Rätebewegung und Klassenkampf*. 89–95. Frankfurt: EVA, 1980 [1919].

———. "Die Sozialisierungsfrage vor und nach der Revolution." *Gesamtausgabe, Bd. 2: Rätebewegung und Klassenkampf*. 161–5. Frankfurt: EVA, 1980 [1919].

———. "Wandlungen des Problems der politischen Arbeiterräte in Deutschland" (1921). In *Ders.: Politische Texte*. 23–32. Frankfurt: EVA, 1974 [1921]. English translation. Accessed at https://libcom.org/library/evolution-problem-political-workers-councils-germany-karl-korsch.

Mandel, David. "The Factory Committee Movement in the Russian Revolution." In *Ours to Master and to Own: Workers' Control from the Commune to the Present*. Edited by Immanuel Ness and Dario Azzellini. 104–29. Chicago: Haymarket, 2011.

Marx, Karl. *Capital: A Critique of Political Economy*, vol. 1. New York: International Publishers, 1967 [1867].

———. "The Civil War in France." In *Marx and Engels Collected Works*, vol. 22. 307–58. New York: International Publishers, 1986 [1871].

———. "First Draft of The Civil War in France." In *Marx and Engels Collected Works*, vol. 22. 437–514. New York: International Publishers, 1986 [1871].

———. "Second Draft of The Civil War in France." In *Marx and Engels Collected Works*, vol. 22. 515–51. New York: International Publishers, 1986 [1871].

Mészáros, Istvan. *Beyond Capital: Towards a Theory of Transition*. New York: Monthly Review Press, 1995.

Ness, Immanuel and Dario Azzellini. *Ours to Master and to Own: Workers' Control from the Commune to the Present*. Chicago: Haymarket, 2011.

Pannekoek, Anton. "Arbeiterräte." In *Arbeiterräte: Texte zur sozialen Revolution*. 515–21. Fernwald: Germinal Verlag, 2008 [1946].

———. *Workers' Councils*. Edited and introduced by Robert F. Barsky. Oakland, CA: AK Press, 2003 [1946].

PFA (Programa Facultad Abierta). *Las Empresas Recuperadas en la Argentina: Informe del Tercer Relevamiento*. Buenos Aires: University of Buenos Aires, 2010.

Ross, Carne. "The Kurds' Democratic Experiment." *New York Times*, 30 September 2015. Accessed at www.nytimes.com/2015/09/30/opinion/the-kurds-democratic-experiment.html.

Schneider, Dieter and Rudolf Kuda. *Arbeiterräte in der Novemberrevolution*. Frankfurt a.M.: Suhrkamp, 1973.

Sitrin, Marina and Dario Azzellini. *They Can't Represent Us! Reinventing Democracy from Greece to Occupy*. London and New York: Verso, 2014.

Strangers in a Tangled Wilderness: *A Mountain River Has Many Bends: An Introduction to the Rojava Revolution*. Excerpted from *A Small Key Can Open a Large Door: The Rojava Revolution*. Oakland, CA: AK Press, 2015. Accessed at www.tangledwilderness.org/a-mountain-river-has-many-bends/.

Vergara-Camus, Leandro. *Land and Freedom*. London: Zed Books, 2014.

Interviews

Jiménez, Atenéa. Red Nacional de Comuneros y Comuneras, Caracas, Venezuela. 14 February 2012.

Ruggeri, Andrés. Universidad de Buenos Aires, Director of the CDER, Buenos Aires, Argentina. 15 January 2015.

Index

Notes are denoted by the letter 'n' and the note number following the page number.

Made in the USA
Monee, IL
13 September 2026

62978980R00149